From Robber Barons
to Courtiers

From Robber Barons
to Courtiers

The Changing World of the
Lovells of Titchmarsh

Monika E Simon

PEN & SWORD
HISTORY

First published in Great Britain in 2021 by
Pen & Sword History
An imprint of
Pen & Sword Books Ltd
Yorkshire – Philadelphia

ISBN 978 1 52675 107 2

A CIP catalogue record for this book is
available from the British Library.

Typeset by Mac Style
Printed and bound in Great Britain by
CPI Group (UK) Ltd, Croydon, CR0 4YY

Pen & Sword Books Limited incorporates the imprints of Atlas,
Archaeology, Aviation, Discovery, Family History, Fiction, History,
Maritime, Military, Military Classics, Politics, Select, Transport,
True Crime, Air World, Frontline Publishing, Leo Cooper, Remember
When, Seaforth Publishing, The Praetorian Press, Wharncliffe
Local History, Wharncliffe Transport, Wharncliffe True Crime
and White Owl.

For a complete list of Pen & Sword titles please contact

PEN & SWORD BOOKS LIMITED
47 Church Street, Barnsley, South Yorkshire, S70 2AS, England
E-mail: enquiries@pen-and-sword.co.uk
Website: www.pen-and-sword.co.uk

Or

PEN AND SWORD BOOKS
1950 Lawrence Rd, Havertown, PA 19083, USA
E-mail: Uspen-and-sword@casematepublishers.com
Website: www.penandswordbooks.com

Contents

List of Illustrations

Acknowledgements

I owe a big thank you to so many people who helped me to get this book written. Too many to personally thank all of them, but there are a few to whom I am particularly grateful to:

First of all, my parents who made it all possible. Secondly, but crucially, my dear friends, Dr Alex Service, Kirsty Hartsiotis, and Michael Gaunt, who helped me stay sane when I was working on my DPhil thesis.

I want to thank all the people who helped with their suggestions and encouragement. To name but a few: my supervisor Prof Mark Ormrod, who sadly is not here anymore to see the book published, Dr Katherine Lewis, Bille Zipperer, Dr Joanna Laynesmith, and all my sisters, in particular my sister Sabine who read through most of the manuscript. A special thank you to Kirsty Hartsiotis (again) for her great help in sourcing the images, and thank you to Sally Baldham for the image of the tomb of John Lovell IX.

Another big thank you to Orderic Vitalis, the countless medieval scribes of administrative records, to the editors of all those fantastic documents, and to the librarians and archivists in England and Germany with a special thanks to the staff of the Bavarian State Library.

Last but not least, I want to thank everyone at Pen and Sword Books who offered me the chance to write about the Lovells, and in particular Danna Messer for her encouragement and support.

The Lovells of Titchmarsh

F rancis Lovell is without a doubt the most famous, if not the only famous, of the Lovells of Titchmarsh. He is often introduced with the well-known and often-quoted doggerel by William Collingbourne:

> The catte, the ratte, and Louell our dogge,
> Rulyth all Englande vnder the hogge

Alongside William Catesby and Richard Ratcliffe, Francis Lovell is described as one of the three most influential men of the realm.[1] Francis Lovell's fame is based on his close association with Richard III (1483–1485). They were intimate friends and companions probably since the days of their early youth when both lived at Middleham, home of Richard, Earl of Warwick, 'the Kingmaker'. Francis Lovell's friendship and devotion to Richard endured even beyond the king's death at the Battle of Bosworth.

Francis Lovell became a part of the closest circle around Richard III since he was a suitable companion for the younger brother of Edward IV (1461–1483). He was the heir of a rich baronial family who over several centuries had accumulated land, wealth, and influence. It is the purpose of this book to chart the history of Francis Lovell's family from their earliest beginnings to his time, and beyond. The Lovells became extinct in the male line in 1489, but lived on in the descendants of the daughters of the family, most notably the Parkers, Lords Morley. Breaking with the tradition of only looking at a family's male descendants allows us to cross the traditional barrier between the Middle Ages and the Tudor period.

A study of this nature, researching a baronial family over several centuries, is at the same time frustrating and rewarding. The scarcity of records, particularly in the earlier centuries, means that sometimes even the most basic facts of their lives cannot be established. As the

Middle Ages progress, the number of surviving records increases steadily. The meticulous records of central administration reveal a plethora of fascinating facts and factoids, particularly for the highest levels of society. By the early Tudor period the amount of records is so great that there is a danger to get lost in details.

Another important source, chronicles, are not without drawbacks. They are often partisan and for most of the period under discussion were written by clerics who had their own particular view on the world. They did not write history in the modern sense but tried to discern a moral of the events described. Their focus was on their immediate world and on the events at the centre of government, focusing on king and court. Unsurprisingly, the Lovells of Titchmarsh are rarely mentioned. However, on occasion chronicles do provide valuable, in fact often unique information about the family (see Chapter 1).

Additionally, both the chronicles and the records of central government, as useful and interesting as they are, never allow us to see beyond the surface to a personal level. This changes towards the end of the Middle Ages when the number of surviving personal records increases. These include the estate records of some noble families which are preserved from the fourteenth century onward. They provide fascinating details of their daily lives, where they stayed, what they ate, and what they spent their money on. A number of personal letters from the later Middle Ages also survive, including for example drafts written by Hugh Despenser the Younger as well as the famous letter collections from the Paston, Stonor, and Cely families.

But these surviving documents are exceptions. For most families the records have disappeared over the intervening centuries. In the case of the Lovells, a few estate papers covering two fiscal years, 1394–95 and 1400–01, exist, but they cover only a part of the Lovell estates. They consist of a summary of income and expenses only and do not include any information about the personal lives of John Lovell VII and his family. Similarly, the handful of letters by the Lovells which have been preserved, deal with routine matters and do not give insights into the writers' minds. From the first half of the sixteenth century a larger number of letters of the Parkers have survived in the *Letters and Papers Foreign and Domestic of the Reign of Henry VIII*. However, interpreting these letters is not always easy, as will be discussed in the last chapter of this book.

Even though the number of records grew immensely over the period covered in this book, as does the variety of what has survived, for most of the time we find ourselves spectators of a mute scene. We can observe what happened, but we can only guess what motivated the people and why they acted as they did. The inner lives of the these men and women remain a closed book.

Despite all these problems, despite the sometimes frustrating gaps in knowledge, and despite the fact that on occasion all that is possible is to speculate, researching a family like the Lovells of Titchmarsh is a very rewarding enterprise. By studying one family over a period of 500 years, from their ancestors in Normandy to their descendants in Tudor times we can not only see how the family's fortunes and status changed over time but also explore how the aristocracy, the society, and the political landscape changed or remained the same.

The long and eventful history of the Lovells of Titchmarsh is well worth studying. Over half a millennium, members of this family participated in a surprisingly large number of pivotal events, crusades, battles, sieges, and revolutions. Though they are not usually found in a leading role, they were representatives of the majority of noble families of this era. Like their peers, the Lovells accumulated wealth and power in the form of ever growing estates and the influence that went with it over the centuries. They were rulers of their estates, participated in the administration of the localities in which their lands were situated, and served as a conduit between the central government and the localities.

To describe the changing lives of an aristocratic family in medieval England, a chronological approach seemed to be the best solution. This allows the history of the family to be followed more easily while, at the same time, addressing several different aspects of the lives of the English nobility: their involvement in war and administration, the profit and perils of service to the Crown, the influence of family tradition and personal choice, of loyalty and opportunism. The only exception to this chronological approach is the chapter looking at the Lovell women. Though little is known about the wives and daughters of the family they were an essential part of the family, and their role in the history of the Lovells should not be ignored.

Several aspects of noble life, marriage, relationships within and outside the family, service to the Crown and the patronage that was its reward, will be a theme throughout the book. It should also be kept in mind that, to some extent, speculation and deduction were necessary.

Like most medieval families, the Lovells were very conservative when naming their offspring. To avoid confusion, the heads of the family bearing the same first names, are numbered, from William Lovell I in the early twelfth century to John Lovell IX in the late fifteenth century. Women are referred to by their maiden name for two reasons. For one, again to avoid confusion. Maud Holland and Maud Burnell would both otherwise become Maud Lovell. Secondly, by using their maiden names their link to their natal families is preserved. This approach is not quite as modern as it may first appear. The Lovells themselves were keeping their wives' families very much in mind in their representation of themselves, as will be seen.

Chapter 1

The Lords of Bréval, the Castle of Ivry, and the Profits of Rebellion

As most English noble families, the Lovells of Titchmarsh were originally from Normandy. Their first known ancestor was Robert, Lord of Bréval, who lived around the middle of the eleventh century and held seigneurial rights near Ivry-la-Bataille on the border between the duchy of Normandy and the kingdom of France. Few facts are known about the earliest ancestors of the family, both because of their relatively low status within the nobility and the scarcity of sources at this time. In the last decades of the eleventh and the first decades of the twelfth century the family came to increasing prominence. It was Robert's grandson, Ascelin Goël, and Ascelin's sons, who initiated the rise of the family in status and fame, or rather notoriety. This rise was the result of gaining possession of the Castle of Ivry in modern day Ivry-la-Bataille (department Eure) to a considerable extent achieved through confrontation and rebellion.[1]

At this time the border between Normandy and France was not a clear line on the map. It was not defined by significant geographical obstacles, nor was there a language barrier. People, then as now, continually crossed and re-crossed these borders, working, trading, and living on either side of it, and noblemen like Robert Beaumont, Count of Meulan, held land both in Normandy and France owing allegiance to both the king of France and the duke of Normandy. The control of the duke of Normandy over his territory – particularly along the border – therefore depended on which of the noblemen were willing to follow his lead rather than that of the king of France. This caused constant friction between the two rulers, giving even smaller lords who held border castles leverage to greatly enhance their power and influence. This made border castles highly desirable places to hold.

As one of the oldest and strongest fortifications on the Norman-French border, the formidable Castle of Ivry situated above the river Eure was one of those highly coveted border castles. It has been argued that Ivry was the model for the White Tower in London and its massive ruins can still be visited today (see plate 1).[2]

The history of the castle is one of betrayal and bloodshed. In the twelfth century, Orderic Vitalis relates that Aubrée, wife of Ralph, Count of Bayeux and half-brother of Richard I, Duke of Normandy, commissioned the castle to be built. The finished castle was so impressive that Aubrée had the architect Lanfred killed to prevent him from building another fortress like it. She herself was in turn killed by her husband who wished to possess the castle himself. Though this tale has all the hallmarks of a sensational legend some fact support the gist of the story. At the beginning of the eleventh century the castle was held by Hugh, Bishop of Bayeux, one of the sons of Ralph, Count of Bayeux until it was taken into the hands of Robert, Duke of Normandy in about 1028.[3]

Though the identity of the wife of the first known Lovell ancestor, Robert, of Bréval cannot be determined with certainty, it is likely that she was Aubrée, daughter of Hugh, Bishop of Bayeux, and granddaughter of Ralph, Count of Bayeux, and his wife Aubrée, who according to Orderic Vitalis's lurid tale had the Castle of Ivry built. If the identification is correct she was also a cousin of William fitz Osbern, a close ally of William the Conqueror (1066–1087). Her son, called Robert like her husband, would have hereditary rights to the Castle of Ivry (see Genealogy 1). This younger Robert appears as castellan of Ivry in 1059, a position to which he must have been appointed by William I the Conqueror when he was only the duke of Normandy. The *Cartulaire de L'Abbaye de Saint-Martin de Pontoise* refers to him as 'Roberto Ibriensi' in the *Vita Dominae Hildeburgis*, a brief life of his wife.[4]

The few facts known Robert d'Ivry's lands come from grants to religious houses since their archives survived the ravages of time better than those of the nobility. These grants to the church of Bréval and rights in Villegats (Eure), Mondreville, and Tilly (both Yvelines) show that his estates were concentrated in the region around Ivry and Bréval both in France and Normandy. The prime possession of the family was Bréval just over 10km or roughly 6.5 miles to the north-east of Ivry.[5] Robert d'Ivry was not a great lord, particularly compared to men like Robert

Beaumont, Count of Meulan or Robert de Bêlleme, but as a lord with feudal rights he was a member of the small land-holding elite.

Robert d'Ivry's wife Hildeburge was the daughter of Hervé de Gallardon and his wife Beatrix, whose lands were in the same region as his own. Gallardon is just over 50km (30 miles) south of Ivry.[6]

Both Robert and his wife Hildeburge entered religious lives in the late 1080s. Robert d'Ivry retired to the Abbey of Bec after a serious illness. It is unknown when Robert died. Hildeburge, who had already founded a hospital in Ivry, spent many years undertaking pilgrimages between different religious houses. She finally settled down as a recluse beside the Abbey of St-Martin-de-Pontoise. She died on 3 June 1115. Hildeburge had acquired the reputation of a saintly women through her many charitable works and her religious life. A brief description of her life was written shortly after her death and the account was the first step of the official road to canonisation. However, no evidence can be found that further efforts were made.[7]

Robert d'Ivry and Hildeburge de Gallardon had three sons: Ascelin, William, and Robert, a clerk. It is unclear why Ascelin assumed the surname 'Goël'. One explanation, given by J. Depoin, is that he adopted the name in honour of his great-grandmother Godeheu or Gohue, countess of Bellême. The suggestion is intriguing, but Depoin unfortunately does not back up this statement with any references or explanations.[8] Considering that his genealogical inferences have been called 'not trustworthy', this should be regarded as speculation.[9]

Ascelin Goël is the first of family who emerges from the records as an individual, not only a name to which a few dates and names can be linked. He was the first to leave his mark on the events of their region. While his mother Hildeburge was renowned for her saintliness, Ascelin Goël was a ruthless and ambitious man, eager to attain more power and influence.

Most of the events surrounding the feud he engaged in to gain possession of the Castle of Ivry are only described in Orderic Vitalis's *Ecclesiastical History*. Fortunately, Orderic Vitalis was well-informed about these events. The monastery he lived in, the Abbey of Saint-Évroult (in modern Saint-Evroult-Notre-Dame-du-Bois) was situated in the heart of Normandy and he was personally acquainted with many of the families he wrote about. Having to rely almost completely on one source has particular drawbacks, as the events often cannot be confirmed, and questions cannot be clarified through other sources. Orderic's narrative style, jumping backwards and forwards in time, makes it sometimes difficult to piece together the exact sequence of events. J.O. Prestwich judges that Orderic 'was remarkably careless of chronology, even of events in his own lifetime. But his history remains of inestimable value for the range, variety, and volume of the information he acquired, and above all for his knowledge and understanding of the lay aristocracy of his day'.[10]

Ascelin Goël is first mentioned when he participated in the 1087 invasion of the Vexin lead by William the Conqueror. The capture of Mantes by William's forces was possible because they discovered that the gates of the town were left open after soldiers and townsfolk had left the city to inspect the damage Ascelin Goël and his Norman forces had caused the previous day. William's troops were able to storm the town and castle, which they plundered and burned to the ground. Ascelin Goël's pillaging of the countryside surrounding Mantes was probably in retaliation for previous raids led by Hugh Esteval and Ralph Mauvoisin on Ascelin Goël's or William de Breteuil's lands. It is unclear in what capacity Ascelin Goël acted, but the raid must have been co-ordinated with William the Conqueror's campaign who reaped its unexpected benefits when he found the gates of Mantes open as a consequence of Ascelin Goël's attack.[11]

The invasion of the Vexin was the final campaign of William the Conqueror. He fell seriously ill and died on 9 September 1087. The death of a monarch is always a time of uncertainty and after the death of William the Conqueror, a considerable number of Norman barons rebelled, hoping to gain greater independence than they had enjoyed under William. Robert de Bellême, William de Breteuil, William, Count of Évreux, and Ralph of Conches all expelled the royal garrisons from their castles.[12]

The honour and Castle of Ivry had remained in the hands of the dukes of Normandy since Duke Robert I had taken them into his custody of in 1028. One of the castellan's appointed by the duke had been Ascelin Goël's father Robert d'Ivry. William the Conqueror gave the castellanship to Roger Beaumont, probably at the time Robert d'Ivry entered the Abbey of Bec. The new duke of Normandy, William the Conqueror's eldest son, Robert Curthose, now granted Ivry to William de Breteuil and in compensation gave the Castle of Brionne to Roger Beaumont.[13] It has been argued that by giving away two important castles, Robert Curthose undermined his own position. However, others have pointed out that Robert had to reward his supporters to retain their loyalty.[14]

The new Lord of Ivry, William de Breteuil, was one of the most powerful noblemen in Normandy. He was the son of William fitz Osbern and grandson of Osbern, steward of Robert the Magnificent, the father of William the Conqueror. The lands William de Breteuil inherited from his father placed him in the top tier of the nobility.[15]

Soon after William de Breteuil gained possession of Ivry he installed Ascelin Goël as its castellan. But Ascelin Goël wanted more than holding the castle for another man. Both Ascelin Goël and William de Breteuil seem to have considered the castle theirs by hereditary right: William de Breteuil's grandmother was Emma, a sister of Hugh, Bishop of Bayeux, while Ascelin Goël's grandmother Aubrée was probably Hugh's daughter, a niece of Emma (see Genealogy 1).

At this time, Ascelin Goël was only a minor border lord. His main residence was Bréval, where, Orderic Vitalis tells us, he built a strong castle and 'filled it with cruel bandits to the ruin of many'. He also held the Castle of Anet and the town of Saint-André. He was by no means poor, but his influence and power were insignificant compared to that of William de Breteuil.[16]

As Orderic Vitalis relates these events, Ascelin Goël decided to take complete control of Ivry from William de Breteuil when he prosecuted Ascelin Goël's younger brother for attacking a woman of Pacy, one of William de Breteuil's towns. Two years after the death of William the Conqueror, Ascelin Goël 'feloniously deprived' William de Breteuil of the castle and handed it over to Duke Robert Curthose.

It is surprising that after taking full control of the castle, Ascelin Goël handed it over to Robert Curthose. Perhaps he hoped Duke Robert would grant the castle to him as the heir with the better claim. If this was the case, his hopes were quickly dashed. Robert Curthose sold the Castle of Ivry to William de Bretuil, for the considerable sum of 1,500 livres, even though Robert Curthose had granted the castle to William de Bretuil shortly before. As his feudal lord, Robert Curthose should have defended William de Breteuil's rights to the castle instead of seeking 'temporary financial advantage'.[17] Having lost the trust in his castellan, William de

Breteuil deprived Ascelin Goël of the castellanship of Ivry and all the property which Ascelin held of him.[18] In his first attempt to gain control of Ivry, Ascelin Goël had gained nothing. In fact, he had also lost the land he had held of William of Breteuil.

However, Ascelin Goël did not abandon his attempt to gain control of the powerful border castle. In 1091, two years after he first deprived William de Breteuil of Ivry, Ascelin Goël captured William de Breteuil with the help of Richard of Montfort and the household troops of Philip I of France (1059–1008). Ascelin Goël held William de Breteuil captive in Bréval for three months, where he and the other prisoners were subjected to various tortures by their captors. Orderic Vitalis reports that Ascelin had his prisoners exposed to the freezing wind clad only in wet shirts until these were frozen solid.[19]

Eventually a truce was arranged by several noblemen, including Richard of Montfort and Hugh Montgomery. It secured William de Breteuil's release but he had to pay a heavy price for his freedom: he had to surrender the Castle of Ivry to Ascelin, give him his illegitimate daughter Isabel as his wife, and hand over a large sum of money, either 1,000 or 3,000 livres as well as 'horses, arms and many other things'.[20]

With his second, ruthless assault Ascelin Goël had gained the price he had fought for, the Castle of Ivry, and a bride from one of the most noble families of Normandy. What his intended wife Isabel thought about being part of her father's ransom was naturally not recorded. Marriages were generally arranged to reinforce existing alliances between noble families, to confirm new alliances, or to end a quarrel. Taking the wishes of sons or daughters into account was usually not a factor. Ascelin Goël's marriage to Isabel was probably an attempt to end the feud between him and William de Breteuil. But, if that was the case, it was not crowned with success.

Only a year after having lost control of the Castle of Ivry and forced to accept humiliating conditions for his release, William de Breteuil attempted to regain it. He fortified the church of St. Mary's Abbey in Ivry, hoping to use it as a base to retake the castle. However, Ascelin attacked, possibly before William had time to finish his preparations, and burned the church and the monastic buildings to the ground. William barely escaped being retaken by his new son-in-law, who again tortured the knights he had taken prisoner.[21]

In the following year and with the support of Robert Curthose and King Philip of France, whom he had to pay handsomely for their help, William de Breteuil made a second attempt to win the castle back. The parish priests, their parishioners, the abbots, and their men also assisted William de Bretuil. Robert de Bellême led the siege of Ascelin Goël's Castle of Bréval. Despite their combined efforts, Ascelin Goël was able to hold the castle for two months, but was eventually forced to surrender and returned the Castle of Ivry to his father-in-law.[22]

Unlike the Castle of Ivry whose massive ruins still survive, the Castle at Bréval has completely disappeared. It was not quite as formidable a fortification as Ivry, but that Bréval withstood a siege, led by the experienced warrior Robert de Bellême and supported by the king of France and the duke of Normandy for a considerable period bears witness to its strength.

The long feud between Ascelin Goël and William de Breteuil that troubled the region for more than three years with 'plundering, burning and slaughter' came to an end after the siege of Bréval and the return of Ivry into the hands of William de Breteuil.[23] Settling property disputes in private wars was typical for the time. A startling aspect of this feud is the almost complete absence of Duke Robert Curthose. As ruler of Normandy it was one of his most important duties to maintain the peace and stop his subjects from waging private wars. As in the quarrel between William de Breteuil and Ascelin Goël, this was a duty at which Robert Curthose often failed.

That peace returned to the troubled region was probably the result of Ascelin Goël's realisation that had no chance of permanently holding the Castle of Ivry against his father-in-law's far greater power base. Indirectly, the marriage between Ascelin Goël and Isabel may also have helped to end this conflict. As William de Breteuil had no legitimate children, Ascelin Goël knew his sons had an even better claim to inherit the castle from Isabel de Breteuil than he himself had. Inheritance laws were not yet precisely defined so William de Bretuil's illegitimate children, Isabel and Eustace as well as more distant relatives, all could all hope to inherit his land or parts of it.

After the death of William de Breteuil on 12 January 1103 the dispute over Ivry erupted again. Next to William de Breteuil's illegitimate son, Eustace, the other claimants were William Gael, the son of William de

Breteuil's sister Emma and Ralph Gael, who had been Earl of Suffolk and Norfolk until 1075, and the Burgundian Reginald of Grancey, a more distant relative of William de Breteuil (see Genealogy 1).[24] Ascelin Goël considered himself to be the rightful heir, both in his own right and in that of his wife.

While one of the rival claimants, William Gael, soon died, Reginald of Grancey was supported by a number of important nobles, including William, Count of Évreux, Ralph of Conches, and Amaury de Montfort. The majority of local barons, however, backed Eustace de Breteuil and advised him to seek help from Henry I. Eustace had married Henry I's (1100–1135) illegitimate daughter Juliana. Eustace had gained the goodwill of the king by participating in the siege of Robert de Bellême's Castle of Tickhill, Yorkshire in 1101, a part of Henry I's strategy to expel Robert de Bellême from England. The king promised to help his son-in-law 'against Goel and all his other enemies'.[25] At least in the report by Orderic Vitalis, Ascelin Goël rather than Robert de Grancey was the main adversary of Eustace de Breteuil, as he is the only opponent Orderic mentions by name. Had Ascelin Goël only fought in support of Reginald de Grancey's claim, it is unlikely that he would have been singled out as the greatest enemy of Eustace de Breteuil.

To solve the crisis, Henry I sent his chief advisor Robert Beaumont, Count of Meulan, to negotiate between the warring factions. He was able to persuade many of Eustace de Breteuil's original opponents to accept his succession. Reginald de Grancey, Ascelin Goël, and a few others remained obstinate and continued to lay waste to the country. However, their ruthlessness and particularly Reginald de Grancey's cruelty further strengthened Eustace de Breteuil's position. Having become 'an object of general hatred', Reginald de Grancey returned to Burgundy where, as Orderic Vitalis recounts with some satisfaction, he soon came to grief. Undeterred, Ascelin Goël continued to fight.

He kidnapped John, a rich citizen from Meulan, when he returned from a meeting with Robert Beaumont at Beaumont and imprisoned him, probably at Bréval, for four months. Unable to rescue John de Meulan despite making several attempts, Robert of Meulan was finally able to arrange a peace with all parties. A 'cunning man', again in the words of Orderic Vitalis, he betrothed his 1-year-old daughter Emma to Amaury de Montfort, appeasing both Amaury and his uncle William, Count of

Évreux, as well as Ralph of Conches, Eustace de Breteuil, Ascelin Goël, and the other feuding lords. John of Meulan was released and peace restored in the region.[26]

Orderic Vitalis does not specify how Robert Beaumont persuaded Ascelin Goël to agree to this settlement, but it is likely that it included handing over the Castle of Ivry. In a later charter, dated after 1115, Ascelin Goël is called 'Goelli de Ibriaco', Goël of Ivry. Gaining possession of the castle could well have been the price of peace Ascelin Goël demanded. At no later date was he in the position to extract such a concession. Perhaps it was at this time as well that Ascelin Goël acquired Saint-André, which he later held 'by gift of' Eustace de Breteuil.[27] Whatever the exact details of the peace brokered by Robert of Meulan were, no major conflict broke out in the following fifteen years, though, according to Orderic Vitalis, Ascelin Goël and his sons continued to plague the region with their violence and cruelty.[28]

After a long struggle, Ascelin Goël had gained what he had fought for: the Castle of Ivry. He had achieved this by pursuing a bloody feud over several decades first with William de Breteuil and then with William's son Eustace. In his single-minded struggle he had shown no respect for the ties of loyalty that were meant to bind a vassal to his lord. Even his marriage was the result of force and coercion. It was his ruthlessness, persistence, and willingness to use force that made him succeed. With the Castle of Ivry he gained a greater position of power for himself and his offspring. His outrageous behaviour not only brought him power and success but was the reason Orderic Vitalis wrote about him. It is one of the oddities of history that people who obey the law and behave impeccably are far less often written about than the villains.

Ascelin Goël died between 1116 and 1119 and was succeeded by his son Robert Goël. He was the eldest of the seven sons of Ascelin Goël and his wife Isabel de Breteuil, who, following the example of their father, 'continually grew in wickedness and caused widows and poor people to weep bitterly by their brutal acts'.[29]

Robert Goël has sometimes been identified as an illegitimate son. One of Ascelin Goël's sons named Robert was certainly illegitimate as he is referred to as 'Roberti Bastardi Rufi'. However, a grant by William Lovell, another son of Ascelin Goël and his wife Isabel, was witnessed by Robert Rufus, his son John, and Richard Rufus, like Robert Rufus a brother of William Lovell. As William Lovell I's wife appears as the first witness the grant was made after his marriage, which took place after Robert Goël's death in or before 1123. The grant is proof that Ascelin Goël had two sons called Robert: an illegitimate son, Robert Rufus, and a legitimate son, Robert Goël, who succeeded him.[30]

Robert Goël probably did not inherit the Castle of Ivry from his father, as it was once again at the centre of renewed conflict. By 1118, neighbouring rulers and Norman magnates had joined forces to try to replace Henry I as duke of Normandy with William Clito, the son of Robert Curthose, who had been a prisoner in England since the conquest of Normandy by Henry I in 1106. The unrest stirred up by William Clito and his supporters engulfed most of the duchy. Robert Goël joined the revolt probably at the end of 1118 or early in the following year.[31] Thanks to the fact that Orderic Vitalis was 'remarkably careless of chronology'[32] it is difficult to put the following events in the correct order, but it is possible to piece together the ensuing conflict.

Early in 1119, Eustace de Breteuil once again raised his claim on Ivry. Orderic Vitalis explains that Henry I was reluctant to grant Eustace de Breteuil's wish and 'put off granting his request for the present but promised to do so at a future date, and won back his support with fair words'. It seems Henry I was not very confident he could trust his son-in-law. To ensure his loyalty an exchange of hostages was arranged: a son of Ralph Harenc, the custodian of the castle, was given into Eustace de Breteuil's custody while two daughters of Eustace de Breteuil and his wife Juliana were handed over in return.

At about the same time, Robert Goël made his peace with the king. He was the first rebel to do so and many other rebels followed his example. As a reward Henry I gave him the Castle of Ivry and to guarantee his loyalty and good conduct his brothers were given to the king as hostages. Orderic Vitalis comments that Ralph the Red of Pont d'Erchanfray was an 'effective security' as he was Robert Goël's brother-in-law and therefore by necessity his ally. Robert Goël was apparently married to a sister of Ralph the Red, one of Henry I's most faithful supporters and a celebrated military commander.[33]

By giving Ivry to Robert Goël, Henry I had secured Robert's loyalty, but at the same time he had deeply disappointed his son-in-law, Eustace de Breteuil. Was it this disappointment rather than the evil influence of

Amaury de Montfort, as Orderic Vitalis claims, the reason for Eustace de Breteuil's rash action of blinding the son of the castellan Ralph Harenc?

The connection of Ralph Harenc to Robert Goël cannot be determined in detailed but his links to the Lovell family is confirmed by his witnessing a grant by William Lovell I to Notre-Dame-de-Gournay.[34] Robert Goël's probably had put Ralph Harenc in charge of the castle, and any attack on Ralph was therefore an attack on Robert Goël, too. The mutilation of Ralph Harenc's son had dire consequences for the hostages guaranteeing Eustace de Breteuil own good behaviour. Ralph Harenc demanded vengeance from Henry I who was obliged to hand over his two granddaughters to Ralph who blinded them and cut off the tips of their noses.

Joining the rebellion against Henry I had very different consequences for Robert Goël and Eustace de Breteuil. While Robert Goël regained possession of Ivry through his expertly timed joining and abandoning of the rebellion, Eustace de Breteuil overplayed his hand. As a consequence, he lost almost all his lands and was the author of the horrible fate inflicted on his daughters. The largest part of the honour of Breteuil was granted to Ralph Gael, brother of William Gael, one of the claimants of the honour in 1103. Only Pacy remained in the hands of Eustace de Breteuil and his wife Juliana.

It was not only Robert Goël who benefited from his well-timed change of allegiance, as Orderic Vitalis points out. By July 1119, Henry I was wiping out the last pockets of resistance and decided to move against Évreux, capital of the Évrecin and the focal point of the resistance of Amaury de Montfort. For this endeavour Henry I employed the help of Robert Goël, instructing him to challenge Montfort to a fight near Ivry on the day the king planned to move against Évreux. As Robert Goël and his men fought against Amaury de Montfort and his knights, Henry I set Évreux on fire. He sent messengers to Robert Goël who instantly informed his opponent of the developments, and a distraught Amaury de Montfort withdrew to his own lands. By winning Robert Goël over to his side, Henry I was able to quickly suppress the revolt and bring peace to the region.[35]

Robert Goël died not many years later, in or shortly before 1123, when Orderic Vitalis relates that his brother William Lovell I had inherited all his estates including the Castle of Ivry.[36] Why Robert Goël's brother

William used the surname Lovell and not Goël as his brother and father had done is unclear. One theory claims that since Ascelin Goël was cruel like a wolf, his offspring was called the little wolves or 'lupelli'. However, I have not found any contemporary source that supports this theory.

In the late eleventh and early twelfth century many families started to use surnames and for a long time the use of these names remained fluid. Many families derived their surnames from their main residence, as for example the Montforts and Beaumonts or used patronyms, like FitzAlan, literally meaning 'son of Alan', which quickly turned into a fixed name for the family. Some families used the title of an office the head of the family held, like Stewart or Butler. Names also could derive from heraldic devices or descriptive nicknames like Rufus, the Red. The name Lovell stems from heraldry where the wolf was a popular device. Several families unrelated to this Lovell family also adopted the surname Lovell, showing that this was a popular choice.

In the later Middle Ages coats of arms had become a symbol of power. Various additions, like animal supporters, helmets, and mantling, were created to form what is called a coat of arms' 'full achievements'. These elaborate coats of arms appear as decorations in many places, from churches to household items, like cups and plates. The full achievement of the Lovell coat of arms, found on Francis Lovell's garter stall plate in St George's Chapel, Windsor Castle, depicts a dog or wolf as the crest of the helmet as a play on their surname (see plate 13).

Parallel with the introduction of surnames, families also started to use the same first names for their children over and over for generations. The Bigod earls of Norfolk for example used the names Roger and Hugh almost exclusively; the Constable family from Yorkshire's names of choice were Robert and Marmaduke. While the Lovell family was firmly based in Normandy, they chose Norman names for their sons, Robert and William. Only after their centre of interest moved to England at the end of the twelfth century did they introduce a new name, John, that was to remain the most popular for centuries.

After several years of peace in Normandy, conflict broke out again as a consequence of the White Ship tragedy in 1120 and the death of Henry I's only legitimate son, William Ætheling. The question of who would succeed Henry I was wide open again. It was a particularly pressing problem in Normandy, since William Ætheling had been made duke of Normandy. William Clito, the son of Robert Curthose, was still attempting to gain the duchy his father had lost in 1106. He found widespread support for his fight as many noblemen who held lands only in Normandy preferred to have their own duke again.[37] Amaury de Montfort, always ready to rise in rebellion, persuaded Count Fulk V of Anjou to marry his daughter Sybil to William Clito and join the attempt to install his new son-in-law as duke of Normandy in place of Henry I. A number of less powerful noblemen also joined the rebellion, including William Lovell I.

To the surprise and consternation of Henry I, Waleran Beaumont, Count of Meulan, rebelled as well. Waleran and his twin brother Robert were the sons of one of Henry I's closest associates, Robert Beaumont, Count of Meulan. After their father's death, Henry I had taken the twins to his court and their lands into his hands. Possibly out of sympathy with William Clito and – as Orderic Vitalis tells it – romantic visions of knightly glory, Waleran threw in his lot with the rebels.[38]

To secure the alliance between the rebels, Waleran Beaumont married three of his sisters to three of his allies: Hugh de Montfort, Lord of Montfort-sur-Risle married Adelina Beaumont; Hugh fitz Gervase, Lord of Châteauneuf married her sister Alberada; and William Lovell I, Lord of Ivry, Matilda Beaumont (see Genealogy 2).[39]

The reasons for William Lovell I joining the rebellion remain unclear. David Crouch speculates that he held a grudge against Henry I because Ivry had been granted to his elder, illegitimate half-brother Robert Goël.[40] However, as discussed above, Robert Goël was Ascelin Goël's eldest legitimate son. After Robert Goël's death William Lovell I inherited the family lands including Ivry.[41] As lord of Ivry, William Lovell I was a valuable ally to the rebels, as his inclusion in the inner circle of the rebellion and, more significantly, his marriage to Matilda Beaumont show.

However, the rebels underestimated Henry I and did not act immediately. The plot against the king and the marriages to cement the alliance between the conspirators must have occurred in 1122, since by autumn of 1123 Adelina and her husband Hugh de Montfort had a son, whom they named Waleran in honour of his uncle. This delay gave Henry I time not only to discover what the rebels planned but also to prepare his defences. In the following months the king besieged several of the rebels' strongholds and devastated the surrounding area. The rebels in turn burned towns and countryside. Waleran Beaumont is reported to have cut off the feet of peasants he discovered collecting wood in the forest.[42]

In the spring of 1123, the rebels achieved a small but important victory when they were able to relieve Vatteville, one of Waleran Beaumont's castles, that was besieged by a royal army. Their movements had, however, not gone unnoticed by the commanders of the royal forces that had been stationed in nearby castles. Ralph of Bayeux, castellan of Évreux, called on Odo Berlong and others, and with a force of approximately 300 knights they met the rebels returning to Beaumont at Bourgtheroulde on 25th March 1124.[43]

Amaury de Montfort wished to avoid a confrontation with the royal troops, but he was overruled by the youthful and impetuous Waleran Beaumont, who wanted to prove his prowess on the battlefield and was contemptuous of the opposing force. However, it quickly became clear that Amaury had been right with his wish to avoid a battle: the royal army slowed down the charge of Waleran Beaumont and his knights by shooting their horses, and the battle turned into a rout of the rebellious forces. Many of the rebels were captured including Waleran Beaumont, Amaury de Montfort, and Waleran's three brothers-in-law, among them William Lovell.[44]

William Lovell I's adventurous escape from captivity after the battle, which Orderic Vitalis describes in some detail, ensures him a place in history books to the present day. He bribed his captor, a 'rusticus', to release him by giving him his arms. He then had his hair cut to look like a squire and made his way to the Seine. To pay for his transportation across the river William Lovell I had to use his boots as payment. He returned home without weapons, barefoot, and probably bedraggled, but no doubt happy to have escaped.[45]

Orderic Vitalis's report that William Lovell I crossed the Seine is intriguing, since Ivry and Bréval, both of which could be called his home, are situated on the same side of the River Seine as Bourgtheroulde. It is possible that Orderic Vitalis named the wrong river. C. Warren Hollister, for example, has him flee across the river Eure instead.[46] It is also possible that William Lovell I did not take the direct route home. Flight across the Seine would have added quite substantially to the length of his journey home but it would also have been much safer since his pursuers would have searched for him on the direct route to Ivry and Bréval, not in the opposite direction. Very shortly after the disastrous battle, William Lovell I made his peace with Henry I.[47]

William Lovell I was indeed lucky to have escaped. Several of the other rebels were not so fortunate and suffered serious consequences: some were incarcerated for long periods of time, including William Lovell I's brothers-in-law, Waleran Beaumont and Hugh de Châteauneuf, who were not released until five years after the battle in 1129. Hugh de Montfort remained imprisoned well into the reign of King Stephen (1135–1154). He rejected a pardon by Henry I and it is possible that his brother-in-law, Waleran Beaumont, also played a role in this prolonged imprisonment as he had gained the Montfort honour.[48] Three of Waleran's captured vassals, Odard du Pin, Geoffrey de Tourville, and Luke de la Barre, were blinded

The rebellion of 1123/24 was the last serious challenge to Henry I's rule in Normandy. In the following, comparatively quiet years little is known about William Lovell I and his family. William continued to be associated with his brother-in-law Waleran Beaumont and, if the *Gesta Normannorum Ducum* can be trusted, he and his brothers were bringing the innocent to ruin 'to the present day'.[49]

Ascelin Goël and his sons Robert Goël and William Lovell I made their names and their fortunes by acts of violence and rebellion. The unlawful and violent behaviour displayed by the three men was not unusual for the aristocracy of the time. Normandy was repeatedly disturbed by violent warfare between aristocratic families, often over disputed inheritance. Whenever an opportunity presented itself, many Norman aristocrats behaved like robber barons.

An all-overriding objective of these noblemen was to possess strategically placed castles and to hold them in their own right rather than as a castellan of the Norman dukes or of magnates like William de Breteuil. The mass expulsion of the ducal garrisons after the death of William the Conqueror was just the largest scale example. Other families, like the Giroie and Grandmesnil, tried to turn their castles into permanent possessions. Indeed, it has been judged that 'Rebellion had a fair chance of success in the duchy and rebels often succeeded in obtaining the lands and castles for which they fought'.[50] Ascelin Goël and his sons are a good example of this: they focused their ambitions on gaining control of the strategically important Castle of Ivry and succeeded because they participated in rebellions against their feudal lord.

However, seeking advantage through rebellion was a strategy with considerable risks that could just as easily have led to the destruction of the family's fortunes. Several of their contemporaries suffered severe setbacks to their careers and fortunes as a result of rebelling. Eustace de Breteuil was not only responsible for his own daughters' mutilation through his own foolishness, he also lost most of his lands, though he eventually regained Henry I's favour and received land in England. Waleran Beaumont and Hugh de Montfort suffered long imprisonment after the Battle of Bourgtheroulde. For Ascelin Goël and his sons, the strategy paid off since they always picked the right moment to concede defeat and make peace.

Through their rebelliousness they also gained valuable allies and status. Ascelin Goël's war with William de Breteuil helped him not only to temporarily secure the Castle of Ivry but also made possible his marriage to Isabel, William de Breteuil's illegitimate daughter and therefore the granddaughter of William I's steward William fitz Osbern. This marriage significantly improved the social standing of Ascelin and his family by creating a link to one of the most powerful noble houses in Normandy. The marriage also strengthened his and particularly his sons' hereditary right to Ivry. Robert Goël's timely change of allegiance ensured he was granted Ivry in 1119. William Lovell I's participation in the rebellion of 1123 was again a boost to his status through his marriage to Matilda Beaumont. She was related to several great noble families in Normandy. Through her grandmother, Adeliza of Vermandois, Matilda Beaumont could trace her family back to Charlemagne, and through her grandfather, Hugh, to the French royal family and to the German king, Henry I (see Genealogy 2). Another crucial factor for the success of the family was, as ever, luck. If William Lovell had not escaped captivity after the Battle of Bourgtheroulde, he may have languished for years in prison like his two brothers-in-law.

In these confrontations Ascelin Goël and his sons often took on men who were by far more powerful and richer than they were. Ascelin Goël waged war against William de Breteuil who was not only his liege lord but also 'one of the most powerful of the Norman magnates'. In the conflict with his brother-in-law Ascelin Goël was not discouraged by the formidable allies of Eustace de Breteuil in his pursuit to gain the Castle of Ivry, and both his sons rebelled against Henry I. In the often unsettled area of the Norman-French border the possession of an important castle, Ivry, allowed the Lovells to exert influence far greater than their wealth and status would otherwise have been possible.[51]

Ascelin Goël and his sons gained influence and wealth through swift changes between rebellion and loyalty to their feudal lord. They laid the foundations for the future prosperity of the family.

Chapter 2

The First Lovells in England

By the end of Henry I's reign, William Lovell I was a nobleman of considerable local importance and a close ally of his brother-in-law Waleran Beaumont, one of the greatest lords in Normandy. William Lovell I naming his eldest son Waleran after the boy's uncle is testament to the importance he placed on this connection. Waleran was not an unusual name at that time, but it had not been used by the family before. It is possible that William Lovell I chose Waleran Beaumont as the boy's godfather to flatter the powerful nobleman. Nonetheless, after the rebellions against Henry I had ended, William Lovell I can no longer be found in the contemporary chronicles.

It was in this time, during the 1120s, that William Lovell I received his first lands in England. Neither the exact date nor the reason for the grant are known. His brother-in-law Waleran Beaumont was released in 1129 from his long imprisonment after the Battle of Bourgtheroulde, when the death of William Clito the previous year had removed any focal point for unrest in Normandy. Waleran Beaumont was quickly reinstated in his former estates and he and his associates were granted land by the king . Possibly William Lovell was among those who profited from this royal largesse.[1]

The only pipe roll surviving from the reign of Henry I, covering the thirty-first regnal year to Michaelmas 1130, records the lands held by William Lovell I: the royal demesne lands of Southmere and Docking in Norfolk, and a rent of 100*s* (= £5) later known as Lovel Soke. Except for Lovel Soke, which William Lovell I lost to Chancellor William Longchamp, the lands remained in the hands of the family for centuries to come. William Lovell I also held land in Oxfordshire, Wiltshire, and Suffolk and was assessed for Danegeld.[2]

Danegeld was originally raised in Anglo-Saxon times to buy off Viking raiders, but it continued to be levied by the Norman kings including Henry I.[3] Danegeld was assessed at 2 shillings per hide. Originally a hide was the land necessary to sustain a household, but for tax reason it was considered to be land worth £1. The sums William Lovell I was assessed for may not appear to be particularly large – 9s (4.5 hides) 54s in Wiltshire (27 hides), 23s 2d in Norfolk (c. 11.5 hides), and 18s in Suffolk (9 hides) – in the terms of annual income, they show that William Lovell I held land worth £52 in England. This was not a great fortune but a substantial income.[4] The Danegeld assessment also shows that William Lovell I's estates were not concentrated in one area but scattered over southern England, which must have made their administration difficult.

William Lovell I founded several small religious houses, so-called cells, near his estates in Minster Lovell (Oxfordshire), in Elcombe (Wiltshire), and Docking (Norfolk). These cells were controlled by the Abbey of St. Mary, Ivry. The abbey already had two cells, Asthall and Fulbrook, which had probably been gifted to the abbey by its founder Roger d'Ivry. In 1183/84 William Lovell I's widow Matilda, with the assent of her son William Lovell II, gave the church of Minster Lovell itself to the St. Mary.[5]

Foundations like these cells controlled by a mother house, in this case the well-established monastery St. Mary, was common practice at this time. The monastic reform movements, like the one originating in Cluny, propagated a stronger centralisation than had been common before. Even though St. Mary was a Benedictine monastery, the reform movements influenced this order as well. Many of these cells, including those founded by the Lovells, were so small, they could not exist on their own. Minster Lovell, for example, was to have two monks at most and was hardly able to sustain itself.

For noble families holding lands in Normandy and in England it was natural to place the cells they established in England under the control of a Norman monastery. The conquest of Normandy by Philip Augustus (1180–1223) in 1204 dramatically altered the situation. The cells were now subject to a foreign authority. It was Edward I who first seized all 'alien' religious houses in 1295. The term 'alien priories' became commonly used for all religious institutions under the control of Norman mother houses. The confiscation prevented that revenue from England was used by a hostile power. This income would instead be at the disposal of the Exchequer. Fear of spies, real or imaginary, was another reason brought forward to justify the measure.[6]

The alien priories continued to be taken into the king's hand during the long wars with France and were finally seized in 1414.[7] As was the fate of many religious houses, the descendants of their founders had little interest in their upkeep. The Lovells profited from the suppression of these alien priories, as Minster Lovell and its cells were on several occasions granted to them.[8] By this time, the Lovells like their noble contemporaries must have lost most if not all emotional connections to the religious houses their ancestors in Normandy supported. To profit from the revenue of alien priories, small as they were, was certainly more in their interest than to see these funds go to Normandy. In 1441, the rent of the alien priory of Minster Lovell and its subordinate cells were bestowed on King's College, Eton, presumably by William Lovell III, who was holding them at this time.[9]

Even though the cell in Minster Lovell was suppressed in the fifteenth century, the memory of its existence was long lasting. By the early eighteenth century the ruins of Minster Lovell Hall were thought to have been the building of the alien priory.[10]

To found these cells and to administer his English possessions William Lovell I must have spent time in England, but his interests remained firmly in Normandy. The general scarcity of records in this period does leave much of the live of William Lovell I in the dark. His appearance in the witness list of a charter of Waleran Beaumont on 5 March 1139 is evidence that William Lovell I was a member of the circle of nobles around his brother-in-law.[11] Keeping good relations with this powerful neighbour and relative was a wise step and profitable for both.

The death of Henry I in 1135 was followed by a long civil war that affected both England and Normandy as Henry I's his daughter the 'Empress' Matilda and his nephew Stephen of Blois fought for the throne. Many noblemen, like William Lovell I's brother-in-law Waleran Beaumont or Roger de Tosny, used the unsettled times to engage in a private war.[12]

No existing record confirms that William Lovell I became actively involved in this conflict. William Lovell I may have been reluctant to risk his life and fortunes in this troublesome time and remained on his estates until the question of succession had been resolved. It is, however, always dangerous to argue from a lack of records. William Lovell I belonged to a society for whom war was a fundamental part of live. Men of his rank were expected to participate in the conflicts around them, their role as warriors was the very reason for their elevated position: they held land in return for military service in war and increasingly administrative service in times of peace. It would have been difficult, though not impossible, for a man of William Lovell I's status to stay aloof from the conflicts. It is more likely that his name does not appear in the chronicles because he held a subordinate role and refrained from committing the kind of outrageous behaviour his father Ascelin Goël had shown and which had attracted the attention of Orderic Vitalis.

William Lovell I probably followed the example of his brother-in-law Waleran Beaumont, who like the majority of aristocrats first supported Stephen of Blois.[13] When Geoffrey of Anjou had conquered Normandy in 1141, William Lovell I supported Geoffrey of Anjou's wife and Henry I's daughter Matilda, once more following Waleran Beaumont's lead.[14] At some time between 1144 and 1150, William Lovell I was employed as a justice by the new duke of Normandy. Together with Guy de Sablé, William was in charge of the bailiwicks of Verneuil and Nonancourt. Another rare record of William Lovell I from this period, is a writ Geoffrey Plantagenet addressed to William Lovell I.[15]

William Lovell I is one of the many supporters of Waleran Beaumont who witnesses a charter of Henry Plantagenet after he had succeeded his father as duke of Normandy in 1150. This was, however, the only surviving charter of the new ruler Waleran Beaumont and his entourage attested.[16] While for the most part William Lovell I profited from being a close ally of Waleran Beaumont this alliance could also be dangerous. Waleran Beaumont's conflict with his brother-in-law Simon de Montfort and nephew Robert de Montfort spread to affect William Lovell I. As part of the retaliation his lands in Normandy and France were devastated by Simon de Montfort, Count of Evreux in 1153.[17] William Lovell I was, for good and for bad, part of Waleran Beaumont's network of allies in Normandy.

No records exist clarifying when William Lovell I died. It is only possible to state, as the *Complete Peerage* does, 'he was living in 1166, but dead in 1170'. His wife, Matilda, outlived him by at least twenty years and died after 1189.[18]

After William Lovell I's death, the family split into a Norman and an English branch. Though the evidence is fragmentary, the bulk of William Lovell I's lands in Normandy and France were inherited by his eldest son Waleran d'Ivry, while most of the English lands were given to his younger son William Lovell II. At this time primogeniture had not yet become the dominant principle of inheritance and estates were often divided along the lines of patrimony, the lands a father had inherited, and acquisition, those estates he had acquired within his own lifetime. The patrimony passed to the eldest son while land that only recently came into the hands of the family were given to a younger son. The most famous example of this form of inheritance is the division of the lands of William the Conqueror: his eldest son Robert Curthose inherited his father's patrimony, the duchy of Normandy, while the second son William Rufus (1087–1100), inherited the conquered kingdom of England. The patrimony of noble families was usually the lands held in Normandy while the acquisitions, the lands that had been granted to them after the Conquest, were situated in England. Effectively, the estates were split along the Channel.

Many Norman nobles followed this principle, for example the Montforts of Montfort-sur-Risle in 1088 or the Montgomerys in 1094. It was not only that a division of the heritage into patrimony and acquisition was a tradition, splitting the estates into a Norman and English part of the lands was also sensible as the Channel 'was a physical barrier' which made administration of cross-channel estates difficult.[19]

However, other factors played a role as well: some families only had one male heir who inherited the entire estates; in other families, as for example the Beaumonts, each son received lands on both sides of the channel. William Lovell I's estates were not divided precisely into an English and a Norman part between his son. William Lovell II also held some lands in Normandy.[20] This separation of the lands was similar to the great estates held by Robert Beaumont, Count of Meulan. His eldest son Waleran Beaumont inherited the majority of his father's lands in Normandy, while the younger twin Robert's inheritance was mainly located in England. Both brothers also were given estates on the other side of the Channel.[21] Since the Beaumont twins were the brothers of William Lovell I's wife Matilda it is possible that he William modelled the division of his own estates on that of the Beaumonts.

It is possible that Minster Lovell, Elcombe and Docking were inherited by Waleran d'Ivry, since according to Robert of Torigni they were confiscated by the Crown after Waleran d'Ivry participated in the revolt of Henry, 'the Young King' against his father Henry II in 1173.[22] However, it is more likely that William Lovell II had inherited these estates and they were confiscated because he had also participated in the rebellion. According to a charter from the time of King John (1199–1216), these estates had been given to William Lovell II by his father and brother. Since William Lovell I had died by 1170, they must have been in the hands of William Lovell II at the time of the 'Young King's' rebellion.

Only a few facts are known about William Lovell II's life due to several factors. First of all, having inherited only a part of the estates held by his father, he was less wealthy and therefore less powerful. None of his English estates were of strategic importance either. It was, after all, the struggle for the powerful border fortress of Ivry that propelled both Ascelin Goël and his sons to prominence. Secondly, many of the government records that provide information about the family in later centuries had not yet been introduced and fewer records have survived.

Unlike his father's and grandfather's wives, who can be identified, all we know about William Lovell II's wife is her name: Isabel. However, it is worth remembering that some of the later Lady Lovells can also not be identified with certainty, even though their husband were of higher rank than William Lovell II and the number of surviving records is greater. A woman who was not an heiress often can only be connected to a specific family if she was granted land from a father or, as in the cases of Isabel de Breteuil or Matilda Beaumont, the circumstances of the marriage was unusual. What can be said with certainty is that Isabel was a member of a noble family of similar rank as William Lovell II, a well-off knight or baron.

William Lovell II was one of the knights who accompanied Richard I (1189–1199) when he joined the Third Crusade shortly after he became king. While no record explicitly states that William Lovell II journeyed overseas with the king, there is strong evidence that he did. When the Abbot of St Edmund was pardoned scutage, the tax that could be paid in lieu for service, for those knights who went to Jerusalem with the king, one of the knights mentioned was William Lovell II.[23]

It was probably at this time that his mother, Matilda Beaumont, granted him the manor Minster (Lovell) (Oxfordshire), which would later become one of the main residences of the family. William Lovell II bestowed Minster (Lovell) on his wife Isabel as her dower. As Isabel gave her assent to a grant of two mills by William Lovell II to the monks of Thame they were either part of her dower or her own estates.[24]

In the grant William Lovell II is styled 'William Lovell of Minster'. The reference to a particular place, made to differentiate between different men with the same surname, was to their main residence. Since Minster was one of the main residences of the Lovell family for centuries it was increasingly associated with them and became to be known as Minster Lovell to differentiate it from other places bearing the same name. While many towns added topographical information, for example the river the town was situated on, several others became identified with noble families who had a strong links to the place. Other examples are Farleigh Hungerford, Acton Burnell, and Ashby de la Zouch. Great Hallingbury in Essex is also known as Hallingbury Morley, a name derived from the Morley family who were descendants of William Lovell II.

Since records are sparse, references to William Lovell II can be found only on a few occasion. Like all noblemen of the time, he must have travelled frequently to visit his estates in various parts of England and, at least on occasion, to attend the royal court. He was at Poitiers in 1199 when he witnessed Queen Eleanor's confirmation for the monastery of St John in Poitiers. In 1201 William Lovell II, like many other noblemen, refused to serve in King John's unpopular expedition to Poitou. In fact, so many of the King's tenants in chief did, that the King was forced to sail with an army of mercenaries.

Just as most of his life is elusive, the date of death is equally uncertain. He was still alive in 1212 and dead in 1213, when his widow claimed her dower. William Lovell II's son and heir, John Lovell I, was a minor at the time of his father's death.[25]

The change of first name from William to John could mean that John Lovell I was a younger son whose elder brother William had died young. However, his name could also have been chosen to honour his godfather, a relative of his mother Isabel for example. Or his parents simply followed the fashion. At this time, John was becoming an increasingly popular name and remained one of the most frequently used names throughout the Middle Ages and beyond.

Since William Lovell II was a tenant-in-chief, holding land directly from the king, it was the king who automatically became the guardian of William Lovell II's minor son. The wardships of his tenants-in-chief were lucrative for the monarch. The guardians had the right to collect the revenue of the wards' estates and also arrange their marriages, if their families had not done so already. The king could either keep the wardship and marriage for his own profit or he could grant them as rewards to his supporters or sell them for a profit. Some guardians ransacked the estates by exploiting the resources of the lands, felling woods without replanting, failing to invest in the upkeep of the property through repairs of buildings or infrastructure to recoup the money they had paid for the wardships.

Often the guardian married the ward to a son or daughter or other close relative. Many nobles feared that low-ranking courtiers who had received the warship and marriage of a noble heir or heiress would marry them to their own daughters or sons. This practice led to complaints that the wards were disparaged by being married to partners below their own status. Complaints both of disparagement of wards and of guardians exploiting estates were common throughout the Middle Ages. They were raised particularly often in the reign of King John.

Since a significant percentage of nobles died when their heirs were still under age the problem of wardships was weighing heavily on the minds of the parents. Almost half of the Lovell heirs were minors and this was not unusual. Nobles therefore tried to ensure the safety of both their heirs and their estates from exploitation in a time when they could no longer do so themselves.

When King John and the rebellious barons came to an agreement that was supposed to end the civil war in 1215, Magna Carta, it included three articles or chapters trying to stop these misuses. Chapter 4 stipulates that the lands of minor wards should not be exploited and only reasonable revenues, customary dues, and services extracted from them. Chapter 5 states that houses, parks, preserves, fishponds, mills as well as all necessary tools have to be maintained in good condition and sufficient quantity. Chapter 6 declares that no heir should be disparaged and that his next of kin had to be informed before the marriage took place.

Despite these provisions in Magna Carta, exploitation of estates and disparagements of heirs remained a problem throughout the Middle Ages. Over time the nobility developed a number of other methods, like enfeoffements to use, to protect their lands if they should die while their heirs were under age. While the fear of disparagement of an heir was always present, a suitable marriage arranged by a guardian could benefit not only the guardian's family who was able to provide a husband of sufficient means for a daughter or a prosperous wife for a son, these matches could also be profitable to the wards, by creating a strong link to another powerful family.

King John granted John Lovell I's wardship to Alan Basset, one of his most loyal supporters. Though Alan Basset himself was not one of the 'most wicked councillors' of King John, Roger of Wendover writes that his elder brother Thomas Basset was.[26] By August 1216 John Lovell I was married to his guardian's daughter. Her name has been given as Aliva but according to later entries in the patent rolls she was called Katherine. (see Chapter 3).[27] The effects this marriage had on the fortunes of the Lovell family became apparent only decades later when Philip Lovell and John Lovell II benefited from the marriage arranged for John Lovell I by Alan Basset (see Genealogy 3).

The connections created between families through marriages could and did influence the behaviour of the individual nobleman, but they did not dictate it. Particularly in political crises their choices were also based on other considerations. When a large number of high-ranking noblemen rebelled against King John, Alan Basset remained a loyal supporter of the king. He and his brother Thomas Basset were named among the counsellors of King John in Magna Carta. His son-in-law John Lovell I joined the baronial opposition against the John and his lands were forfeited in 1216.[28] No further evidence survives about John Lovell I's involvement in the civil war. The death of King John allowed the minority government of Henry III (1216–1272), headed by William Marshall, to expel the French army which occupied considerable parts of southern England and to restore peace. John Lovell I probably also regained his estates after the end of the war.

The following years were still troubled by violent conflicts. Some of the men who had gained power and influence in the final years of John's reign, as well as neighbouring princes, hoped to extend their influence during the minority of Henry III. In 1223, Llewelyn ap Iorwerth, King of Gwynedd (1195–1240), besieged Builth Castle. The government summoned all tenants-in-chief, but John Lovell I refused to comply so that his lands were forfeited again.[29] However, it seems that his lands were restored to him after only a short period of time. The renewed confiscation of his lands probably had a sobering effect on John Lovell I. When the nobility was called out again to the siege of Bedford Castle, where William de Bréauté had retreated after kidnapping a royal official the following year, John Lovell I followed the order.[30]

In the reign of Henry III the scope and breadth of surviving records of the royal administration is already quite extensive. Since the Lovells were still only of minor importance, it is often impossible to ascertain which Lovell family is referred to in the government records. Lovell was a name used by various families and the popularity of the first names John and William increase the possibility of mistakes. Grant G. Simpson writes about his difficulties in trying to identify several members of Roger de Qunicy's *familia*. William Lovell 'proved impossible to trace, since his name is so common'.[31] This William Lovell from Chalton (Beds.) was not related to the Lovells of Titchmarsh since they did not hold any land in Bedfordshire.

This difficulty also occurs in later periods, but the richer and more powerful the Lovells of Titchmarsh became the easier it is to identify them. Even the royal administration occasionally mixed up men with the same name. As late as 1388, John Lovell VII's goods and lands were confiscated although it was a different John Lovell from Yorkshire who should have been distrained.[32]

In the middle of the thirteenth century, the Patent Rolls repeatedly mention John and William Lovell, sometimes styled 'king's huntsmen'. In some cases it is possible to deduct which Lovell is referred to, in others it is impossible to make a clear identification. Did John Lovell I receive two stags and six hinds from the royal Forest of Brayden (Wilts.) or was it one of the king's huntsmen? The royal huntsman may seem the more likely recipient. However, by this time, John Lovell I's younger brother Philip Lovell was serving in the royal administration and received similar gifts. It is therefore possible that John Lovell I benefited from his brother's position at court and he was the recipient of these stags and hinds.[33]

Keeping these difficulties in mind, John Lovell I can be identified on several occasions when fulfilling his role in the local administrations of Oxfordshire. When the Charter of the Forests was reissued in 1225, he was one of the twelve men appointed to the perambulation of the forest in Oxfordshire.[34] On two occasions, in the years 1236 and 1249 John Lovell I was granted the tallages of his manors of Southmere and Docking. The latter case specifies that it was a reward for the services of his men.[35] John Lovell I may also have served as a justice at an assize of novel disseisin held at Wilton (Wiltshire) in 1230.[36]

John Lovell I died shortly before 23 December 1252 when the writ to hold the inquisitions post mortem was sent out.[37] John Lovell I's widow, Katherine Basset, did not marry again though she outlived him by at least 15 years (see next chapter).

William Lovell II and John Lovell I are relatively obscure to us, particularly in comparison to their Norman ancestors, Ascelin Goël, Robert Goël, and William Lovell I. Their landed wealth was smaller, they were less powerful, and were therefore of only little interest to the royal administration and the chroniclers of the time. Their relative obscurity and the popularity of both their surname and their first names makes it difficult to trace them.

While little as is known about their lives, William Lovell II and his son were still members of the small elite ruling the country. Already in the next decades the Lovells become more visible, thanks to a combination of a larger number of surviving records as well as the closer involvement with the royal court by John Lovell I's younger brother Philip Lovell and son John Lovell II.

Chapter 3

Law and Connections

Philip Lovell entered the church and made a career as a royal administrator and justice. He was not the only Lovell to do so, but he had the most successful, if turbulent, career. Although entering the church and advancing through its ranks was one way of advancement common at the time for younger sons, for Philip Lovell this was not the path he initially took. He had married Alexander de Arsic's widow, whose name is unfortunately unknown. They had two sons, Philip Lovell the younger and Henry Lovell, and one daughter, Amicia, wife of Richard de Curzon of Derbyshire. At some time after his wife's death, Philip Lovell entered the church. In 1231 he was rector of Lutterworth in Leicestershire, a position he was given by Nicholas de Verdun, a rich landowner with property in Leicestershire.

It is likely that Nicholas de Verdun also helped Philip Lovell to a position in the service of Roger de Quincy, Earl of Winchester, Lord of Galloway, and Constable of Scotland whose subtenant he was.[1] Philip Lovell served as steward of the earl's English estates and was one of the men who frequently witnessed charters by him.[2]

To advance in the service of a great nobleman, it was necessary to prove one's capabilities. Grants of lands or appointments to offices were not simply handed out, they had to be earned. Men like Roger de Quincy wanted their estates run efficiently and without disturbances. Philip Lovell's further career shows that he was an able administrator who won the respect of two kings, but was possibly greedy enough to break the law.

Philip Lovell came in contact with other important men in the service of Roger de Quincy, and his ability to win their respect and friendship helped his career. As de Quincy's steward, Philip Lovell travelled to Scotland where he met and won the friendship of King Alexander II (1214–1249) and his wife, as Mathew Paris reports. It also brought Philip Lovell in contact with the English royal court. That there were frequent meetings of the royal household and that of the earl of Winchester is attested by the fact that several members of de Quincy's *familia* entered royal service. Philip Lovell soon profited from this connection as by 1247 he had gained the confidence of William Mauduit, chamberlain of the English royal Exchequer. William Mauduit gave him the rectorship of the church of Henslope.[3] This position provided him with a good income and, it seems, like many other noblemen and administrators of the time, he tried to extend this income. After Philip Lovell's death an inquest came to the conclusion that he had unlawfully appropriated the right of view of frankpledge from William Mauduit.[4]

Philip Lovell also made the acquaintance and gained the support of John Mansel. It was Mansel, an administrator and royal councillor, who brought Philip into royal service. Philip Lovell was appointed a justiciary of the Jews by 1249, but was dismissed only two years later, in 1251, after being accused of taking bribes in return for reducing their taxes. He was also fined 10 marks of gold. John Mansel came to his aid and paid this hefty fine. Additionally, Mansel arranged a petition by King Alexander III (1249–1286) of Scotland to restore Philip Lovell to royal favour, which he did for his parents' friendship with Philip Lovell.[5] Mansel may have felt responsible for the man he himself had introduced to royal service, but he would not have spent his energy and a considerable sum of money had he thought Philip Lovell unworthy of the efforts. The accusation must have been credible, but was possibly exaggerated as the result of a dispute within the royal administration.

John Mansel's attempt was certainly successful, as only a year after being dismissed as a justiciary, in 1252, Philip Lovell became Treasurer of England.[6] As treasurer, Philip Lovell was at the centre of royal administration and his name is appears constantly in the administrative records. The *Liberate Rolls*, the writs ordering the money to be paid out of the royal treasury, contain fascinating information about Philip Lovell's role as treasurer. Most frequently, he is the person who authorised the reimbursement of expenditure on behalf of the king. These include purchases of wine for the royal household, wax for candles, jewellery, and clothes. The size of the royal household was substantial, and the orders for items for consumption staggering. For Christmas 1254, over 10,000 pounds of wax, 385 pounds of pepper and 386 pounds of ginger were purchased. In October Philip Lovell bought 8,600 pounds of wax. He also ordered money to be paid out to sheriffs for expenditure on buildings or transporting treasure or household goods for the king. He oversaw the payments of dower money from Ireland to Eleanor, Countess of Leicester, the sister of Henry III and wife of Simon de Montfort. Occasionally, the rolls also report that Philip Lovell himself purchased items for the royal household, including gold-wrought cloths for the queen, large numbers of gold rings bought from various sources, or embroidered copes for the king to donate to a church. He also received an allowance of £40 for his own expenses in service to the king. Among his other duties Philip Lovell delivered wine to various royal residences on several occasions. The role of treasurer was varied, often hands-on, and required continuous travelling, both with the royal court and independently of it.[7]

The king was the greatest patron, and royal service was very lucrative. Philip Lovell was granted the wardship and marriage of the heirs of Vivian de Staundon, free pasture in several royal forests, and prebends and benefices worth 200 marks annually.[8] On occasion he was also gifted deer and wood from royal forests. Constant contact with the king also meant that trespasses were more easily forgiven, as in 1250, when Philip Lovell was pardoned for hunting in the royal forest of Sherwood while he was passing through.[9]

As treasurer Philip Lovell was a man whose goodwill was worth cultivating. Hugh de Marshall made him keeper of his lands, and Hugh de Mancetter granted Philip Lovell lands in Dunton, Warwickshire.[10] He also acquired, most likely by purchase, the manors of Little Brickhill in Buckinghamshire, Littlebury in Essex, and Snotescombe in Northamptonshire.[11]

Philip Lovell's nephew John Lovell II most likely profited from his uncle's career at court and his closeness to the king. Another and stronger influence on John Lovell II was the family of his mother Katherine Basset. Most of her numerous brothers were actively and closely involved with the royal court. Her eldest brother, Thomas, was a Crown servant. Gilbert Basset was a household knight and served on many campaigns. He rebelled against Henry III but was restored to grace and continued actively serving at court until his death. Fulk Basset was elected bishop of London in 1241, possibly against the wishes of Henry III. The king and Fulk did on occasion quarrel about a variety of issues but generally they were on good terms. Another brother, Philip Basset, had also rebelled against the king in the 1230s, but regained Henry III's favour. After accompanying Richard of Cornwall on crusade Philip Basset became an important administrator and justiciar. Yet another brother, Henry Basset, was in royal service in Ireland. The Bassets were a family dedicated to royal service, though the relationship was on occasion tempestuous.[12]

Having several uncles already at court certainly facilitated John Lovell II's entry into royal service. His relationship to his mother's family was very close and can be seen in the coat of arms he adopted around this time. Though royalty and nobility had displayed coats of arms on seals and armours for more than a century at this time, they became more common in the thirteenth century. Their use had not become regulated yet and coats of arms were not regarded as the exclusive property of one family. Sometimes different members of one family used different coats of arms, sometimes one person used different coat of arms at different times, and some men adopted the arms of their lord. Often some difference was added to distinguish them from their lord's, but not always.[13]

The coat of arms of the Lovells, *barry nebuly or and gules*, is an adaptation of the Basset arms. The arms of Justiciar Philip Basset are recorded in a number of heraldic rolls as *barry undy or and gules* (Camden Roll, c. 1280, and Charles' Roll, c. 1285, as well as in the St. George's Roll, c. 1285, and Heralds Roll, c. 1279). The earliest existing version of the Lovell arms is John Lovell II's seal on a grant dating from the last years of Henry III's or the early years of Edward I's reign (1272–1307). The seal shows three bars *nebuly* with a three-pointed label. Later his arms are recorded in the Camden Roll and the Charles' Roll as *barry undy or and gules, a label azure*.[14]

Another indication of the influence of the Basset family on the Lovells at this time is that Katherine Basset and John Lovell I may have named their younger son Fulk in honour of his uncle Fulk Basset, Bishop of London. A Fulk Lovell entered the church around 1242 and came to some prominence within the hierarchy. His relationship with the Lovells of Titchmarsh cannot be firmly established, but there is some evidence that make it possible, even likely. In 1277, Fulk Lovell was named as proctor of Ivry Abbey for its estates in England. The Lovells had endowed several cells of the abbey near their lands (see previous chapter). By ensuring that a younger son was appointed proctor for the motherhouse they secured him an income and ensured the estates were properly supervised.

Like his Basset relatives and his uncle Philip Lovell, Fulk Lovell entered royal service. He served as king's clerk, archdeacon of Colchester, canon of York, and more. In 1272, he was appointed guardian of the spirituality of the bishopric of London and in 1280, after the death of John de Chishull, he was elected bishop of London but resigned. Richard of Gravesend was elected instead.[15] Fulk Lovell and Philip Basset endowed a chantry in St Paul's in London together. Though the joint endowment could have been two royal administrators working together, it certainly supports the theory that they were nephew and uncle.[16]

John Lovell II did follow his relatives into royal service, but unlike them he took the more traditionally noble route of military service. He was in the service of Henry III's eldest son Edward by 1255, when he was accompanied him to Gascony. Two years later he participated in the unsuccessful campaign against Prince Llewelyn of Wales (1246–1282).[17]

At some unspecified time, possibly even before his father's death, John Lovell II married Maud de Sydenham. She was the heiress of William de Sydenham, who had died before 1233. Little information exists about her family. They held the manor of Titchmarsh in Northamptonshire, which passed to the Lovell family and became the main residence of the family. As an heiress, Maud de Sydenham was a desirable bride for any aspiring minor nobleman or younger son. It is possible, even likely, that this profitable match was arranged or at least helped along by one of John Lovell II's relatives at court. An interesting note is that the Lovells continued to use the coat of arms of the Sydenhams, *gules, three padlocks or,* in decorations, as in the Lovell Lectionary, but also quite prominently as on the tomb of John Lovell IX in Minster Lovell. The family continued to proudly show their connection to the Sydenhams, long after that family disappeared.[18]

The discontent with the partiality of the rule of Henry III, which had increasingly alienated a large number of barons, turned into an armed conflict towards the end of the 1250s. The causes of this conflict are complicated, but two interrelated problems were at the heart of it: the king's favouritism of a particular group of administrators and his family, and his inability or unwillingness to reign them in when they bullied others or even broke the law. In the middle of the 1250s the critics of the king found a charismatic and skilled leader in Simon de Montfort, Earl of Leicester and husband of the king's sister Eleanor. Eleanor and her husband also had their personal grievances against Henry III, mostly about Eleanor's dower from her first marriage to William Marshall the younger and other outstanding debts. As treasurer Philip Lovell assured the payment of the king's debts to Simon de Montfort in 1257, and it is therefore unsurprising that he was one of the courtiers singled out for criticism.[19]

In 1258, Philip Lovell was arrested and charged with plundering the royal forest of Whittlewood. Shortly afterwards, in November the same year, he was removed from office on the demands of the barons. Philip Lovell retired to his church in Hamestable and died in the following year, according to Matthew Paris, 'of grief and bitterness that the king, whom he had served so much, was unforgiving'.[20]

Philip Lovell was a controversial figure. While Matthew Paris calls him a prudent, eloquent, and magnanimous man, his position within the government and the way he fulfilled his post provoked the hostility of his contemporaries. It is their judgement that is often repeated by modern historians. J.R. Maddicott, for example, describes him as 'a man with a bad reputation for corrupt and oppressive behaviour'.[21] It is hardly surprising that opinions about Philip Lovell were so divided in his own time. As treasurer it was his duty to collect as much money for the royal treasury as possible. Naturally, the more diligently he went about his work, the more people were upset with his conduct and accused him of performing his inquiries into the king's revenues too harshly.[22] Additionally, in times of political crises it was a standard tactic to attack those close to the king and blame all the ills in the country on them. The king was badly advised, the men leading his administration were corrupt and self-serving and had to be replaced. While often true, these attacks were also used to settle private scores or to avoid criticising the king himself (see also Chapter 5).

Philip Lovell's dismissal from court did not discourage John Lovell II from service to the Crown. In fact, it may have strengthened his support, since his uncle was dismissed on the insistence of the barons, not the king. Like his Basset relatives he remained a staunch loyalist. In the following years of crisis, he was appointed to several offices. In 1261 and again in 1264, he was appointed sheriff of Cambridge and Huntingdon. In 1264 he was also appointed constable of Northampton Castle.[23]

Though John Lovell II was slowly rising within royal service, it is sometimes still difficult to determine whether it was John Lovell II or another John Lovell who was receiving a royal grant, as in 1261, when a John Lovell was granted £20 from the king, or when a John Lovell was given the right to hunt not only cats, badgers, foxes, but also deer in a string of counties in southern England (see also previous chapter).[24]

When the conflict between the king and the disaffected barons turned into outright war, John Lovell II fought on Henry III's side in the disastrous Battle of Lewes. He was taken prisoner by the victorious barons, as was the king's brother Richard of Cornwall and John Lovell's uncle Philip Basset. To pay his ransom, John Lovell III had to lease three of his manors in Norfolk, Titchwell, Southmere, and Docking, in 1265.[25] That John Lovell II granted the marriage of his eldest son John Lovell III to Warin de Bassingbourne in October 1265 could have been a result of his indebtedness.[26]

The Barons' War lasted another two years until the Battle of Evesham on 4 August 1265 and the death of Simon de Montfort. Among the other casualties was Hugh Despenser, who was married to Philip Basset's daughter Alina. Despite his father-in-law's close allegiance with Henry III, Hugh Despenser fought and died on the side of the barons. Philip Basset had not been able to persuade his son-in-law to follow his political course, but the ties to his daughter and her family were not permanently ruptured. After Hugh Despenser forfeited his estates, they were granted to Philip Basset. He in turn gave them to his daughter Alina, Hugh's widow, who in turn gave them to her son.[27]

Among the rebels who continued to resist the victorious king after the Battle of Evesham, holding a castle (probably Kenilworth) against him, were John, Robert, and Thomas Lovell. In August 1265, Henry III ordered the persistent rebels to leave, hand over the castle to Henry III, and to rebel no more.[28] It is tempting to assume that John, Robert, and Thomas Lovell were the sons of John Lovell II. His eldest son was called John and he had a younger son called Thomas. Despite the fact that John Lovell II remained Henry III's loyal supporter throughout the war, his sons may not have followed his course. Even Henry III's eldest son and heir Edward had for a time sided with the disaffected barons. However, John Lovell II's sons were almost certainly too young. John Lovell III would have been about 10 years old in 1265, as he was said to be 32 or 30 at his father's death in 1287. Though the *Inquisitions post mortem* are often vague about the ages of heirs as long as they were of full age, they were not completely off the mark. Boys in their teens could be caught up in a civil war, but they generally did so only when accompanying their father or other close relative, as happened to Thomas Lovell and his young sons in 1327, rather than being found fighting on the opposing side of the conflict (see next chapter).

The Barons' War caused widespread disturbances that did not only affect those who fought in battles. According to the sheriff's report, in 1266 several malefactors broke a chest which was stored at the Abbey of Sulby in Northamptonshire and, since it did not contain any of the precious objects they had expected, they threw the chest that contained deeds belonging to Katherine Basset into the water outside nearby Welford.[29]

For his faithful service to the king, John Lovell II received rewards. He was granted the lands forfeited by James Savage for his participation in the rebellion. James Savage redeemed his lands by paying John Lovell II a fine in 1266, which must have been welcome particularly in light of the financial problems he had experienced.[30] After the end of the Barons' War John Lovell II took on more administrative duties. He was appointed to a commission to confiscate the lands of the defeated rebels in Northamptonshire in the immediate aftermath of the war, and in 1267, he was among the men appointed to find royal land that had been illegally seized during the Barons' Wars and restore it to the king.[31] Royal patronage helped John Lovell II to overcome his financial difficulties. In 1268, he was granted weekly market in Docking and a yearly market in Docking, Southmere and Elcombe.[32]

A few years after the end of the Barons' Wars, in 1268, Edward, Henry III's son and heir, his brother Edmund, and a large number of noblemen decided to join the crusade. Pope Urban IV had promoted this crusade since 1263, and King Louis IX of France (1226–1270) had already taken the cross the year before.[33] Among the numerous noblemen who joined the crusade now was John Lovell II. He received license to lease the manors of Southmere, Docking, and Elcombe to raise money to pay for his expenses. One of the lessees was Henry Lovell, the son of Philip Lovell. His status as a crusader his estates alone should have protected his estates from attacks and spoliation by neighbours who remained behind during his absence, but John Lovell II also received protection from the king to go abroad for four years, officially sanctioning his absence and confirming the king's protection of the Lovell estates.[34]

The crusade against Tunis was led by Louis IX. Edward and the English contingent were delayed several times and when they arrived in Tunis, Louis IX had died and the campaign was over. The English crusaders continued to Acre, where they achieved some victories. However, the crusade did not prevent the collapse of the remaining crusader territories that followed not long afterwards.

It is hardly surprising that we know nothing about John Lovell's participation in the crusade, or even when he returned to England. Not all crusaders returned at the same time. Both Edward's brother, Edmund of Lancaster, and William de Valence, Earl of Pembroke, left the Holy Land before Edward himself.[35] John Lovell II may have been abroad between 1272 and 1275, since he is not mentioned in either the Patent or the Close Rolls in those years.

That fact that John Lovell II's eldest son, John Lovell III, went on campaign in Wales in his father's place in 1276–77, could be an indication that John Lovell II, who was by then about 54, returned from the crusade in poor health. In 1282 two 'servants' fulfilled John Lovell II's military service in his stead.[36] John Lovell II continued to receive gifts of deer and wood from Edward I.[37] Even though, as before, it is not certain that the John Lovell who received the gift was in fact John Lovell II, it is quite possible that Edward I would favour a companion from crusade, particularly if that crusade had ruined his health.

From 1280 onward, John Lovell II was excused from almost all administrative tasks, like attending the eyres and the eyres of the forests.[38] In these entries he is often styled John Lovell 'the elder' to differentiate him from his son and namesake John Lovell III. John Lovell II died in summer of 1287.[39] His wife Maud de Sydenham survived him, but no information seems to exist on the date of her death.

Both Philip Lovell and his nephew John Lovell II made their career in royal government. It is the reason that Lovells become more visible to us in the surviving records from the middle of the thirteenth century. The two men used the two different options available: administration and military service. Philip Lovell was a career clerk and lawyer, advancing to one of the highest positions in the government as treasurer. John Lovell II chose military service, but later in life, he also served in the administration of the localities in which his estates were situated. Military service was the traditional role of the nobility, but their administrative work in the localities was of vital importance as well. They brought the decisions of the central administration to the localities and reported back problems and grievances from the areas of influence (see also Chapter 5).

Personal relationships are very difficult or impossible to trace at this time, but they played an important, sometimes vital role. Philip Lovell and John Lovell II were helped by their connections to powerful men in their advancement at court. Philip Lovell was aided by John Mansel and once even by King Alexander III of Scotland. John Lovell II could rely on his relationship to both his paternal uncle Philip Lovell as well as his maternal uncles, the Bassets, for help and aid.

However, family relationships themselves did not necessarily and automatically create advancement. They provided an opportunity for those who were interested and capable of seeking it. Nor did family ties dictate which side a nobleman took in political controversies. There are good reasons why civil wars are often decried as pitching members of the same family against each other. This was the case for Alina Basset, daughter and heiress of Philip Basset, who was married to Hugh Despenser. During the Barons' War, Hugh Despenser fought on the side of the Barons, while Philip Basset remained stoutly loyal to Henry III.

Royal service allowed the nobility to participate in royal government. Philip Lovell's prominence in the administration of his time is a good example of the opportunities a career in the law could give a younger son from a minor noble family. The most obvious benefit of royal service was that the royal court was the centre of patronage. Both Philip Lovell and John Lovell II reaped the rewards for their work in the form of gifts from the royal government of deer and wood and grants. Philip Lovell acquired a number of estates during his time as treasurer, which were divided after his death between his children and John Lovell II. John Lovell II also gained from his service and felt affluent enough to provide for his younger son Thomas with the manor of Titchwell in Norfolk and his illegitimate son, also called John Lovell, by granting him the manor of Snotescombe, which had formerly belonged to Philip Lovell.

We have seen, though, that royal service was not only profitable but also could be dangerous. Philip Lovell's career shows both the possibilities for advancement and the pitfalls. He rose high in the administration only to be dismissed and die disgraced and exiled from court.

The history of the Lovells in the next few decades was influenced by both sides of royal service: its chances of advancement and its dangers.

Chapter 4

The Profits and Perils of Service

W hen John Lovell III inherited the Lovell estates after his father's death, he was in his 30s, a widower with a daughter, and possibly already remarried. He also had already been in royal service when fulfilled his father's military service in Wales with Edward I in 1276–77.

His first wife, Isabel du Bois, the daughter of Arnold du Bois, had died in 1280. Her uncle William du Bois had been a household knight of Roger de Quincy, Earl of Winchester in whose household Philip Lovell had started his career. Philip Lovell and William du Bois had died when John Lovell III was only a little boy of about 5, and Philip Lovell had left Roger de Quincy's service even earlier. It is therefore unlikely that either of them played a role in the arrangement of the marriage. The nobility was, after all, a rather small group of people, and John Lovell II and Arnold du Bois must have known each other from court and campaign.

John Lovell II settled a part of his estates jointly on John Lovell III and Isabel. However, some of the lands Isabel and her husband held jointly must have been hers. John Lovell III continued to hold the estates, but they did not pass to his son from his second marriage. They were inherited by Maud, his daughter from his first marriage, and her husband William de la Zouche after John Lovell III's death in 1310. Three years later, in 1313, Maud also inherited the estates of her uncle William du Bois (see Genealogy 4). Several years before he died William du Bois had already settled a large part of his estates on his niece Maud and her husband William de la Zouche.[1]

After his first wife's death and before 1288 John Lovell III married again. Unfortunately, his second wife cannot be identified with complete certainty. The *Complete Peerage* confines itself to saying that she was probably Joan de Ros, daughter of Robert de Ros and Isabel d'Aubigny. John Lovell III's second wife was certainly called Joan, as later records show, and as John Lovell III knew Joan's father Robert de Ros and her brother William de Ros from the councils they were summoned to and from participating in the same royal campaigns. As such, it is possible that his wife was Joan de Ros, though she cannot positively be identified. Though the evidence is sparse, she will be referred to as Joan de Ros in the following to avoid confusion.

John Lovell III and his second wife had at least two sons, his heir John Lovell IV and William Lovell. John Lovell III and Joan de Ros probably also had a daughter, Isabelle Lovell who married Sir Walter Calthorp. According to a description of Norfolk, she was the daughter of John, Lord Lovell of Titchmarsh. A link certainly existed between the families: John Lovell V, the grandson of John Lovell III and nephew of Isabelle, later held some land of Walter de Calthorp in Docking (Norfolk). As Maud Lovell was the sole heiress of William du Bois, Isabelle was not her full sister but a daughter of John Lovell III and Joan de Ros.[2]

In 1287 John Lovell III was serving in Edward I's Welsh campaign under the earl of Gloucester, Gilbert de Clare. He was accompanied by his illegitimate brother, John Lovell of Snotescombe. In the following year both John Lovell III and Master John Lovell, presumably John Lovell of Snotescombe, were going on campaign 'beyond seas' and received protection during their absence.[3]

A less law-abiding side of John Lovell III is revealed in 1290 when he, together with Gilbert de Clare, Earl of Gloucester, and a number of others, was accused by Humphrey Bohun, Earl of Hereford and Essex, of attacking his land at Brecon, committing homicides, and robberies. What actually happened, the reasons behind the attack and the outcome of this suit is unknown as is so often the case.[4]

Two years later, his half-brother John Lovell of Snotescombe sued John Lovell III in an assize of *mort d'ancestor* in which he claimed that John Lovell of Titchmarsh had illegally deprived him of some lands in Bromwych by Coleshill which should be his by right of inheritance. Unfortunately, the outcome of this suit is again unclear.[5] Since both the plaintiff and the defendant were called John Lovell the royal Chancery started to add 'of Titchmarsh' to John Lovell III's name to differentiate between the two men. Even though Titchmarsh did not remain the main residence of the family, they continued to be identified as the Lovells of Titchmarsh.

Like his uncle Philip Lovell, John Lovell of Snotescombe entered the royal administration. He became a judge and is frequently called a king's clerk. As a judge he was often appointed to commissions dealing with judicial matters, as in 1289 when he was sent with three colleagues to view the property of John de Vescy and seize all his writing, or when he was appointed to goal deliveries.[6] In 1295, he was among the judges summoned as 'Master' John Lovell to parliament.[7]

John Lovell III's service to the Crown diversified when he became a member of a diplomatic mission. In 1294, he went abroad on an embassy with Hugh Despenser the Elder, who, as the son of Alina Basset, was John Lovell III's second cousin.[8] A year later, John Lovell III, accompanied by his brother Thomas Lovell of Titchwell, was on campaign in Wales under the leadership of Gilbert de Clare, Earl of Gloucester.[9] Up to this point, John Lovell III had not held any important roles in military or administrative service. This changed in 1296 during the Scottish campaign of Edward I in which John Lovell III was marshal of the army that successfully defeated and deposed the Scottish king, John Balliol (1292–1296).[10] John Lovell III must have shown considerable skill and responsibility in fulfilling his military duties in the previous years to be appointed marshal of the army, which was both a prestigious role and a position of great responsibility.

Shortly afterwards, John Lovell III received his first individual summons to parliament as John Lovell of Titchmarsh.[11] According to later use, he was now a peer, Lord Lovell of Titchmarsh. At this time the issuing of individual summonses to parliament had not yet become standardised and the list of men receiving individual summonses fluctuated from parliament to parliament. It had not become a right that one's sons automatically inherited. It was the time of 'military summonses': the same group of noblemen who were called upon to serve on campaigns received summonses to parliament.[12] Parliament itself was still developing as an institution and the individually summoned nobles and the elected knights of the shire still sat in one room. John Lovell III's inclusion in what would become the House of Lords, and his continued receipt of individual summonses to future parliaments, is proof that he was a reliable supporter of Edward I.

1297 was a particularly busy year for John Lovell III. In June he was summoned to serve in Scotland, in July he was summoned to accompany the king to Flanders, in September he was to attend a military council, and in November he was to be in Newcastle to serve in Scotland. Additionally, he was one of the barons ordered to collect the recognizances and inquire about disturbers of the peace. It is possible that he did not fulfil all these roles himself as he did not join the campaign in Scotland in 1298 and may have appointed deputies for some of the duties he had been assigned.[13]

In the same year, John Lovell of Snotescombe was sent abroad by Edward I on a diplomatic mission to France. Among the men accompanying him was 'John Lovell the younger'. Since John Lovell III's son John Lovell IV was only about 10 years old at this time, too young to have been included in a such a mission, 'the younger' was another way to differentiate between John Lovell III and his half-brother. On this mission, John Lovell of Snotescombe met King Philip IV of France (1285–1314) to confirm a truce between England and France, an important mission and sign of trust in the competence of John Lovell of Snotescombe.[14]

As reliable a supporter of the king as John Lovell III was, he did not always agree with Edward I's policies. When Roger Bigod, Earl of Norfolk and Earl Marshal, and Humphrey Bohun, Earl of Hereford and Constable of England appeared at the Exchequer on 22 August 1297 to protest against taxes raised by Edward I, John Lovell III was among Roger Bigod's household. For this offence John Lovell III later received a royal pardon. The continuous wars against the Welsh, the Scottish, and on the Continent, and the demands for yet more taxation had started to irritate parts of the nobility, as can be seen with John Lovell III's own involvement in the 1297 protest.[15]

His presence at this protest against Edward I was certainly, to a considerable extent, due to his close links to Roger Bigod. Bigod had been the second husband of Alina Basset, the daughter of Philip Basset and cousin of John Lovell II (see Genealogy 3). John Lovell III witnessed several of the earl's charters, once together with his younger brother Thomas. Roger Bigod granted John Lovell III the manor of Wilton in Yorkshire. In 1304, John Lovell III requested to be allowed to grant the manor to John de Heselarton and his heirs, possibly because he considered the manor too distant from his other lands which were in the south and the midlands.[16] As important as his ties to Roger Bigod were,

John Lovell III's status and position was strong enough that he did not need to accompany the earl if he did not agree with the protest.

This moment of opposition to Edward I's policy is remarkable because it stands in curious isolation. Both before and immediately after the protest, John Lovell III was by all evidence on best terms with Edward I. John Lovell III accompanied Edward I on his unfortunate campaign in Flanders from where he and William de Gainsborough were sent back to England to request the additional funds necessary for Edward I's return to England. Despite the recent protest, Edward I still regarded John Lovell III as one of his most loyal men and entrusted him with this difficult mission. John Lovell III and William de Gainsborough must have been also been highly respected by their peers to persuade them to forward the required funds.[17]

As the war with Scotland continued, John Lovell III served in many of the campaigns. In 1300 he mustered in Carlisle and served at Dunfermline. In 1304 he participated in the 'the show-piece siege' of Stirling Castle. After three months of fierce fighting, the constable of the castle, Sir William Oliphant, surrendered the keys of the castle to John Lovell III, who must have held a high position in the royal army to be given this role in the dramatic event.[18] On this campaign John Lovell III was serving in Scotland in lieu of a hefty fine of 2,000 marks (a little over £1,330) for illegally hunting in the royal forest. This was hardly a grave punishment for John Lovell III since he had participated in most of Edward I's campaigns without the added incentive of cancelling his debts to the Crown. The pardon John Lovell III received in 1304 extended to his wife, his heir John Lovell IV and his younger son William.[19]

One of the few glimpses on John Lovell III's personal life is that his second wife Joan was on campaign with him in 1303, since a plea between Robert de Bytering and John Lovell and his wife was held until their return from Scotland. Unfortunately, we do not know whether Joan de Ros accompanied her husband on other occasions as well. Her presence is an indication that their marriage was amicable, as otherwise Joan would not have undertaken the hardships that travelling to Scotland and army life entailed.[20] During their absence in Scotland Walter de Pavely, Richard de Avene, and others attacked John Lovell III's men and lands at his manor in Elcombe, Norfolk, causing serious damage. This attack highlights the downside that prolonged military service could have, particularly when, as in this instance, both husband and wife were absent. Usually wives acted in their husbands place while the husbands were serving with the king, administering. managing, and protecting the family's estates. The royal protection John Lovell III had received did not deter the attackers. A commission of oyer and terminer was appointed on the complaint of John Lovell III, but whether he ever received any compensation for the damages is unknown.[21]

At least on occasion John Lovell III also took his fowler with him on campaign. In 1306, when John Lovell III was serving in the royal army as lieutenant of the earl marshal of England, Robert le Fughelere, fowler of John Lovell of Titchmarsh, received protection from Edward I for catching cranes and other birds for the king.[22] Alongside his service in Scotland, John Lovell III also was engaged in advising the king, in parliament. While it is probably that he did not attend all parliaments summoned in this period, he certainly was present in some of them, as in 1301, when he was one of the noblemen who witnessed a letter to Pope Boniface VIII.[23]

Though he was on campaign for long periods of time, John Lovell III had the time and resources to improve his home. In 1304, he received licence to crenellate his manor in Titchmarsh. In the same year he was granted a weekly market and an annual fair in Titchmarsh, as reward for his service (see also Chapter 6).[24]

The war with Scotland was far from over when Edward I died on 7 July 1307 in Brugh by Sands. This conflict was going to have a profound impact on the reign of his heir Edward II and on the Lovell family.

John Lovell III was summoned to Edward II's (1307–1327) coronation on 25 February 1308.[25] Though he was not a young man, John Lovell III continued to be actively involved in royal government. His position in the first of the series of crises that characterise Edward II's rule is unclear. John Lovell III's younger brother Thomas Lovell, however, was in the retinue of Gilbert de Clare, Earl of Gloucester, at the tournament in Dunstable in 1309. Edward II had expressly forbidden this tournament to be held.[26] Tournaments often were used as a pretext to allow dissatisfied members of the nobility to gather in force and discuss their grievances and how to address them. With what slender evidence there is, Thomas Lovell was one of Gilbert de Clare's retainers. He was in the earl's company again in 1310. In March 1310 John Lovell III was one of the magnates declaring that the appointment of ordainers should not be taken as a precedent nor prejudice the king or his heirs.[27]

John Lovell III died later that year, before 1 October when the escheators were ordered to inquire into the land he was holding and who his heir was.[28]

His second wife, Joan de Ros, survived her husband by thirty-eight years, outliving not only her son but also her grandson. As dower, the manors of Elcombe and Bluntesdon (Wiltshire) were assigned to her. Despite her long life she seems to have remained unmarried after her husband's death. She died on 13 October 1348, possibly of the plague, which first appeared in England in June 1348. Considering she was at least in her 60s but probably in her late 70s, it is equally possibly that she died of natural causes.[29]

Like his father John Lovell II, John Lovell III's advancement in the social hierarchy was firmly based on military service to the Crown. Though John Lovell III's relationship to the king was not always amiable, his continuous service, particularly his dedicated military service, in Flanders and Scotland, allowed John Lovell III to rise in status and ensured his advancement into the peerage. He was also rewarded directly, by gifts of deer or the grant the right to a weekly market and an annual fair in Titchmarsh. That he was allowed to participate in Edward I's campaign in Scotland instead of paying a substantial fine for illegally hunting in the royal forest was nothing short of a royal favour. How much the family had gained in wealth can be gauged from the fact that many decades later Reinald Fyfide testified that John Lovell IV was called 'John Lovell the Rich'.[30]

When John Lovell III died his eldest son John Lovell IV was about 21 or 22 years old. John Lovell IV had entered the service of Aymer de Valence, Earl of Pembroke, in 1308 and had served overseas with him in 1309. Though the indenture does not specify which John Lovell, father or son, became the earl's retainer, it was certainly John Lovell IV, since his father was an older, well-situated nobleman who had no need to seek employment or advancement. Moreover, the same John Lovell can be found in Aymer de Valence's retinue after his father died.[31]

Several relatives of John Lovell IV also served in the earl's retinue: his younger brother William Lovell, his uncle William de Ros, and

William de la Zouche, husband of his half-sister Maud. The nobility was a relatively small group of people, but to find so many relatives in the same retinue is an indication that those already retained by Aymer de Valence recommended the service of the earl or advanced the case of their relative to be included in his retinue.[32]

John Lovell IV married Maud Burnell before 1312. She was the daughter of Philip Burnell and Maud FitzAlan, sister of Richard FitzAlan, Earl of Arundel. Philip Burnell's uncle, Robert Burnell, Bishop of Bath and Wells had been chief justice of Edward I and 'the leading figure' of Edward I's reign.[33] The marriage between John Lovell IV and Maud Burnell linked two families serving at the royal court and who had gained considerably from this service. The marriage of John Lovell IV and Maud Burnell was probably arranged by John Lovell III through his excellent connections at court.

Maud Burnell's father Philip Burnell had inherited the eighty-two manors his uncle Robert Burnell had collected during his life. Since Philip Burnell was heavily in debt, the estates his son Edward Burnell inherited were much reduced. Nonetheless, the size of the inheritance was still considerable and Edward was the first Burnell to receive an individual summons to parliament in 1311.[34]

John Lovell IV's involvement in the stormy politics of Edward II's reign is hard to assess. Edward II saw himself faced with an increasingly hostile nobility, who were infuriated by Edward's blatant favouritism for Piers Gaveston. In this conflict, Aymer de Valence had long been among the more moderate of Edward's critics. However, when Piers Gaveston was executed by several noblemen led by the king's cousin Thomas of Lancaster, while under the protection of Aymer de Valence, he threw his full support behind Edward II. As a retainer of Aymer de Valence, John Lovell IV probably followed his course.

While Edward II struggled with his own nobles, the war in Scotland continued. Robert the Bruce (1306–1329) had been crowned King of Scotland in 1306 and became a formidable opponent. In 1314, the Scottish forces besieged the Castle of Stirling. To prevent this important castle being taken by the Scottish army, Edward II led a large army north. Aymer de Valence joined the army with his retinue, including John Lovell IV and his younger brother William Lovell. According to William Wollaston's deposition in the Lovell-Morley dispute John Lovell IV's brother-in-law, Edward Burnell, also participated in this campaign (see Chapter 5 for the dispute).

The Battle of Bannockburn on 24 June 1314 ended in a devastating defeat of the English army. Among the many noblemen who were killed in the battle were the king's cousin, Gilbert de Clare, Earl of Gloucester, Edmund de Mauley, the king's steward, and John Lovell IV. His younger brother William Lovell was lucky enough only to be taken prisoner by the Scots.[35]

John Lovell IV's early death was a severe setback to the fortunes of the Lovell family. The inquisitions held after John Lovell IV's death found that his heir was his 2-year-old daughter Joan. As heiress of a tenant-in-chief, Joan became a ward of the king.[36] The inquisitions in all counties in which John Lovell IV had held land took several months and during this period, as late as 26 November, an individual summons to parliament was sent to John Lovell IV.[37] His widow Maud Burnell gave birth to a posthumous child, John Lovell V, during this period, probably in September 1314. As son, he replaced his sister Joan as his father's first heir.[38]

What happened to Joan is not known. She may have died young. She may have married and lived a long life. Since she did not inherit any of the Lovell estates, it is possible that she is mentioned in governmental records without being identified as Joan Lovell, daughter of John Lovell IV.

John Lovell V's was the longest minority in the history of the Lovell family. As was the fate of numerous underage heirs John Lovell's wardship and marriage passed through several hands over the next years. The Lovell lands were granted to Edward II's Italian financier Antonio de Pessagno in August 1314. On 2 October the wardship and marriage of John Lovell V was sold to Aymer de Valence for the considerable sum of 1,200 marks. After the death of Aymer de Valence in 1324 the wardship of John Lovell was released as part of the payment of his debts to the Crown by Mary de St. Pol, Aymer de Valence's widow. In 1326 the marriage of John Lovell V was granted to Joan Jermye, the sister-in-law of Thomas, Earl of Norfolk, the king's half-brother.[39]

It is unfortunate but unsurprising that nothing is known about John Lovell V's life during his minority. Since he was born after his father's death he may have stayed with his mother for a period of time, but probably he was soon handed over to his guardian, perhaps at the time of his mother's remarriage.

Maud Burnell, John Lovell IV's widow, received her dower after February 1315.[40] Her fortunes changed dramatically again when her brother Edward died on 24 August 1315. Since he and his wife Alina Despenser had no children, Maud Burnell became his heiress. Though a third of the estates were held as the dower by Edward Burnell's widow Alina Despenser, the Burnell inheritance and the dower from her marriage to John Lovell IV made her a very attractive prospective wife for a second husband.

It is unsurprising that Maud Burnell did not remain a widow for long. By December 1315 she had married the widower John Haudlo (or Handlo). As the widow of a tenant-in-chief and a tenant-in-chief herself, Maud Burnell was not allowed to marry without the king's permission. In fact, she had sworn an oath not to marry without the king's license when she received her dower. However, like many other women in her position Maud Burnell remarried without first receiving Edward II's permission. Isabella FitzAlan, widow of Patrick Chaworth, and Hugh Despenser the Elder had married without royal license (see also Chapter 7).[41]

Maud Burnell probably met her second husband John Haudlo through her sister-in-law, Alina Despenser, a daughter of Hugh Despenser the Elder. John Haudlo was a long-time retainer of Hugh Despenser the Elder and can be found in Despenser's service as early as 1300. By May 1314 John Haudlo had become such an important supporter of the Despensers, that Hugh Despenser the Younger requested John Haudlo to be replaced as sheriff of Kent to be able to accompany his lord.[42] Maud Burnell and her sister-in-law must have met each other on numerous occasions and may have felt a kind of bond, both being widowed at a young age.[43]

In light of John Haudlo's close connection to Hugh Despenser the Elder and both Hugh and his son's reputation for using force and threat to get what they wanted it is tempting to conclude that Maud Burnell was pressurised into this marriage. However, in 1315, Hugh Despenser the Younger was not yet the royal favourite he was to become, and his father, as a loyalist, had less influence during the ascendancy of Thomas of Gloucester. Maud Burnell probably choose her second husband because he was a man whom she knew and who, she hoped, would be able to protect her interests. After the fall of the Despensers, Maud Burnell did not raise a complaint against her marriage. She also accompanied her husband on his pilgrimage to Santiago de Compostella, which is most likely a sign that the relationship between Maud Burnell and John Haudlo was affectionate.[44]

Having married without the king's permission, Maud Burnell's lands were declared forfeit and taken into the king's hands. After paying a fine of £100 in February 1316, the lands were restored to her and her second husband. Another, for the Lovells unfortunate, consequence of Maud Burnell's second marriage was that they did not inherit the majority of the Burnell estates when Maud Burnell died at some time before 17 May 1341. She and her second husband had entailed the largest part of the estates on their joint sons. After John Haudlo's death on 5 August 1346, their second son Nicholas Haudlo – his elder brother Thomas had died – inherited these estates and assumed the surname Burnell. Four years later, in 1350, he received his first individual summons to parliament.[45]

While John Lovell V grew up, the Lovells did not disappear completely from the political scene. His uncle William Lovell and his father's uncle Thomas Lovell of Titchwell became entangled in the mounting crises of Edward II's reign. For some time they found themselves on opposing sides of the conflict. William Lovell had received as his endowment the manor of Docking (Norfolk) and remained in the service of Aymer de Valence, one of Edward II's most steadfast supporters.[46] Thomas Lovell, the younger son of John Lovell II was in service of Thomas of Lancaster, Edward II's cousin and most outspoken critic, from 1317 onwards.[47]

He remained in the service of Thomas of Lancaster even as the conflict between the Earl of Lancaster and Edward II worsened. A large number of Thomas of Lancaster's supporters, deserted him when it became obvious that an armed conflict with the king was imminent, including the earl's most trusted confident and protégé Robert Holland. Thomas Lovell remained loyal to his lord and fought on at Thomas of Lancaster's side in the Battle of Boroughbridge on 16 March 1322. A large number of those taken prisoner were executed, including the king's former retainers John Mowbray and Bartholomew Badlesmere. Others were imprisoned indefinitely and often their families suffered the same fate. Thomas Lovell escaped from the battle itself, but was apprehended as a traitor and his lands declared forfeit.[48]

Thomas Lovell's return to favour was surprisingly easy. Soon after the battle, on 11 July 1322, he was pardoned and charged a fine of £200, half of which was pardoned in 1324. In 1325 the last part of his lands were returned to him.[49]

It is possible that Thomas Lovell's rehabilitation was part of the move toward a reconciliation with the party of Thomas of Lancaster, which Edward II tried to achieve at that time.[50] Thomas Lovell's return to favour may also have been the result of his entering the service of Hugh Despenser the Younger at this time. Evidence for this can only be found a few years later, but it is possible that with this move Thomas Lovell earned the protection of the younger Despenser. One may also speculate that Thomas Lovell employed the help of Maud Burnell, widow of his nephew John Lovell IV, and of her husband John Haudlo to gain entrance into the Despensers' service.

William Lovell also joined the service of Hugh Despenser the Younger after the death of his pervious patron Aymer de Valence in 1324. William Lovell claimed in 1333 to have been forced by Hugh Despenser the Younger to enter his service.[51] In fact, the Peruzzis, bankers of Hugh Despenser the Younger, had paid William Lovell £20 out of Despenser's account as a loan in 1325. It is possible that Despenser used these debts to pressurise William Lovell to enter his service. It was strong-arm tactics like that which were a major reason for the Despensers' unpopularity. It is equally possible that William Lovell tried to explain away his association with the disgraced family. However, since Edward III had already appointed William Lovell sheriff of Northamptonshire and keeper of Northampton Castle in 1331, he already had the king's trust and no great need to prove it.[52]

Thomas Lovell may have first entered Hugh Despenser's service as a means to gain a royal pardon, he certainly took his allegiance to the younger Hugh Despenser as seriously as he had for his loyalty to his former lord. Just as he had not deserted Thomas of Lancaster, Thomas Lovell did not abandon Hugh Despenser's cause like many others did when Queen Isabella returned to England in autumn 1326. Even after the death of the Despensers, Thomas Lovell and his young sons, Gilbert and Ralph, were among the troops under Sir John de Felton holding Caerphilly Castle against Queen Isabella and Roger Mortimer, protecting Hugh Despenser the Younger's son, also called Hugh. The siege lasted until 20 March 1327 when John de Felton surrendered Caerphilly Castle after Isabella had agreed to spare the life of young Hugh Despenser.[53] Thomas Lovell's lands were declared forfeit again. They were soon returned, and he and his sons were pardoned.[54]

Thomas Lovell died before 11 August 1331. There was considerable confusion about the age of Thomas Lovell's heir Gilbert. The *inquisition post mortem* for Thomas Lovell stated that his son Gilbert was 25.[55] This was clearly a mistake and the inquisition is described as 'defaced' in the calendar. Five years later, in 1336, Gilbert Lovell's younger brother Ralph showed the escheator that he was of age. Until then his father's estates had been in the king's hands since Ralph's older brother Gilbert had died a minor in the king's wardship.[56] If Ralph was declared of age when turned 21, he must have been only 12 years old when he had been with his father and older brother during the siege of Caerphilly Castle.

After the deposition of Edward II and the fall of Despensers, William Lovell found a new lord in Henry, Earl of Lancaster. Henry, a cousin of Edward II and younger brother of Thomas of Lancaster had first joined Roger Mortimer and Queen Isabella and had been instrumental in the deposition of Edward II in favour of his son Edward III (1327–1377). But by 1328 he had fallen out with Roger Mortimer and the queen and his lands were confiscated.[57] In 1330 William Lovell received a pardon for 190 marks of the 200 marks he had been fined for participating in Henry of Lancaster's rebellion.[58]

In politically volatile times like the reign of Edward II members of one family could easily find themselves on opposite sides, as Thomas Lovell of Titchwell and his nephew William Lovell did. Thomas Lovell was a retainer of Thomas of Lancaster, the king's harshest critic, while William Lovell was in the service of Aymer de Valence, one of Edward II's most loyal supporters. These two groups of noblemen were not clearly defined. There was considerable fluctuation, as the fate of the two Lovells shows, but both eventually served in the retinue of Hugh Despenser the Younger. They as many other nobles 'perforce performed such contortions', as Goodman describes them, changing their alliances depending on the current political fortunes of the quarrelling sides to survive the political upheavals.[59]

Family connections could be employed but they also could be ignored. In fact, in such troubled times like the 1320s, to be present on both sides of a quarrel could be of advantage for a family. Whoever found himself on the winning side then could use their influence to help their relatives who had backed the losing side.

Thomas Lovell of Titchwell was the founder of the only cadet branch of the Lovell family that lasted for several generations. His great-grandson William Lovell died without male heirs in 1415, probably at the Battle of Agincourt. William Lovell, John Lovell III's younger son, seems to have died without heirs, since Docking manor was later held by John Lovell VII.[60] This was not an uncommon phenomenon. The failure of younger sons to found families may be due to the fact that they married later than the heirs of the family.

John Lovell V's long minority ended in 1333 when Edward III ordered the escheators to hand over the lands to him.[61] Since John Lovell V was born late in 1314, he was given control of the family's estates before he reached his twenty-first year. John Lovell V must have impressed the king to be worthy of this favour or he had an unknown advocate at court.

As no estate records of the Lovells have survived it is impossible to judge whether the long minority had a negative impact on the Lovell lands. Considering the length of the minority and the frequent changes of guardian it seems almost inevitable that some reduction of value occurred. Part of the Lovell estates were in the hands of two Lovell dowagers who were still alive in 1333: John Lovell V's mother Maud Burnell and his grandmother Joan de Ros. Though long-lived dowagers have been seen as a problem and hindrance to the family heir by keeping control over part of his inheritance, often for a considerable time, their reputation has recently undergone a much-needed revision. By holding part of the family's estate as dower, they kept it out of the hands of possibly greedy guardians (see also Chapter 7).

In the following years, John Lovell V served on campaign in a variety of regions under different leaders. First, in 1334, he was in Scotland in the company of Thomas Ughtred.[62] Two years later John Lovell V was guarding the Islands of Jersey, Guernsey, and Sark with Hugh Balle.[63] From 1340 on, John Lovell V was also appointed to more administrative duties, like arresting suspected felons, or on the commission to collect wool in Norfolk. A task they must have regarded as too tiresome and were reluctant to perform, since John Lovell V and his fellow commissioners were reprimanded for being remiss in their duties.[64] He served in France with Henry of Lancaster in 1344 and in the company of the earl of Warwick in 1346–47.[65] John Lovell fought in the Battle of Crécy in 1346 and participated in the long siege of Calais together with his father's cousin Ralph Lovell of Titchwell.

At or before the Battle of Crécy a dispute erupted between Nicholas Burnell, John Lovell V's younger half-brother, and Robert Morley about the right to bear the arms *argent, a lion rampant sable, crowned and armed or.* As Edward III feared that unrest would threaten the campaign if more conflicts like the Burnell-Morley clash broke out between other nobles, he ordered that a decision about the right to these arms would be taken later in the campaign. The case was heard before the earl of Northampton, as earl marshall, and the earl of Lincoln, as constable during the protracted siege of Calais. The trial was eagerly followed by those present, as a welcome distraction from the routine and boredom of the siege, as was later recalled by Thomas Blount (see next chapter).[66]

John Lovell V was fulfilling the role of a noblemen serving the king in war and peace, but it is obvious that he was not given the prestigious roles his grandfather had held and his appearances in the government records are considerably less frequent. Unlike his father and his grandfather John Lovell V never received an individual summons to parliament, a clear indication of this reduced status. Though he was frequently abroad on campaign, it is unlikely that he would never have received a summons to parliament for this reason alone.

John Lovell V died only a year later, on 3 November 1347 at the age of 33.[67] It is possible that he had been the victim of an attack as he already had been assaulted before. In 1344 John Lovell V was attacked by William Belgrave, his son John Belgrave and others, who had imprisoned John Lovell V, carried away his goods, and assaulted his servants. The surviving records do not allow us to reconstruct either the cause of this attack or the outcome of his lawsuit. In 1349, when the keepers of the peace in Norfolk were appointed they were charged in particular to deal with 'many evildoers indicted before them of the death of John Lovell'.[68] That this commission was only appointed two years after John Lovell V's death does not exclude the possibility that the murdered John Lovell was John Lovell V since legal processes were notoriously slow at this time. However, the existence of several John Lovells makes a positive identification impossible.

Dower was assigned to John Lovell V's widow Isabel on 22 January 1348.[69] She outlived her husband only by two years. The date of her death is recorded as 2 July in Somerset, the feast of St Margaret (20 July) in Northampton, and 6 November in Norfolk.[70]

Nothing is known Isabel except her first name, whom she married, the names of some of her children, and when she died. Who her parents were can only be guessed at. According to the *Complete Peerage* she may have been Isabel de la Zouche of Harringworth, sister of Eon de la Zouche. If this is correct, Isabel was the great-granddaughter of Isabel du Bois and John Lovell III (see Genealogy 4). While one reason for Isabel's obscurity is the lessened status of the Lovell family, more importantly, she did not inherit nor was she granted any land from her natal family. Often the only proof allowing the identification of a woman is if she inherited or was granted lands from her family. If she received no lands or records of such transactions have been lost over the centuries, such a connection cannot be made (see Chapter 7).

John Lovell V and Isabel had at least three children, two sons who were both called John and a daughter, Elizabeth. When John Lovell V died, his son and heir, John Lovell VI, was only about 6 years old, and about 9 when his mother died.

Like his father's, John Lovell VI's wardship passed through a number of hands during his minority. First, it was given to John de Beauchamp, and later to Richard Talbot.[71] Richard Talbot sold the wardship to John de Pulteneye, except for Elcombe and Blunsdon Gay (Wiltshire). John de Pulteneye died and left the wardship to William Clinton, Earl of Huntingdon.[72] Edward III retained some parts of the Lovell estates, including the advowson, the right to present clerics, of several churches, which he did for example in Chiriton and Elcombe.[73] After the deaths of Joan de Ros, widow of John Lovell III, in 1348, and John Lovell V's widow Isabel in 1349 the whole Lovell estates were in wardship. The lands Isabel had held were granted to Isabel, the king's daughter.[74]

Just as during the own minority of John Lovell V, nothing is known about the fate of his children nor can the effect of this second prolonged minority within a few decades be measured. It is hard to imagine that the efficiency and profitability of the estates did not suffer, particularly since the wardship of John Lovell VI again changed hands repeatedly. Further deterioration of the lands value was caused by the plague which swept through England in 1348. In 1350, it was reported that the Lovell lands, at the time in the hands of Richard Talbot as guardian of John Lovell VI, had been devastated by the plague. The farm had to be reduced by a quarter from 160 marks to 120 marks per annum.[75] At Titchmarsh only four of the eight tenants had survived the plague, and even Titchmarsh Castle, which used to be the family's main residence, was reported to be in a severe state of disrepair in 1361.[76]

John Lovell VI died unmarried on 12 July 1361, still a minor. His heir was his younger brother, also called John.[77]

Based on the foundations laid by his father John Lovell II and great-uncle Philip Lovell, and through his own dedicated and long service to the Crown in war and peace, John Lovell III reached new levels of prominence. His higher rank was reflected in his inclusion in the ranks of noblemen who received individual summonses to parliament and rewards for this service both in gifts and grants of offices.

The short life of his son John Lovell IV shows the dangers and risks of royal service and in particular of military service to the Crown. His early death and the long minority of his posthumous son John Lovell V was a severe crisis for the family. John Lovell V never achieved the rank of his father or his grandfather in the king's service. The fact that John Lovell V never received an individual summons to parliament is clear evidence for his reduced status. Between the parliament summoned on 24 October 1314, in the immediate aftermath of the Battle of Bannockburn when an individual summons was sent to John Lovell IV even though he had been killed in the battle, to 1375 when John Lovell VII, John Lovell V's son, received an individual summons for the parliament in spring of 1376, none of the lists of summonses mention a John Lovell. Though the right to an individual summons was slowly becoming hereditary during the fourteenth century, there was still a considerable flexibility in the ranks of the lords. After his long minority, John Lovell V was not automatically included as he would have been in later centuries, but had to earn his right to an individual summons. His younger half-brother Nicholas Burnell was summoned to parliament four years after he had inherited the Burnell estates and after serving for long periods in France. If John Lovell V had lived longer it is possible but not certain that he would also have been summoned to parliament as a lord as well.

Instead, his early death was the start of another long period of wardship, which was further prolonged by the death of his older son John Lovell VI when he was still a minor. In the middle of the fourteenth century, the fortunes of the Lovells of Titchmarsh were at a distinctly low ebb. They were about to improve rapidly with the younger brother, John Lovell VII, who would achieve and surpass the status that any of his ancestors had achieved.

Chapter 5

Luck, Service, and Opportunism

John Lovell VII was declared of age on 8 June 1363, almost exactly forty-nine years after his grandfather John Lovell IV died at the Battle of Bannockburn on 24 June 1314. For almost two-thirds of these forty-nine years, the heirs of the family had been underage, and the Lovell estates partially or completely under the control of a guardian. The long minorities, the frequent changes of guardian, and the plague reduced the value of the lands, the prosperity, and the status of the family. It was only after more than ten years of dedicated service to the Crown, a very advantageous marriage, and a considerable portion of luck, that John Lovell VII regained the status his grandfather held, and receive an individual summons to the House of Lords.

In the first few years after John Lovell VII was invested with the Lovell estates he appears only on a few occasions in the government's records, again a clear sign of the family's still reduced status. In 1366, John Lovell VII was appointed to a commission of array in Middlesex. This is a somewhat unusual appointment since the Lovells did not hold any land in this county, but they had lands in the surrounding counties, including Berkshire and Buckinghamshire. A year later John Lovell VII was appointed to commissions of array in Middlesex and Northamptonshire where the Lovells held considerable estates, including the manor of Titchmarsh.[1]

During the following years John Lovell VII spent long periods of time abroad in military service. He served in Brittany in 1367 and in the following year he was in Milan in the company of Lionel, Duke of Clarence, for the duke's marriage to Violante Visconti.[2] John Lovell VII was granted protection for serving abroad again and it was probably during this time that he went to Prussia and the eastern Mediterranean on crusade.[3] In 1374 he was in Brittany in the retinue of Edmund Mortimer.[4]

It was also around this time John Lovell VII married. His wife Maud Holland was the heiress of her grandfather Robert Holland. This marriage was a turning point for the Lovell family. Maud Holland's inheritance approximately doubled John Lovell VII's estates. No record exists that would shed light on who arranged this momentous marriage. Robert Holland's brother Thomas Holland had been the first husband of Joan of Kent. Robert Holland's son and Maud Holland's father, another Robert Holland, was therefore the cousin of John and Thomas Holland, the half-brothers of Richard II. The marriage created a link, if only indirectly, between the Lovells and the royal family (see Genealogy 5).

However, connections established through marriages could but need not influence a nobleman's career. Maud Holland's relationship to the king's half-brothers was distant, and John Lovell VII had to rely on his own efforts to advance his career. He and the king's elder half-brothers can be found working together only on rare occasion as in 1484 when he was one of the six men who stood guarantee for Thomas Holland, Earl of Kent, when he was given the marriage of Edmund Mortimer's heir Roger Mortimer. In this case, John Lovell VII's involvement may be explained by the fact that he had been on friendly terms with the boy's father (see below). However, he must also have trusted that Thomas Holland was able and willing to pay the money he had pledged for the marriage of young Roger Mortimer.[5]

Though the date of John Lovell VII's marriage to Maud Holland is unknown, it probably took place in 1371 when Maud Holland was about 15 years old. At this time, John Lovell VII transferred considerable lands to her grandfather Robert Holland, estates that the couple later held in jointure.[6] Considering Maud Holland's great inheritance, John Lovell VII may have had a powerful patron who supported this match. However, the marriage may have been arranged before Maud Holland became her grandfather's heir. It is even possible that John Lovell V and Robert Holland had planned the marriage between their young children as early as 1346/7 during the campaign in France in which both participated. However, such a prearranged marriages could have been easily set aside, when Maud Holland became her grandfather's heir.[7]

John Lovell VII himself knew how important his marriage to Maud Holland was. Over the years he settled a significant part of the Lovell estates in jointure on himself and his wife to ensure that Maud Holland would be able to live comfortably and retain her status if or when she became a widow and as a sign of appreciation. By giving their second son the name Robert, a name that had not been used by the Lovells before, John Lovell VII and Maud Holland also honoured her family.

Several years after his marriage, John Lovell VII began to add her title to his own, styling himself 'Lord Lovell and Holland'. John Lovell VII was in fact the first baron to use a double-barrelled title.[8] He also combined the coats of arms of both families, the Lovell arms, *barry nebuly, or and gules*, and the Holland family's arms, *azure, semy de lis a lion rampant argent*. On the earlier seals the two arms were impaled but soon the Holland and Lovell arms are shown as quartered, implying the equality between both.[9] John Lovell VII was as proud of his own family as he was of his wife's. This combined coat of arms was displayed not only on the seals of John Lovell VII, Maud Holland, and their sons (see plate 4), but also as decorations in places like the cloister and chapter house of Canterbury Cathedral, the windows of St Kenelm's church in Minster Lovell, or St Mary's, Everdon.[10] The significance of coats of arms had increased substantially since the late thirteenth century, when coats of arms had become widespread but were not yet seen as the property of one family and their use was not yet regulated. The dispute between Nicholas Burnell and Robert Morley during the siege of Calais in 1347 is one indication of this change. By the late fourteenth century the title and coat of arms of a noble family were more than just a symbol. They were also a claim to the estates themselves. Nicholas, Maud Burnell's son from her second marriage to John Haudlo, used both the surname Burnell and the Burnell coat of arms as a public statement that he was now holding the Burnell barony.

In contrast, Thomas Holland, Maud Holland's great-uncle, did not use the Holland coat of arms in the 1350s. He probably tried to distance himself from his father Robert Holland who had deserted his lord Thomas, Earl of Lancaster prior to the Battle of Boroughbridge. Robert Holland had been Thomas of Lancaster's most trusted confident and protégé and his betrayal was a shocking break of feudal ties. The reputation of treachery was still tarnishing the name of Holland in the 1350s to the extent that Thomas Holland did not use the family's coat of arms.[11] When John Lovell VII married Maud Holland, the name had lost this taint. Thomas Holland had redeemed the family honour by his glittering military career and through his marriage to Joan of Kent.

John Lovell VII received his first individual summons to parliament after his wife had inherited her grandfather's estates and it is tempting to conclude that his inclusion in the parliamentary peerage was a consequence of his increased wealth and status.[12] While this certainly played a role, it was not the only and perhaps not even the most important reason. At this time John Lovell VII had already spent many years serving in the king's wars and had made the acquaintance and gained the respect of several influential noblemen. The most important of them was Edmund Mortimer, Earl of March. Crusading in Prussia and the Eastern Mediterranean certainly raised his reputation as well. Therefore, John Lovell VII's elevation into the parliamentary peerage was the result of a combination of his own efforts and work and of his acquisition of a second barony through marriage. The fact that his grandfather John Lovell IV and his great-grandfather John Lovell III had been members of this parliamentary peerage had not been enough for John Lovell VII to be included in their ranks, but it certainly counted in his favour.

John Lovell VII made his first experiences in his new role in one of the most famous parliaments of the late medieval period: the Good Parliament. The government in general and a court clique including William Latimer and the king's mistress Alice Perrers were attacked for misgovernment, mismanagement, and their appropriation of public funds. John Lovell VII's former commander, Edmund Mortimer, was among those who severely criticised the court, and it was his steward Peter de la Mare who headed the proceedings of impeachment against the accused. Despite his close connection to Edmund Mortimer, John Lovell VII did not join the critics of Alice Perrers, William Latimer, and the other courtiers. Along with a number of bishops, earls, and other lords, John Lovell VII stood surety of William Latimer, the king's chamberlain.[13] Though William Latimer and the others accused were found guilty by parliament, the decision was overturned within a year.

Already in the first parliament he attended John Lovell VII displayed his ability to understand the political machinations at court and in parliament, as well as his aptitude for remaining on good terms with opposing sides of a conflict. His relationship with Edmund Mortimer was not damaged by his support of William Latimer. The Good Parliament was John Lovell VII's first experience of the dangers of court politics, but it was certainly not his last. His understanding of court politics and his ability to keep on good terms with men on both sides of a political conflict would stand him in good stead in the years to come.

Edward III died on 21 June 1377, and was succeeded by his 10-year-old grandson Richard II (1377–1399). John Lovell VII attended the young king's coronation on 16 July 1377 and swore fealty to him.[14]

In the years following this first foray into politics, John Lovell VII's career was again dominated by service in various military campaigns. He participated in the siege of Berwick in 1378 under the command of Henry Percy, Earl of Northumberland. In 1379 and 1380 John Lovell VII served in Ireland, once more under Edmund Mortimer, Earl of March, who had been appointed lieutenant there.[15]

The relationship between Edmund Mortimer and John Lovell VII was closer than that of a commander and a noblemen serving under him. Edmund Mortimer gave John Lovell VII his lordship in Newbury (Berkshire) and the manors of Ducklington and Finmore (Oxfordshire) free of rent for life. In his testament, written in 1380, Edmund Mortimer bestowed a cup with the cover of a blue stone on John Lovell VII.[16] John Lovell VII was also rewarded for his service by the Crown, as in 1378 when he received the commitment of some of the lands formerly held by Edward III's mistress, Alice Perrers.[17]

1381 saw the first major upheaval of Richard II's reign, the so called Peasants' Revolt.[18] Though John Lovell VII was probably not directly involved in the conflict itself, he was one of the many men who dealt with the repercussions of the revolt after it had been subdued. He was appointed to several commissions dealing with crimes committed during the revolt, including the lynching of Simon Sudbury, Archbishop of Canterbury, Robert de Hales, Prior of the Hospital of St John of Jerusalem, and John Cavendish. He also served in a commission to arrest certain rebels in Berkshire and the commissions of peace in Oxfordshire and Berkshire.[19] Perhaps as a reward for his service John Lovell VII was appointed as keeper of the Castle of Devizes, the forests of Melkesham, Chippenham, and Pensham and the manor of Roude. He was also granted the keeping of the hundred of Catsash (Somerset) for ten years.[20]

Having gained respect and experience through his service in war, John Lovell VII became increasingly involved in the administrative side of service to the Crown. One of the most important roles of the nobility was to act as a link between the centre of government around king and court and the localities. Noblemen were appointed to commissions in the areas where their estates were concentrated and where they were respected by their neighbours. Here they could exert their influence to implement the decisions of the centre of government. They brought news from court to the localities and in turn informed the government of the reaction to its policies. John Lovell VII's area of greatest influence was in Oxfordshire and Berkshire where he had considerable estates, where he was appointed to a large number of commissions.[21] Though it is impossible to judge how much noblemen like John Lovell VII were personally involved in the work of these commissions, later evidence shows that many took the work seriously. They added weight to the commissions and ensured that the decisions made were implemented.

Through his work on these commissions John Lovell VII became well acquainted with a number of noblemen and gentry whose interests where in the same areas as his own. Many of them served at court as well, including Chief Justice Robert Tressilian, the king's knight Philip de la Vache, and Richard Abberbury. Being appointed to the same commissions only demonstrates that the landed interest of John Lovell VII and these men were in the same areas. Whether friendships developed between them while working together is not easy to determine.

When war broke out between Scotland and England in 1385, Richard II led one of the largest armies ever assembled north. In this campaign John Lovell VII, together with William, Lord Botreaux and Richard, Lord Seymour, was in command of a contingent of 100 men-at-arms and 200 archers.[22] The war in Scotland saw no large military engagements but was considered a success.

During the campaign two disputes broke out about the right to bear a particular coat of arms: between John Lovell VII and Thomas, Lord Morley, about the right to bear the arms *argent, a lion rampant sable crowned and armed or*, and between Richard Scrope and Robert Grosvenor about the right to bear the arms *azure, a bend or*. The opponents probably encountered each other displaying the same coat of arms they used in the unusually large army assembled for Richard II's campaign, just as Nicholas Burnell and Robert Morley's dispute about their coat of arms had erupted in the large army assembled for the French campaign of Edward III in 1346 (see previous chapter).

The Scrope-Grosvenor controversy is undoubtedly the most famous dispute about a particular coat of arms but many similar cases were heard before the Court of Chivalry. They include the cases of Warbletone *versus* George over the arms *lozengy or and azure*, and Aton *versus* Boynton over *or, a cross sable surmounted by five bulls' heads argent*.[23] While no records exists for most of these proceedings, for three cases substantial records have survived: the disputes between Richard Scrope and Robert Grosvenor, John Lovell VII and Thomas Morley, and the slightly later case between Reginald, Lord Grey of Ruthin and Sir Edward Hastings.[24]

Taking a dispute over a coat of arms to the Court of Chivalry was no trivial matter and could have serious consequences. When Sir John Hastings lost the case against Reginald, Lord Grey of Ruthin, he was sentenced to pay the costs of the trial. Hastings appealed but was arrested as a debtor in 1416 and kept imprisoned for nearly twenty years. Coats of arms had become much more than mere decoration or a means to identify an armoured man. They represented the estates, titles, and honour of a family. John Lovell VII had adopted the Holland arms as a visible sign of his control of the barony when the Holland inheritance had come into his hands. Sir John Hastings's claim to the Grey of Ruthin coat of arms for himself was also as a claim to the Pembroke estates the majority of which had been inherited by Reginald Grey, his opponent in the trial. But more than just rights to lands and riches were involved in these quarrels. As Andrew Ayton phrases it: 'These disputes were pursued with the utmost vigour and determination because armorial bearings were at the heart of the aristocrat's sense of identity, at once marks of social status and symbols of family honour.'[25]

Given the serious nature of starting a dispute about a coat of arms, it is interesting that John Lovell VII took the risks involved to quarrel with Thomas Morley. The case is particularly intriguing since the coat of arms he claimed was not that of the Lovell family. The Lovell coat of arms was *barry nebuly or and gules*, as a number of deponents in favour of Thomas Morley were only too happy to point out. Not only that, two deponents who spoke in favour of Thomas Morley's claim, Richard Cosyn and Thomas Gerberge, state that John Lovell VII had seen Morley bear the disputed arms in Brittany in 1374 and had not raised a complaint then.[26]

The coat of arms that John Lovell VII now claimed as his own was in fact that of the Burnell family. The Lovell-Morley dispute was effectively a rerun of the quarrel between Nicholas Burnell, half-brother of John Lovell VII's father John Lovell V, and Robert Morley, grandfather of Thomas Morley, during the siege of Calais in 1347. Many of the witnesses recalled that they had been at Calais and had observed the quarrel themselves or, as in the case of the injured Thomas Blount, had been told by a friend. Unsurprisingly, deponents like 86-year-old John Breke, a witness in favour of John Lovell VII, remembered that the coat of arms had been awarded to Nicholas Burnell, while those who spoke in favour of Thomas Morley, like William King, claimed that they had been awarded to Robert Morley.

To establish who of the two men, John Lovell VII or Robert Morley, had the right to the coat of arms the deponents were not only questioned about the events at Calais but also where they had seen either claimants or their respective ancestors displaying the coat of arms over the years. To prove they had the older right the opponents found witnesses who were of very advanced age. Reginald Fyfide, for example, was 85 and remembered that Edward Burnell wore the disputed coat of arms at the Battle of Bannockburn. William Wollaston was even older. He stated that he was 96 years old, and recalled not only Edward Burnell bearing the coat of arms fighting at Bannockburn, but also that Edward's sister Maud first married John Lovell IV and that their first born son and heir was the father of the John Lovell VII, the author of the dispute.[27] Several of the deponents claimed that the family they spoke in favour of used the disputed arms since before the Norman Conquest, like Hugh Camoys and Thomas Morley himself.[28] That the coat of arms was used that early was obviously an exaggeration. To claim a right or custom existed as long ago as or even before the Norman Conquest was commonplace and was often used interchangeably with 'from time immemorial'.

The depositions of the Lovell-Morley dispute reveal fascinating details about the men who John Lovell VII and Robert Morley associated with, their military service as well as interesting facts about the way the medieval nobility used their coats of arms as decorations and to display their wealth. One aspect that cannot be thoroughly examined is the relationship of the deponents to the Lovell family. Most of the deponents who spoke in support of John Lovell VII's claim were of relatively low status and are therefore difficult or impossible to trace. Even men like Hildebrand Barre, Thomas de la Mare, John de Ipres, and Thomas Wake who appear in the records in other circumstances together with John Lovell VII, when they were appointed to the same commission or witnessed a grant together, only do so on one or two occasions. Nonetheless, the depositions for this case certainly would deserve to be studied in greater detail as they reveal interesting aspects of the lives and careers of the deponents.[29]

Though the verdict of the Court of Chivalry in the case Lovell v. Morley is not recorded later rolls of arms indicate Thomas Morley won the dispute. His coat of arms is depicted as undifferenced, while Hugh Burnell's arms are recorded as *argent, a lion rampant, crowned or, a border azure*.[30] John Lovell VII continued to use the Lovell arms quartered with the Holland arms. He had not gained the right to add another coat of arms to the two he already held. Unlike the unfortunate John Hastings, John Lovell VII suffered no serious consequences for his attempt. He was rich enough to pay the costs when he lost the case as seems likely.

The question remains why John Lovell VII started this dispute with Thomas Morley in 1385. The coat of arms *argent, a lion rampant, crowned and armed or* was not the one he used himself. The family who had regularly used the coat of arms was the Burnells. For John Lovell VII this quarrel was a public claim not only on the coat of arms, but also on the lands which were in the hands of Hugh Burnell. John Lovell VII had not pursued his claim when he had seen Thomas Morley wear the disputed coat of arms in 1374, as witnesses for Thomas Morley had pointed out, because he had been a young man of little influence and wealth just starting to make his career in royal service. When he did claim it in 1385, he had not only taken his seat in the House of Lords, he had gained considerable influence at court and in the localities. He was now in a much stronger position than ten years earlier.

In light of the importance of coats of arms for the identity and honour of a noble family, for Hugh Burnell the dispute between John Lovell VII and Thomas Morley was one in which he lost whoever emerged as victor. He would lose if the right to the arms was granted to Thomas Morley, but he would also lose if it was awarded to his half-cousin John Lovell VII as it would have confirmed he had a claim to the Burnell estates. The relationship between the descendants of Maud Burnell's two marriages had been distant at best, this dispute must have strained it further. While witnesses in the Lovell-Morley dispute remembered that John Lovell V was at Calais with his 'cousin' Ralph Lovell of Titchwell, none of them mention that Nicholas Burnell was John Lovell V's half-brother. Several of the deponents stressed the fact that John Lovell V was the first-born son and heir of Maud Burnell. William Montague, Earl of Salisbury, one of the Morley deponents even referred to Nicholas Burnell, the father of Hugh Burnell, as 'a man called Haudlo', the surname of Nicholas Burnell's father. Reginal Fyfide stated that Maud Burnell and her second husband had a son, Nicholas 'apelle' Burnell. Both statements can hardly be interpreted as a sign of appreciation for Nicholas's claim to the Burnell barony.[31]

In the late 1380s, John Lovell VII became a mainstay of the administration at court and in the localities. He became a king's knight and was a banneret at the royal household. He was repeatedly appointed to commissions of oyer and terminer and to commissions of the peace in Wiltshire, Berkshire, and Oxfordshire as well as to many other commissions which dealt with a variety of problems from ascertaining common pasture in the forest of Braden to dealing with a counterfeiter of money in Marlborough.[32] He was also actively engaged in the work of parliament, as in April 1384 when he was one of the noblemen appointed to confer with the commons.[33]

Being close at hand and engaged in the royal administrations brought its rewards. In 1387 he was awarded the custody of Elizabeth Mautravers, the heiress of John Mautravers. However, John Lovell VII was expressly forbidden to marry Elizabeth to his own son.[34] No such restriction was placed on him when he received the marriage of the heiresses of the Bryan barony, Philippa and Elizabeth, in the following year.[35] John Lovell VII arranged for Philippa, the older of the two girls, to be married to his second son Robert. Together with Alice Bures, Lady Bryan, the mother of Philippa and Elizabeth, John Lovell VII was put in charge of several manors in Somerset until the lawful age of Elizabeth and Philippa, formerly held by their uncle Philip Bryan.[36]

It seems strange now that the medieval nobility treated the marriage and wardship of their children or grandchildren as a business. However, they were able to combine caring about the welfare of their children or grandchildren with financial considerations, making provisions for their economic security in the future. Sir Guy Bryan, the grandfather of Philippa and Elizabeth, had been a close personal friend of Edward III and a trusted and important administrator during this reign. Though he had swapped his role of active administrator for that of elder statesmen after the death of Edward III, in that role he was still present at court and parliament where he would have met and worked with John Lovell VII. By entrusting his granddaughters to the care of John Lovell VII, Guy Bryan showed he had confidence in John Lovell VII's financial acumen and trusted him to keep his side of the bargain.[37]

For an ambitious and dedicated man like John Lovell VII, court was lucrative and opened many opportunities. In 1388, John Lovell VII discovered that it could also be dangerous. As Richard II took on the role of an adult monarch, he promoted his close friends and supporters, rewarding them with grants and new titles. Most famous or notorious among them was Robert de Vere, Earl of Oxford, who was made Marquess of Ireland. Several high-ranking members of the nobility, including Richard II's youngest uncle, Thomas, Duke of Gloucester, and Richard FitzAlan, Earl of Arundel, were deeply offended by the king's actions. In their opinion the king favoured and rewarded the wrong people. The situation became increasingly confrontational from 1386 onwards.

The conflict between the king and his critics reached its climax in the 'Merciless Parliament' in 1388, in which Richard II's closest friends and advisers were accused of treason. Those of the accused who escaped to exile abroad like Robert de Vere and Michael de la Pole, Earl of Suffolk were lucky. With the exception of the clerics, those who were apprehended like the chief justice Robert Tressilian or the king's former tutor Simon Burley were executed.

Though John Lovell VII had been trusted by both the king and his opponents in early stages of the conflict and had been employed as intermediary, he was now seen as an ally of the king.[38] John Lovell VII was one of fifteen courtiers who were ordered to leave the court, since they were considered to have abused their position and influence. They had to swear not to return without permission by parliament, and are referred to as the abjurers. Two of the abjurers were bishops, John Fordham, Bishop of Ely, and Thomas Rushok, Bishop of Llandaff. Five were peers, John Lovell VII, John, Lord Beaumont, Thomas, Lord Camoys, Hugh, Lord Burnell, and William, Lord Zouche of Harringworth. Another five abjurers were knights, namely Sir Richard Abberbury, Sir Baldwin Bereford, Sir Thomas Clifford, Sir Aubrey de Vere, and Sir John Worth. The last three were ladies, Margery, Lady Moleyns, Joan, Lady Mohun, and Blanche, Lady Poynings. In short, the abjurers were a cross section of the people who made up the royal court.

No specific accusations are recorded against the abjurers. Though John Lovell VII had received a number of grants in the years leading up to his banishment from court, they were not extravagant considering the service he had given. Whatever his actual or alleged crimes were, John Lovell VII was regarded as one of the people at court who had considerable influence over the king.

Examining the abjurers as a group, as John L. Leland did in a detailed study, reveals a multitude of ties between them.[39] As already discussed, John Lovell VII was Hugh Burnell's half-cousin (see Genealogy 6). William de la Zouche had sat with John Lovell VII on various commissions and was probably his cousin (see Genealogy 4). Sir Richard Abberbury, like the unfortunate chief justice Robert Tressilian, had been on numerous commissions with John Lovell.

As courtiers they were bound to work together, even if, like John Lovell VII and Hugh Burnell, they did not seek each other's company in their private lives. These men and women were all members of the aristocracy, which was a small group of people. It would be more surprising, to not find connections between most of them in some way, either through family or shared experience in war or administration. In the end what mattered to their critics and led to their expulsion from court was not the ties between them but their influence at court which, at least in the eyes of their critics, they had abused.

Many of the people banished from court also had ties, often close ties to the critics of Richard II. John Lovell VII was on very close, indeed friendly terms with Thomas Arundel, Bishop of Ely and brother of Richard FitzAlan, Earl of Arundel. Historian Margaret Aston calls John Lovell VII 'a lifelong friend' of the bishop. John Lovell VII was Thomas Arundel's most frequent visitor, after his sister Joan, Countess of Hereford, and the two men frequently exchanged gifts. John Lovell VII was one of Thomas Arundel's retainers and probably a member of the bishop's council at this time.[40] It is only thanks to the rare survival of some of the bishop's account books that the closeness of the relationship between Thomas Arundel and John Lovell VII is revealed. Many other friendships and fellowships between the noblemen, gentry, and clergy remain untraceable in the absence of similar records. Most of the time it is impossible to decide whether two men employed each other as witnesses or guarantors simply because they were working together at court or in the same locality or because they were friends.

Despite his friendship to Bishop Thomas Arundel, John Lovell VII was expelled from court. Just as family ties did not automatically direct a man's behaviour, neither did a man of the rank of John Lovell VII necessarily adhere to the political position of the man whose livery he had received. John Lovell VII's banishment from court revealed their political differences. Nonetheless, John Lovell VII and Thomas Arundel remained on friendly terms for the rest of their lives.

His friendship with Thomas Arundel may have been one reason why John Lovell VII's banishment was of short duration. Already in 1388, shortly after his banishment, he was on a naval expedition in the company of Lord Welles under the command of Thomas Arundel's brother Richard, Earl of Arundel.[41] By 1389 John Lovell VII had returned to court and was appointed to the commission to sell the land of those people who had been condemned by the Merciless Parliament.[42] Indeed, far from being discouraged by his expulsion from court, John Lovell VII's involvement in all aspects of central government increased after his banishment.

As before John Lovell VII did not only attended parliament, he was actively involved in its administrative work. He was appointed as one of the triers of petitions for Gascony and the other lands beyond the sea in the next four parliaments. In 1397, he was appointed as one of the triers of petitions for England, Scotland, Wales, and Ireland. John Lovell VII attended all parliaments between 1388 and 1399 with one exception. He was absent from the parliament of 1395 when he was in charge of shipping troops to Ireland in preparation for Richard II's expedition there.[43]

During the last decade of the fourteenth century, John Lovell VII gained an even higher position at court. He became a regular member of the king's council from the early 1390s, and in 1395 Richard II retained him for life. John Lovell VII had witnessed royal charters already in the late 1380s, but the number of charters in which he appears as witness increases significantly in the period from 1396 to 1398.[44]

While he continued to be appointed to administrative commissions in the localities, he now also sat on commissions which were dealing with issues arising at the central government. Several of these were appeals against decisions taken by the Court of Chivalry, including a case about a coat of arms between Thomas Baude and Nicholas de Syngleton, an argument over prisoners of war, and a suit between Henry, Bishop of Norwich and William, Baron Hilton about the military service of the latter in Flanders.[45]

His role at court did not stop John Lovell VII from protecting and enlarging his estates. Like many of his contemporaries he was involved in violent attacks, both as perpetrator and as victim in disputes over lands. In 1391, Thomas Manston accused John Lovell VII of unlawfully expelling him from his manor of Manston (Dorset). In his petition to parliament Thomas Manston complained that he had not been able to gain justice at the local level, since John Lovell VII had 'threatened the jurors empanelled at an assize to hear the case so that they did not dare to appear'. Unsurprisingly, John Lovell VII denied all charges. A commission was empanelled to hear Thomas Manston complaints and was renewed in 1393.[46] The outcome of Thomas Manston's suit is once more unknown, but the manor does not appear to be in the possession of the Lovell family later.

In the same year in which he was accused of expelling Thomas Manston, John Lovell VII was himself the victim of crime. A commission of oyer and terminer was empanelled on the complaint by John Lovell VII that William Wakelyn and a large number of other men had tried to prevent him from reaching his home at Minster Lovell and kill him. That they assaulted his men, servants and tenants, and caused the enormous damage of £1,000.[47] As in the case of John Lovell VII's quarrel with Thomas Manston neither the cause nor the outcome of this case is known.

Over the years John Lovell VII considerably enlarged the family's possessions. In 1389, he purchased the reversion of Bridzor from the abbess and convent of Shaftesbury. Between 1386 and 1393 he acquired the manors of Knook, Wardour, and Knighton (Wiltshire) and Sutton Waldron (Dorset), which were part of the former estates of Sir Laurence St. Martin, from Thomas Calston, one of the co-heirs. Whether John Lovell VII purchased these estates or they were part of a family settlement is unclear. Thomas Calston was the grandson of Maud of

London, whose brother Robert of London was married to John Lovell VII's sister Elizabeth. John Lovell VII quitclaimed his rights to the manor of Littlecote, previously held by Robert of London, to Thomas Calston possibly as part of the same settlement.[48]

More than ten years later, in 1405, Henry Popham, the co-heir of Thomas Calston, tried to regain possession of the lands. He procured a writ of *novel disseisin* against John Lovell VII, his wife Maud, their sons John Lovell VIII and Robert Lovell, as well as a whole list of other men, including Thomas Calston. Henry Popham claimed that they had unlawfully seized his manors of Knighton and Upton. The assize was revoked since credible witnesses had stated that the claim was false. Another assize of *novel disseisin* against John Lovell VII, his wife 'and others' regarding Sutton Waldron and Wardour was put on hold as John Lovell VII was about to go campaigning with the king in Wales.[49] Only after extended litigations, which lasted till 1410, did Popham drop his claim on the estates.[50]

John Lovell VII received a licence to crenellate Wardour in 1393 and had a spectacular new castle built.[51] Old Wardour Castle, as it is known today, is unusual for its hexagonal shape showing an idiosyncratic streak in John Lovell VII's personality. Though the castle was badly damaged during the Civil War the ruins are still impressive and well worth a visit (see plates 6–8).

While overtly the conflict between Richard II and his critics ended in 1389, neither side forgot their grievances or injuries. The mistrust and mutual suspicion led to a number of crises in the 1390s. As a royal counsellor John Lovell VII was witness to many of these, as in 1394 when Thomas Talbot confessed his plan to assassinate the dukes of Lancaster and Gloucester in the presence of Henry, Earl of Derby, John Lovell VII, and others, not mentioned by name.[52]

John Lovell VII often acted as one of the moderating forces at court. For example, he vouched for the good behaviour of Richard, Earl of Arundel, who had angered Richard II by arriving late at the funeral of Queen Anne and immediately asking to be allowed to leave again. A number of high-ranking men, headed by the earl's brother Thomas Arundel, by now archbishop of York, and including Roger Mortimer, Earl of March, Thomas Beauchamp, Earl of Warwick, Hugh Burnell, and John Lovell

VII stood surety for the enormous sum of £40,000 Richard FitzAlan pledged for his good behaviour.[53]

When Richard II went on campaign in Ireland in 1394, John Lovell VII was in charge of shipping the troops to Ireland,[54] a task in which he could use his experience of campaigning in Ireland gained in 1379 and 1380. John Lovell VII's second son Robert Lovell participated in the Irish campaign as well, serving in the company of Alexander de Balscot, Bishop of Meath. A more distant relative, Thomas Lovell of Titchwell was in John Lovell VII's company on this campaign. John Lovell VII and Hugh Burnell were on better terms now, as John Lovell VII appointed Hugh Burnell as one of his attorneys while he was abroad. Thomas Arundel, now archbishop of York, headed the list of attorneys of John Lovell VII. The two men were obviously still on excellent terms with each other.[55] During the campaign in Ireland, John Lovell VII was granted the manor and lordship of Rounde and the borough and town of Devizes, where he was already constable of the castle, free of rent for life. This was a considerable gift and a sign of appreciation for John Lovell VII's service on the campaign.[56]

In 1397, Richard II took his revenge on the main instigators of the destruction of his friends in the Merciless Parliament ten years earlier. Richard FitzAlan, Earl of Arundel was accused of treason and executed, and Thomas, Duke of Gloucester died under suspicious circumstances while imprisoned in Calais. Thomas Beauchamp, Earl of Warwick and Thomas Arundel were exiled. Often this has been seen as the start of the king's so-called 'tyranny', though doubt has been cast on this assessment.[57] In the following years the circle of people around Richard II shrank steadily. During this time, John Lovell VII's ties to his wife's Holland relatives became closer, particularly to Thomas Holland, Duke of Surrey, the son of the king's half-brother Thomas Holland. Thomas Holland appointed John Lovell VII as one of his attorneys while he was in Ireland and as one of his feoffees.[58] The two men trusted each other, perhaps developed a friendship, during the time they were together at court.

By relying on only a small group of people Richard II estranged large parts of the nobility who felt left out of the political process. When he took the lands of his uncle John of Gaunt, Duke of Lancaster into his own hands and turned the exile of his cousin Henry of Bolingbroke into a life sentence, many nobles saw this as an attack on the very principle of inheritance law. For Richard II to leave for another campaign in Ireland immediately afterwards, a campaign both John Lovell VII and his eldest son John Lovell VIII joined, turned out to be the gravest mistake of his reign.[59] Henry of Bolingbroke used Richard II's absence to return from exile, march through England and attract a considerable following. Richard II aggravated his mistake by remaining in Ireland while sending his troops back, before he eventually sailed to Wales in the company of a his remaining troops and household including John Lovell VII.

Though several chronicles describe the momentous events of this autumn they are frustratingly vague. What is clear is that soon after arriving in Wales John Lovell VII, Thomas Percy, Earl of Worcester, Edward, Duke of Aumale, and John Stanley, controller of the royal household, left Richard II's side and joined Henry of Bolingbroke either in Chester or Shrewsbury where they 'put themselves at his mercy'.[60] At first glance this may look like a blatant case of four ungrateful chancers abandoning their king, who had shown them great favour, when his situation became difficult and he had most need of them. However, one should not forget that these men vividly remembered the fate of Richard II's favourites at the Merciless Parliament. Of those who had been appealed or impeached all but the clerics had been sentenced to death; only a lucky few escaped abroad and avoided execution. It is quite possible that these men tried to avoid a similar fate by throwing themselves at Henry's mercy.

John Lovell VII did abandon the cause of Richard II very quickly. When a few months later, in autumn of 1399, Richard II was deposed, and Henry of Bolingbroke became king he was supported by the vast majority of parliament, including John Lovell VII. He also agreed to the parliament's decision to imprison Richard II.[61]

During Henry IV's (1399–1413) first parliament, Edward, Duke of Aumale and cousin to both Richard II and Henry IV, was questioned about his position to Richard II's withholding the inheritance of Henry of Bolingbroke. Edward declared that he had always been opposed to it, that he had advised the treasurer William Scrope to try and dissuade Richard II from this 'evil purpose', and that he told John Lovell VII that the whole world would be astonished by Richard II's acts. To confirm the veracity of his statement he asked Henry IV to examine John Lovell VII. While John Lovell VII's reply was unfortunately not recorded, the fact that he was called upon as a witness shows that he was a trusted and well-known courtier.

A few months after Richard II's deposition, his half-brother John Holland, his nephew Thomas Holland, Thomas Despenser, and their associates attempted to restore him to the throne and to assassinate the new king and his entire family. The rising collapsed remarkably quickly and the ring leaders were executed.

While his old acquaintance Richard Abberbury joined the rebels, John Lovell VII was not involved. He had already gained the trust of the new king and did not want to jeopardise his position. A few weeks later, he was appointed on the commission to deal with all treasonous dealings in London and Middlesex. John Lovell VII was briefly appointed castellan of Corfe Castle in 1400. The position had been previously held by Thomas Holland and his wife, Joan Stafford. It was restored to her in 1401.[62]

A particular honour and sign of trust was bestowed on John Lovell VII when he was one of the four noblemen considered as possible tutors for Henry, Prince of Wales. Only men who had the complete trust of the king would be considered for a role as important as the upbringing of the heir to the throne. The other three candidates were Thomas Percy, Earl of Worcester, Sir Thomas Erpingham, and the steward of the household William Heron, Lord Say.[63] John Lovell VII and the young Henry knew each other since Henry had been taken as a hostage on Richard II's Irish campaign in 1399. In the end John Lovell VII was not chosen for the position as the prince's tutor, which was given to Thomas Percy. Despite the faith the king placed in him, Thomas Percy joined the rebellion against Henry IV led by his nephew Henry 'Hotspur' Percy only a year later.

While John Lovell VII was one of many courtiers whose careers were hardly affected by Richard II's deposition, few were as successful in keeping their position and rank as John Lovell VII was. He was able to immediately slip back into his former position as a courtier and reliably administrator under the new king. His friendship with Thomas Arundel, who had returned from exile with Henry of Bolingbroke, no doubt helped John Lovell VII to find Henry IV's favour but his experience and abilities certainly also played a role.

John Lovell VII continued to be appointed to commissions dealing with problems that reached the court, for example a commission of appeal against a decision of the lieutenant of the constable of the king's military court at Bordeaux or a commission to inquire into the misdeeds of the prioress of Amesbury.[64] In 1403, John Lovell VII was among the men sent by the king to Southampton to organise the defence against the threat of a French invasion.[65] He was again appointed as trier of petitions for England, Wales, Scotland, and Ireland in the parliaments that sat in 1402, both parliaments of 1404, the parliaments in 1406, and 1407.[66] In 1404, John Lovell VII was appointed to the continual council of the king.[67]

He was reappointed to the council in 1406, but excused himself due to a pending lawsuit with William Doyle over the possession of the advowson and manor of Hinton in the Hedges. This dispute shows that John Lovell VII continued to bend or even break the law to achieve his ends. John Freeman, one of his servants, had stolen a bundle of feet of fines concerning Northamptonshire between 1331 and 1336 from the Treasury of Receipt in connection with this dispute.[68] Even though this was a serious crime, John Freeman and his lord seem to have escaped punishment. The dispute was considered in parliament and in 1406 an agreement between John Lovell VII and William Doyle was enrolled that they would submit to arbitration. The case was not resolved in John Lovell VII's lifetime.[69]

Though John Lovell VII's attendance at the continual council was infrequent compared to that of administrators like the treasurer, he was an active and involved councillor. The councillors appointed in Henry IV's reign were men who had acquired administrative skills and who had proven their loyalty to the king. They were, however, not men who were personally close to Henry IV. John Lovell did indeed witness no charters during the reign of Henry IV as he had done during the reign of Richard II nor was he styled a king's knight any longer. It seems that while John Lovell VII retained his position at court and was valued as an experienced administrator with considerable skill, his relationship with Henry IV was less friendly than his relationship with Richard II had been.[70]

However, Henry IV held John Lovell VII in high regard, and in February 1405 John Lovell VII's long service to the Crown was rewarded in a public and highly prestigious way when he was made Knight of the Garter.[71] He was also richly rewarded when the custody of the park of Fremantle (Southampton) and the castle and lordship of Ludlow were granted to him for life in 1402. John Lovell VII continued to serve in the king's campaigns, as in 1405, when he went on campaign to Wales, though he must have been about 63 years old.[72]

According to later tradition, John Lovell VII was called both the 'Great Lord Lovell' and 'Lord Lovell the Rich'.[73] How wealthy he was is almost impossible to determine. The nobility were inventive in finding ways to avoid taxes, and official records often underestimated their income. Parts of their land was entrusted to feoffees or held in jointure, so that the inquisitions taken after a nobleman's death did not include all the land he had held. In their private records they often kept separate accounts for different parts of their estates.

The two account rolls from John Lovell VII's time kept at Magdalen College, Oxford from the fiscal years 1394–95 and 1400–01 concern only a part of the Lovell estates.[74] The later and longer roll records income of £415 18s. 8d. and expenses of £367 5s. 10d. for eleven manors. Most of the expenses were money paid directly into the 'lord's coffer'. Based on *inquisitions post mortem* of John Lovell VII his annual income was almost £480.[75] Maud Holland's income, according to the *inquisitions post mortem* was almost £200. Both figures most likely underestimated their income.

His wealth allowed John Lovell VII to lend Henry IV 500 marks in 1404.[76] Today still visible proofs of his wealth are his great castle at Wardour or the coat of arms at Canterbury Cathedral paid for by his donations to the cathedral fund. Most of the improvements of churches or his own residences that John Lovell VII paid for have been lost over time or cannot be attributed to him, but it is certain that he, like his fellow noblemen, used his wealth for these purposes. He was certainly one of the richest barons under the rank of earl.

John Lovell VII also commissioned an expensive book for Salisbury Cathedral, the Lovell Lectionary.[77] This large book was illuminated by John Siferwas and at least two other painters. Though it only survives in fragmentary and damaged form the Lovell Lectionary is a marvellous example of late medieval craftsmanship. The most impressive artwork is a large presentation scene. The two figures shown in the picture are John Lovell VII receiving the book from the illuminator John Siferwas (see Cover). Both its size of a 'small panel painting' and the portrait-style are singular for its time.[78] John Siferwas is identified by the inscription on the lower frame (ffrater Johes Sifer Was). John Lovell VII, wearing a fur-collared red gown and a black hat, is shown as an elderly man with a pointed beard. The inscription on a scroll wrapped around a column at the left reveals the recipient of the book and requests prayers for John Lovell VII and his wife: '*Orate pro anima domini iohannis louell qui hunc librum ordinauit ecclesie cathedrali Sarum pro speciali memoria sui & uxoris*'. Pray for the soul of John Lord Lovell, who had ordered this book for the cathedral church of Salisbury for the special remembrance of him and his wife.

Another purpose of the book was the commemoration and celebration of the union between John Lovell VII and Maud Holland. Two miniatures in the margins of the manuscript depict both John Lovell VII and Maud Holland (see plate 3). The illustrations also repeatedly depict the Lovell and Holland arms in a variety of forms, both separately and combined. Golden padlocks, the Sydenham badge, are also shown. The dog, a pun on the family's name Lovell makes an appearance as well. As the Lovell Lectionary was held by Salisbury cathedral and even though it was not the public who would see it, it was a celebration of John Lovell VII's illustrious marriage and ancient lineage and shows his pride in his family. It was, in Janet Backhouse's words, 'a memorial offering'.[79]

John Lovell VII died on 10 September 1408 at the age of about 66 after a long and profitable career at court. For more than forty years he had been at the very heart of royal government. He had participated in the workings of parliament, survived a number of violent conflicts, including the deposition of Richard II, and had been councillor to two kings. He had increased his lands and showed his wealth to the world by building a spectacular castle at Wardour.[80]

John Lovell's success was based on three interdependent factors: luck, dedicated service, and skill. Luck came to him in the form of being born into the nobility and inheriting the estates of a baronial family, his marriage to Maud Holland, who brought him more land and interesting connections, and his longevity. His marriage doubled his wealth and turned him into a very rich landowner, a man with influence in the localities. It was, however, his willingness to serve, at first in the military, later in administration, that truly advanced his career. John Lovell proved himself to be a man of considerable skills in a variety of fields. Though it may be exaggerated to call him, as A. Emery did, 'probably Richard's most able commander', he became a military commander of experience and standing.[81] John Lovell VII was also a skilled administrator, who was repeatedly appointed to important and difficult commissions. That he was chosen, along with Henry Percy, Earl of Northumberland, to mediate between the bitterly opposed camps in 1388 shows particularly clearly that, at this point, he was trusted by both sides of this quarrel. It is clear evidence of his skill in making and retaining friends and allies on different sides of a conflict. Though in a group as small as the royal court or the nobility, links can be found between all of its members, the connections John Lovell forged, for example with Thomas Arundel or Richard II, were strong enough to withstand considerable stress. It was these abilities, his friendships and alliances, and his skill in service, that allowed John Lovell VII to not only survive but to flourish in these turbulent times. His dedicated service was rewarded when he was made a Knight of the Garter.

Due to lack of personal records, the nature of his relationships with Maud Holland can only be judged by a few indicators. While John Lovell VII's adoption of the title and coat of arms of her family may only reflect their material importance to him, the fact that he made his wife one of the executors of his will and left the disposal of his goods in her hands shows that he had absolute confidence in her (see also Chapter 7). As a final symbol of how important his marriage had been to John Lovell VII, he decided to be buried in the church of the Hospital of St. James and St. John near Brackley (Northamptonshire) where Robert Holland, Maud's grandfather, and his father, another Robert Holland, were buried.[82]

John Lovell VII's life was a success, but luck was running out for the family.

Chapter 6

Family Tradition and Individual Choices

John Lovell VIII was about 30 years of age when his father died. He was given seisin of his lands in 1409.[1] He was not a courtier like his father had been and it was his younger brother Robert Lovell who became closely involved with court and in military service. While John Lovell VIII's only recorded military service is on Richard II's campaign in Ireland in 1399, Robert Lovell was on campaign in Ireland with his father in 1394 and again from 1395 to 1397, first in the company of Alexander, Bishop of Meath and then under the command of Roger Mortimer, Earl of March. Robert Lovell probably stayed in Ireland until 1399. In 1404 and again in 1406, Robert Lovell served in the company of Prince Henry in Wales.[2] John Lovell VII's connection to court surely eased Robert Lovell's way into royal service. What is surprising is that his elder brother did not follow his father's and brother's example.

One explanation could be that John Lovell VIII suffered from ill-health, but there is no evidence to that. No exemptions from commissions or for attending parliament were issued. In fact, John Lovell VIII attended parliament in 1410 when he agreed to a special assize held on petition of William Doyle.[3] He also attended the coronation of Henry V (1413–1422). It is more likely that John Lovell VIII simply did not have the inclination to seek advancement at court. He was the owner of considerable estates with a large income and, unlike his younger brother, did not need to make a career as a courtier. His lack of involvement is also reflected in the appointments to commissions of the peace. While John Lovell VII was regularly appointed to the commissions in Oxfordshire and Wiltshire, John Lovell VIII was only appointed to the commission of peace in Oxfordshire once, in 1413.[4]

Surprisingly, when John Lovell VII received the wardship and marriage of Philippa and Elizabeth Bryan, the co-heiresses of Guy Bryan, he married Elizabeth to his second son Robert, not his heir John Lovell VIII (see Genealogy 8). John Lovell VII also settled considerable land on

Robert, including the manors of Upton Lovell, Knighton, and the new, splendid castle at Wardour.[5] This endowment was probably part of the marriage arrangements for Robert Lovell and Elizabeth Bryan. With her share of the Bryan barony, Robert Lovell should have been financially secure.

When Guy Bryan died in 1390, Elizabeth was already married to Robert Lovell and her sister Philippa to John Devereux. Guy Bryan's two granddaughters inherited not only his estates but also the lands of their uncles, Philip and William Bryan, who had died shortly after Guy Bryan the younger.[6] William Bryan had tried to claim the Bryan estates for himself after the death of his two elder brothers, being vigorously, and sometimes violently opposed both by his father Guy Bryan as well as John Lovell VII and John Devereux, the future fathers-in-law of the two Bryan heiresses.[7]

Though Elizabeth Bryan is called the wife of Robert Lovell in the inquisitions taken after her grandfather's death, she was only 9 years old. According to the inquisition that proved that she was of age in 1400 she was born on 13 March 1381.[8]

Philippa Bryan's husband, John Devereux, died in 1396. Shortly afterward she married Henry Scrope of Masham. Henry Scrope was to become a close companion of Henry of Monmouth, son and heir of the future Henry IV. This was an additional link that tied Robert Lovell to the circle around the prince of Wales. In light of his father's courtier life and particularly the fact that his father was considered as tutor for the prince of Wales, it seems unlikely that Robert Lovell owed his place in the retinue of the prince of Wales solely to his wife's brother-in-law, as J.S. Roskell argues.[9]

While his younger brother's wife was the heiress of a considerable fortune, John Lovell VIII's wife was not and her identity is therefore a matter of conjecture. All that is certain is that she was called Eleanor. It is possible that she was the daughter of William de la Zouche of Harringworth.[10] If Eleanor was the daughter of William de la Zouche this would be the third intermarriage between the two families (see Genealogy 4).

This identification is strongly supported by the fact that the Zouche coat of arms appears in the Lovell Lectionary, where it is impaled with the quartered Lovell and Holland arms. On the same folio the same coat of arms appears impaled with the Bryan coat of arms. These heraldic decorations probably commemorate the marriages of the two eldest sons of John Lovell VII and Maud Holland. Robert Lovell certainly married Elizabeth Bryan and the combination of the Lovell and Holland arms with those of the de la Zouche family would be the equivalent for John Lovell VIII's marriage to Eleanor de la Zouche.[11] The heraldry of the tomb in St Kenelm's Church in Minster Lovell on which the Zouches' coat of arms is depicted on four of the escutcheons also points to a close connection between the two families. John Lovell VIII and his wife Eleanor gave their eldest son the name of her father William. John Lovell VIII's marriage to Eleanor de la Zouche shows that John Lovell VII considered that strengthening the ties to this neighbouring family was more important to him than securing a wealthy heiress for his eldest son.[12]

In 1406, Philippa Bryan died childless and her part of the Bryan estate was inherited by her sister Eleanor.[13] Though Robert Lovell did now hold the entire Bryan barony, he was never summoned to parliament as Lord Bryan, as at this time, there was considerable lee-way in who was allowed to succeed a lordship in right of his wife.

By 1410 Robert Lovell was described as esquire of the prince of Wales. When Henry Scrope became treasurer of the Exchequer in the same year, Robert Lovell was appointed clerk of works at Clarendon, a position he held until 1424.[14] In the same year the King's Council, headed by the prince of Wales, met at Robert Lovell's house in Old Fish Street, which was only a few minutes' walk from Lovell Inn in Paternoster Row.[15] That the council met in Robert Lovell's house is proof that he was one of the group of young nobleman surrounding the prince of Wales.

During these years Robert Lovell incurred enormous debts on the prince's behalf, which he was never able to recover. He had already been in debt by 1,000 marks to Henry Scrope and also owed 200 marks to John Storton and William Coventre.[16] By 1413 he was in severe financial difficulties and made quitclaim of all estates in Wiltshire and Dorset, including Wardour Castle, to his mother and his elder brother John Lovell VIII.[17]

Henry IV died on 20 March 1413, and both Robert Lovell and his elder brother attended the coronation of Henry V on 9 April 1413. They received scarlet cloth for the occasion, John Lovell VIII as peer received eight ells and Robert Lovell five ells.[18]

Robert Lovell no doubt hoped that as king Henry V would repay his debts. However, repaying his outstanding debts was obviously not a priority for the king not even to Robert Lovell who had been a close companion since 1404 and remained one of his confidents.[19]

A year after attending Henry V's coronation, on 18 or 19 October 1414, John Lovell VIII died. He was about 36 years of age. There is no indication that he had been ill, and he was still summoned to parliament in September 1414.[20] No record of dower being assigned to John Lovell VIII's widow Eleanor exists, but she was still living in Titchmarsh in 1430. The date of her death is unknown.[21]

In 1415, Robert Lovell was indentured for the first French campaign of Henry V. This campaign started with the treason and execution of Henry, Lord Scrope of Masham. He was not only married to the sister of Robert Lovell's wife but was his close acquaintance and probable sponsor. However, Robert Lovell was not implicated in the plot. He took part in Henry V's campaign in France and fought in the Battle of Agincourt.[22]

By 1420 Robert Lovell was chronically in debt. The Patent Rolls record several instances in which Robert Lovell received pardons of outlawry after not appearing to answer for his debts.[23] In 1419 he lost several manors for outstanding debts to John White, clerk.[24] Despite his financial difficulties, Robert Lovell actively participated in the administration of the localities, particularly in Dorset. In 1421, he was one of the men called to organise the defence in Dorset against a threatened attack by the kings of Aragon and Castile, and Leon, and was one of the men appointed to supervise the muster of the men serving under the duke of Bedford in Southampton on their way to join Henry V in France. Robert Lovell also served in this campaign. In 1423, he was in France again, possibly happy to escape the people in whose debt he was. Between campaigning in France, in 1421 and 1422, he was elected to parliament as one knight of the shire for Dorset. He was also appointed to the Commission of Peace in Dorset.[25]

During the parliament of 1422, Robert Lovell was granted the marriage and wardship of John FitzAlan, Lord Mautravers, Earl of Arundel, who later married Robert Lovell's only daughter and heiress Maud Lovell. Even though Robert Lovell was on the edge of complete financial breakdown, his wife's inheritance made this advantageous match possible.

In addition to the Bryan barony Elizabeth Bryan inherited estates worth approximately 700 marks a year from her mother Alice Bures, sole heiress of the Bures estates.[26]

In 1427, Robert Lovell made another attempt to recover his outstanding debts by a petition to parliament, explaining that Henry V had owed him £2,330. He does not seem to have succeeded in recouping his debts and was outlawed when he died in 1434, and his goods and chattel were confiscated.[27]

Robert Lovell was one of the few younger sons of the Lovell family who made a significant career of his own. In fact, it was him rather than his elder brother John Lovell VIII who followed in their father's footsteps and pursued a career both in military as well as administrative service to the crown. Though John Lovell VIII died only six years after his father, in this time he had not shown any enthusiasm for joining military campaigns or serving in administration. His brother Robert Lovell had already spend several years on campaign in Ireland and was in the service to the prince of Wales when their father died.

John Lovell VII had certainly supported his second son's career. He ensured that Robert was both endowed with lands by his own family as well as by marrying him to a rich heiress. It is also likely that John Lovell VII's involvement at the court of Henry IV introduced Robert Lovell to Henry, Prince of Wales. However, Robert Lovell's service did not result in gaining status and riches, quite the contrary, he suffered 'from the vicissitudes and parsimony of royal gratitude and patronage', and over the next three decades might have slid down to join the *nouveaux pauvres* had it not been for his wife's substantial property'.[28] It was his wife's wealth the allowed their daughter Maud to marry John FitzAlan, Earl of Arundel.

Robert Lovell is unusual in as far as one of his personal letters survives. He wrote the letter to his mother-in-law in 1396, when he was on service in Ireland with Roger Mortimer. Written in elegant French, the letter demonstrates that John Lovell VII ensured his sons were well-educated and as fluent in French as in English. French was becoming a foreign language for the nobility in the second half of the fourteenth century, though the use of either French or English must have differed widely between families.[29]

Though the letter 'was little more than a charming "bread-and-butter" letter', it sheds an interesting and unique personal light on Robert Lovell.

He sends his mother-in-law an abundance of wishes for her health and good estate, thanks her profusely for her many kindnesses to him, a recommends himself humbly to her. By all evidence, Robert Lovell was on very good terms with his mother-in-law. Though it is not clear whether he himself or one of his household paid a visit to Alice de Bures, Lady Bryan in 1410, he did help her with the administration of her estates by occasionally collecting rents from one of her manors.[30]

John Lovell VIII's son William Lovell III was under age when his father died. As he was about 17, his minority would be relatively short. For the last 200 years, the heirs to the family were all called John, and the sudden break with family tradition confused the royal administration. In one instance William Lovell III was referred to erroneously as John.[31] While it is possible that William Lovell III was the second son and had had an elder brother named John who died young, he may have been named after his maternal grandfather William de la Zouche.

William Lovell III's wardship and marriage were granted to Henry Lord FitzHugh of Ravensworth.[32] A considerable part of the Lovell estates were held in dower and jointure by his grandmother Maud Holland. Minorities were a regular occurrence in the Lovell family, as they were for most noble families. As young as he was William Lovell III participated in the campaign in France in 1415. Two years later, in 1417, he was leading his own company in France, serving under Humphrey, Duke of Gloucester.[33]

After the death of Hugh Burnell on 4 February 1420 William Lovell III came into a large inheritance. Hugh Burnell was grandson of Maud Burnell, widow of John Lovell IV, and her second husband John Haudlo. While his heirs general were his three granddaughters, Joyce, Katherine, and Margaret, his male heir was William Lovell III (see Genealogy 6). The descendants of Maud Burnell's two marriages mostly had kept at a distance, though John Lovell VII and Hugh Burnell seem to have developed a relationship of trust after several years of working together at the royal court. The Lovells of Titchmarsh certainly had not forgotten their relationship to the Burnells even after a century had passed since Maud Burnell and her second husband John Haudlo had settled the larger part of the Burnell estates on their own offspring, but in the male line only.

Hugh Burnell, to use Roskell's words, 'possessed not a single acre of which he was free to dispose'.[34] Nonetheless, he arranged advantageous marriages for his three granddaughters. Sir Walter Hungerford married Margaret to his younger son, Edmund, Katherine was engaged to John Talbot, Lord Furnival, and Joyce married Thomas Erdyngton.[35] These marriage arrangements seem to have been made under the pretence that they would inherit his considerable estates.

Was he deliberately misleading his granddaughter's spouses by claiming they were his heirs? It seems unlikely that Hugh Burnell was unaware he held the estates in tail male. He may simply have chosen to ignore the fact and hoped that William Lovell III, who was still under age, was unaware of the entail. Once his granddaughters' husbands had been given seisin of his lands, it would be considerably more difficult for William Lovell III to reclaim the estates. The *inquisitions post mortem* of Hugh Burnell in 1420 indeed described his heirs to be his three granddaughters: 'Joyce wife of Thomas Erdynton junior, Katherine Burnell and Margery wife of Edmund Hungerford, the daughters of his son Edward Burnell, knight, are his kinswomen and next heirs. Joyce is aged 24 years and more, Katherine 14 years and more and Margery 11 years and more.'[36]

However, Hugh Burnell's attempt to divert his lands to his granddaughters was not successful, and William Lovell inherited the estates. John Talbot, Lord Furnival dissolved his contract to marriage with Katherine Burnell when he discovered that his wife was not the heiress he had thought her to be. He must have become aware of the problem early since Katherine Burnell was not married when her grandfather died. Katherine eventually married Sir John Ratcliffe, who after twelve years of lawsuits managed to secure three manors in Norfolk as his wife's inheritance (Billingford, Thurning, and East Ryston), as well as the two other Norfolk manors of Docking and Southmere.[37]

An amicable settlement was reached between William Lovell III and Edmund Hungerford. William Lovell granted the manor of Rowland Ryght (Oxfordshire) and the manors of Estham Burnell, Westham Burnell, and Hilhowse (Essex) to Margaret Burnell and Edmund Hungerford.[38] The Hungerfords and Lovells were neighbours in Oxfordshire and continued to keep on friendly terms even after the quarrel about the Burnell inheritance.

1423 brought even greater changes for William Lovell III: he inherited all the estates his grandmother Maud Holland had held in jointure after her death on 7 May. In July he was given control of his inheritance.[39] He also married Alice Deincourt who, like Maud Holland, was an rich heiress.

Alice and her sister Margaret had become the co-heiresses of their brother William Deincourt when he died at the age of about 19 on 5 September 1422. They inherited both the Deincourt barony and the Grey of Rotherfield barony, as their mother Joan had been the heiress of Lord Robert Grey of Rotherfield (see Genealogy 7). Margaret and Alice received seisin of their share of the estates in February 1423. As they were not married the land was to be given to them.[40] Both married soon afterwards. When their grandmother Elizabeth de Bermingham died later the same year, the land she had held in dower was divided between her granddaughters Alice and her husband William, Lord Lovell and Holland and her sister Margaret and her husband Ralph, Lord Cromwell of Tattershall.[41] As befitted a wife of Alice Deincourt's status, William Lovell III provided generously for her. According to an estimation based on her *inquisition post mortem* Alice Deincourt held land worth more than £256 at the time of her death.[42]

In the years after his marriage William Lovell III became involved in local administration. From 1424 on he served on various commissions, mostly in Oxfordshire and Berkshire, but also in many other parts of the country. The Lovell estates had always been spread over several counties, from Norfolk to Somerset. Now they covered an even larger part of the country: the Burnell barony had added a cluster of estates in Shropshire, the Holland barony included many manors in Lancashire and Leicestershire, and the Deincourt and Grey of Rotherfield lands stretched from the manor of Rotherfield Greys in Oxfordshire to Askham Bryan in Yorkshire. Occasionally William Lovell III is referred to as Lord Lovell, Burnell and Holland, reflecting the multiple baronies he held.[43]

The baronies he inherited and the lands of his wife Alice Deincourt, which increased again after the death of her grandmother Alice Neville in 1433, made William Lovell III one of the richest peers below the rank of earl. For the income tax of 1436 William Lovell III was assessed at exactly £1,000. This tax assessment was certainly an undervaluation and probably did not include the estates of his wife.[44]

William Lovell III was appointed to a larger number of commissions of the peace than his father and grandfather. While John Lovell VII had only sat on the commissions on Oxfordshire and Wiltshire, William Lovell III was appointed to the commissions of peace in Berkshire, Leicestershire, Northamptonshire, Oxfordshire, Staffordshire, and Wiltshire. In later years he was no longer on the commission in Staffordshire, but was added to the commission in the North Riding of Yorkshire and Shropshire.[45] To some extent this is due to the fact that high-ranking noblemen were appointed to an increasing number of commissions even without increasing their holdings. However, William Lovell III's appointment to these commissions does reflect on how widespread and large his estates were.

In 1430 William Lovell III was again in France when supplies of bows and oil bottles were sent to him. A year later he returned to England, as recorded in Annals of St Albans. That the annalist thought this was an event worth recording shows that William Lovell III was a known personality and probably that the position he had held was of some importance.[46]

It is possible that William Lovell III's heir, John Lovell IX, was born while his father was serving in France. Letters of denization for a 'John Lovell born in the duchy of Normandy' were enrolled in 1452.[47] Though the *inquisitions post mortem* after William Lovell III's death in 1455 states that his heir was 22 years old it is possible that John Lovell IX was 25 when his father died, since the exact age of an heir was not important for this inquest as long as he was of age.

Looking at the life of William Lovell III it is interesting to note that his involvement in the royal court or the war in France was limited. As part of the military elite, William Lovell III had served in various campaigns in France, but ended his military service in 1431 when he was only about 34 years old. Most noblemen, like William Lovell III's grandfather John Lovell VII, served into their 60s or longer. He seems to have lacked the ambition or inclination to pursue a career at court. He avoided the dangers of both court and military life, but also missed the opportunities such career offered.

A good contrast to William Lovell's quiet life is that of Ralph Cromwell, husband of Margaret Deincourt, William Lovell III's sister-in-law, which highlights both the possibilities and dangers of a career at court. He used his position, sometimes quite ruthlessly, to enlarge his wealth and estates. He has been described as 'devious, dishonest and, even judged against the standards of his own age, more than commonly rapacious'.[48] In 1449, he even was the target of an assassination attempt by William Tailboys, and the last years of his life were spent in a struggle against attempts to besmirch his name as well as a bitter conflict with John Holland, Duke of Exeter, over land.[49]

William Lovell III's life is a good example to show that while there were certain expectations of and limits to a nobleman's public life, they had considerable leeway in how they choose to fulfil their role. Perhaps the fate of his uncle Robert Lovell persuaded him to avoid the perils of being too close to royalty beyond those of execution for treason and death or captivity in war.

William Lovell III did occasionally participate in the administration of the country. He was trier of petitions for Gascony and other overseas territories in the parliament of 1433.[50] After his effective retirement from military service, William Lovell III appears regularly on commissions, particularly for Oxfordshire. Here he was repeatedly appointed to commissions trying to persuade the notables of the county to lend the king considerable sums of money for the defence of the realm. William Lovell III himself was one of the people who opened their purses for a loan. In 1435, he was to be repaid 500 marks (£333 6s. 8d.), a considerable sum and demonstration of his wealth.[51]

A consequence of William Lovell III's distance from court, the centre of patronage, was that he received few rewards, except occasional favours, as in 1440 when he was allowed to impark some fields close to Minster Lovell, though they were within the royal forest of Wychwood.[52]

But even a retiring man like William Lovell III was part of the ruling elite. William Lovell III was granted the offices of constable of Wallingford Castle and of steward of its honour and lands after the banishment and murder of William de la Pole, Duke of Suffolk in 1450 who had held it before. If William Lovell III had not been regarded as a steady and reliable administrator he would not have received the grant.[53] Later the same year, Richard, Duke of York considered William Lovell III the most influential nobleman in Oxfordshire as he sent his auditor to talk to him about the elections of knights of the shire.[54]

William Lovell III continued to be appointed to commissions until 1454 but in 1453 he was excused from attending parliaments and councils, due to his bad health.[55] William Lovell III died on 13 June 1455. His eldest son and heir John Lovell IX was at least 22.

John Lovell IX married Joan Beaumont, daughter of John, Viscount Beaumont and Elizabeth Phelip. Though William Lovell III himself was not a courtier he had many links to the royal court and his peers. He worked together with Ralph Cromwell, who was married to the sister of William Lovell III's wife, as in 1447 when they were two of the founders of the Guild of St Christopher in Thame.[56] Through his wife Alice Deincourt he was also related to John, Viscount Beaumont, whose sister Elizabeth Beaumont, was the widow of Alice Deincourt's brother William, Lord Deincourt. William Lovell III and John Beaumont had interest in the same localities and served occasionally on the same commissions. They attended parliament together and occasionally acted together as when they both were feoffees of William Ferrers of Groby. The match of John Lovell IX to Joan Beaumont was a prestigious one and linked the Lovells to another influential and rich family.[57]

William Lovell, the second son of William Lovell III, did not serve in any prominent position in either local or central administration. Only once, in the parliament of 1459, he sat as knight of the shire for Oxfordshire. Possibly it was his mother Alice Deincourt who helped him to gain this position. She was the governess of the prince of Wales at this time (see next chapter).[58]

William Lovell married Eleanor Morley before 1465. As the only daughter of Robert Morley and Eleanor Roos she was the heiress of the Morley and Marshal baronies. It was Eleanor Morley's grandfather's grandfather Thomas Morley whose right to the arms *argent, a lion rampant sable, crowned and armed or* John Lovell VII had challenged before the Court of Chivalry eighty years earlier (see previous chapter). After the death of her grandmother Isabel, daughter of Michael de la Pole, Earl of Suffolk in 1467, William Lovell and his wife Eleanor were also given seisin of the land she held.[59]

Little is known about William Lovell III and Alice Deincourt's two younger sons, Robert and Henry. Both were provided for handsomely by their father in his will. Since these lands were later in the hands of

Francis Lovell, they must have died without children. It is possible that Robert Lovell married Eleanor Roos. He must have died before 1466 when Eleanor Roos was married to Thomas Prout.[60]

William Lovell III was buried in Greyfriars Convent in Oxford. Just as he did not follow his grandfather's example to pursue a career at court, he chose not to be buried in the same place as John Lovell VII. His decision did not only break family tradition it also does not conform with historians' expectations of noble families' behaviour.

It has been argued that the arrival of a noble family in a certain area was symbolised by and strengthened through their establishment of a *caput honoris* and a family mausoleum. The *caput honoris*, the main residence of the family, was a symbol of the family's power in the area. A place successive generations would enlarge and modernise to demonstrate to the public their presence and importance. Close to the main residence, 'the foremost symbol of status' of a noble family, would be a church in which successive generations of the family were buried. Like the main residence the church would be endowed repeatedly and improvements or even whole rebuilding programmes financed by the family. Just as a magnificent residence demonstrated the wealth and grandeur of a noble family, the richness and size of their family mausoleum would be a public display of their power, piety, and generosity. Its interior would be a celebration of the nobility of the family in the stained glass windows and ornaments showing the family's coat of arms and their ancient lineage by the growing number of splendid tombs, equally lavishly decorated with the family's coats of arms.[61]

The noble family's castle and mausoleum at the *caput honoris* would become the centre of administration and remembrance. As Chris Given-Wilson sums up: 'Here [at his *caput honoris*] he would build his castle, the symbol of his lordship ... and nearby would be the chief religious house patronised by the family, often indeed founded by it, where successive generations of lords and their families would be buried.'[62]

While many families followed this pattern, the Lovells of Titchmarsh did neither have a favourite castle nor a mausoleum where succeeding generations were buried. Since the burial places of only three Lords Lovell are known for certain, it may be dangerous to draw conclusions, but it is remarkable that all three men were buried in different churches. John

Lovell VII decided to be buried in the Hospital of St. James and St. John in Brackley (Northamptonshire). His grandson William Lovell III was buried in in the church of the Greyfriars Convent in Oxford. William Lovell III's son John Lovell IX was buried in St Kenelm's, Minster Lovell (see plate 11). Each site reflects personal priorities and a personal choice. Why these particular churches appealed to them can only be answered for John Lovell VII. The Hospital of St. James and St. John in Brackley was the traditional burial place of the Hollands and represented his gaining the Holland barony through his wife Maud Holland.[63]

While John Lovell IX's tomb survives to the present day in Minster Lovell, the tombs of John Lovell VII and of William Lovell III no longer exist. Like so many other tombs, they were destroyed either during the Reformation or in one of the many waves of iconoclasm during the next two centuries that did not spare even the tombs of kings who were buried in monastic buildings, like Henry I's in Reading Abbey.

It is possible that another Lovell tomb still exists in the parish church St Mary the Virgin in Titchmarsh. The fourteenth-century tomb in the south isle of the church has been tentatively identified as that of one of the Lords Lovell.[64] Since the church is right next to where Titchmarsh Castle once stood it is a plausibly theory, but the tomb could just as easily be that of another well-off nobleman or knight. Even though most of the burial places of the Lovells are unknown, the existing evidence shows that the family was not interested in creating a family mausoleum. For John Lovell VII, William Lovell III and John Lovell IX, as well as presumably the other Lovells, personal piety was more important than family tradition.

The Lovells did not only not establish a family mausoleum, they also did not have a single castle that was their preferred residence over several generations on which they spent their energy and money to enlarge, modernise and embellish. Minster Lovell Hall comes closest to achieving this distinction. Its convenient location, less than 20 miles from Oxford and not too distant from London made it a good place to stay for men who had to regularly attend court. It's pleasant setting was also no doubt part of its charm.

William Lovell III rebuilt Minster Lovell Hall as a fortified manor house during the 1440s. It was mainly designed to provide for the comfort of the lord and his family. Even the quarters of the lord's personal attendants included fireplaces. Though Minster Lovell Hall is now in ruins, its size and lavishness still give an impression of the magnificent residence it once was. Some details of its former ornate decorations remain, like the elaborate tracery in the room under the chapel, the decorated vaulting of the entrance porch, and the patterned path leading to the porch. The building displayed the wealth of its builder to all who visited or passed it (see plates 9 and 10).[65]

However, Minster Lovell Hall was not the only castle that served as a major residence. Titchmarsh (Northamptonshire) became the main residence of the Lovells in the later thirteenth century, when its name was used to differentiate John Lovell III from his half-brother John Lovell of Snotescombe (see Chapter 4). In 1304, John Lovell III received a licence to crenellate his castle in Titchmarsh. However, it did not remain the main residence of the Lovell family for long. Already in 1361, the buildings had fallen into disrepair.[66] Titchmarsh Castle was later restored, probably by John Lovell VII, since archaeological excavations have found traces of a rebuilding programme.[67] Today, Titchmarsh Castle has completely disappeared. Only a few stones peeking out of the soil in the remnants of the moat and a small rise called chapel mount are still visible (see plate 2).

Wardour Castle (now Old Wardour Castle, Wiltshire) is the most eccentric residence linked to the Lovell family. It was the project of John Lovell VII who received license to crenellate his manor at Wardour at the beginning of 1393.[68] The castle he decided to build was a large, hexagonal tower house. Like Minster Lovell Hall, Old Wardour Castle is now in ruins. Like Minster Lovell Hall, the ruins are still imposing and give the visitor an impression of its former splendour. Wardour Castle looks more like a traditional castle than Minster Lovell Hall. However, it was also built primarily as a family residence, with large, comfortable private lodgings. The outfacing walls were decorated with flowers and animals' heads. The vaulting of the entrance corridor is an early example of fan-vaulting.[69] The grandeur, lavishness, and eccentricity of Wardour Castle is a testament to John Lovell VII's taste in architecture and a demonstration of his wealth (see plates 6–8).

Though I have previously called Wardour Castle John Lovell VII's favourite residence it is unlikely that he spent long periods of time there.[70] Since building only started around 1393, Wardour Castle must have been a construction site for many years and not a comfortable place to stay.

Moreover, John Lovell VII spent a large part, if not the majority of his time at the royal court or on campaign, and Wardour was a considerable distance from London and thus too far away for any short visit to the countryside.

To attend court, noble families who could afford it also invested in houses in London. The Lovells owned a house in Paternoster Row, close to St Paul's Cathedral, called Lovell's Inn, part of the inheritance of Maud Holland.[71] Robert Lovell's house was situated in Old Fish Street not far from Lovell's Inn. Once, as mentioned above, the Privy Council headed by Prince Henry was held in Robert Lovell's house in London.

To supervise their estates barons and greater lords led itinerant lives, not only staying in London to attend parliament but also visiting different estates to supervise their management and assert their authority. There are only a few instances in which there is concrete evidence of one of the family staying at one of their residences. In 1393, John Lovell VII was on his way to Minster Lovell when he was attacked by William Wakelyn and his associates. Richard, Duke of York, expected to find William Lovell III at Minster Lovell Hall as he sent his auditor there in 1450. On his progress through England after his coronation Richard III stayed in Minster Lovell in the company of Francis Lovell in 1483. John Lovell IX wrote to his father-in-law from Rotherfield Greys (Oxfordshire).[72] The manor, part of the inheritance of Alice Deincourt, had been 'exceedingly derelict' in 1422. It must therefore have been rebuilt by William Lovell III, to allow John Lovell IX and his mother to stay there in the mid-1450s.[73]

Though Minster Lovell emerges as the main residence of the Lovell family which was also used for the longest time, it was not the only residence and perhaps calling it their *caput honoris* would be stretching the term. For the Lovells personal preferences were as important a factor as family tradition. This may at least in part be a consequence of the long minorities, particularly during the fourteenth century. If they had been raised with their guardian's family they may have established new relationships that seemed more important than the connection to their own family residence and burial place.

John Lovell VII had held a high respected position in the governments of both Richard II and Henry IV, which had brought influence and riches to the family. His son John Lovell VIII and grandson William Lovell III were noticeably less involved at court and in military service. The death of John Lovell VIII only six years after his father's death may be part of the reason why he did not distinguish himself. However, in the time he was head of the family, John Lovell VIII had shown little interest in gaining a position at court as did his son William Lovell III, who fulfilled his duties by participating in several campaigns in France as a young man and by serving on commissions in the localities, but for most of his life was content to live the life of a rich landholder without seeking promotion through service at the royal court.

Several noble families served with distinction in war in peace over several generation, but the Lovells followed a different path. While some Lords Lovell, like John Lovell III or John Lovell VII, did pursue careers at court, others, like John Lovell VIII and William Lovell III did not. Medieval noblemen were influenced by the traditions of their family, but they did not determine the way they lead their lives.

This was not the only point in which the Lovell family showed less regard for family traditions than other noble families. They neither established a family mausoleum nor did they have one single favourite residence on which they concentrate their building efforts. A reason for this lack of continuity may have been the repeated long minorities that interrupted their history. Wardships may have created new connections to different families or locations and estranged them from the traditions and connections of their own family. Though, in the same circumstances others may have felt a particular need to hold on to their family's traditions to confirm their identification with them.

Since their arrival in England in the twelfth century, the Lovells had risen from being a family at the lower end of the nobility, holding only a few manors to enormously rich barons whose estates were spread far and wide across almost all of England, from Wiltshire to Yorkshire and from Kent to Chester.[74] They had accumulated five baronies, Lovell, Holland, Burnell, Deincourt, and Grey of Rotherfield. The five coats of arms are proudly displayed for example on the tomb in Minster Lovell and on the garter stall plate of Francis Lovell in St George's Chapel in Windsor (see plate 13).

William Lovell III's income rivalled that of the poorest earl. His reluctance to serve at court and in war was probably the reason why the family did not rise into the titled peerage. But service at court could also be a ruinous business, as Robert Lovell discovered. It could also be dangerous. This aspect of noble life may have persuaded William Lovell III to eschew career and promotion in favour of a quieter life.

The family's rise in wealth was only in part due to service, another equally important factor that made this rise possible were the heiresses who married into the family and the land they brought with them. These heiresses and the female offspring of the family have so far been left to the side-lines. They deserve a closer look.

Chapter 7

Wives, Widows, and Daughters

In his last will, William Lovell III decreed that his wife Alice Deincourt was to be the surveyor of the will. As heiress of the Deincourt and Grey of Rotherfield baronies, Alice was already a very rich woman. She held significant parts of the Lovell estates as her dower and in jointure. Her wealth made her one of the richest and most powerful women of her time.

In short, Alice Deincourt was one of the 'tough, dower-clutching widow[s]' of the later Middle Ages.[1] She outlived her husband William Lovell III by almost nineteen years, became governess of the prince of Wales, married a second time, and outlived her second husband, too, if only by ten months. The long-lived dowagers fascinate due to their longevity and have all too often been viewed as a nuisance. Holding a significant part of the family's estates they have been regarded as hindering the careers of their sons, particularly if they remarried. It was judged that 'the mere survival of dowagers could and did cause havoc', and that heiresses like Alice Deincourt 'had a nasty habit of surviving their husbands, sometimes for decades, to keep the heir out of the promised land'.[2]

Just as our interpretation of history has been too royalist for a long time, as K.B. McFarlane pointed out decades ago, so our view on women in general and widows in particular has for a long time been too patriarchal.[3] While viewing family history in the Middle Ages and beyond primarily from the perspective of the male head of the family does reflect how these families saw themselves, criticising these women for outliving their husbands does not take into account that they were valued members of the family who were as interested in the good of the family as their male kin.[4]

While some of the problems when researching noble men and women in this period are the same, researching noble women is even more challenging because even fewer records exist. This is due to the fact that for the major part of their lives women were not considered to be individuals by law. Young unmarried women were represented or 'covered' by their fathers. Wives were considered to be part of their husbands' legal person. Only widows or unmarried heiresses were legally considered to be a separate person, a 'feme sole'. Despite these difficulties it is worthwhile to explore the lives of the women as well since they were an important, in fact an essential part of noble families.

Taking Alice Deincourt's life as a guide this chapter addresses various aspects of women's lives in the Middle Ages. The first and most obvious is the identity of the women marrying into the family and the arrangements of the marriages including the provisions made for them in case they outlived their husbands. We also look at whether it is possible to assess the quality of the relationship between husbands and wives and how the women's contribution to the family's fortunes was valued. After discussing Alice Deincourt's role at court, a distinction she shares with her granddaughter's granddaughter Jane Parker, the question of second marriages and how the long-lived dowagers impacted on the lives of their sons will be addressed. The chapter will also briefly look at the lives the daughters of the family.

Several important aspects of the role of noble women for their families cannot be discussed in context of the Lovell family due to a lack of sources, for example their role as administrators and representatives of their husbands during the often long periods they were absent in the king's service either at court or in war.

From Isabel de Breteuil who married Ascelin Goël around 1100 to Grace Newport who became the wife of Henry Parker the younger in the 1530s, seventeen women married into the family. How little is known about these women is already apparent by the fact that the identity of four of them cannot be established with certainty: Isabel, the wife of William Lovell II, Joan, second wife of John Lovell III and another long-lived dowager, as well as Isabel and Eleanor, the wives of John Lovell V and John Lovell VIII, respectively. Since these four women were neither heiresses nor did their marriages occur under unusual circumstances like the marriages of Ascelin Goël and William Lovell I they left hardly any trace in the records. It is only from the fifteenth century on that women who were not heiresses, like Anne FitzHugh and Alice St John, can be identified with certainty. While there is no hint of who Isabel, wife of William Lovell II, could have been, tentative identifications were made for the other three. In the following I will consider these identifications as correct and refer to them as Joan de Ros, Isabel de la Zouche, and Eleanor de la Zouche.

Nearly all the women who married into the family came from families of a similar rank. Relatives of John Lovell III's two wives received their individual summonses to parliament at the same time he did; John Lovell V's wife was from a neighbouring baronial family. As the Lovells became richer, more powerful and of higher status, the rank of the women they married rose as well. William Lovell III, who had just inherited the Burnell estates, married Alice Deincourt, herself a rich heiress. When John Lovell IX married Joan Beaumont, daughter of John, Viscount Beaumont, the income of his father William Lovell III was equal to or even surpassing that of the of the poorest earl.[5] William Lovell III's grandson, Henry Lovell, Lord Morley even married into the royal family. His wife Elizabeth de la Pole was the niece to Edward IV. He was, however, the only Lovell to marry directly into the royal family. Though his father had been a second son, his mother was the sole heiress to the Morley barony. The considerable estates he inherited from his mother made him an attractive spouse. Moreover, his elder cousin, Francis Lovell, was a close friend of the king's younger brother, Richard, Duke of Gloucester, and Henry Lovell himself was a henchman of Edward IV which brought him into close contact with the king (see following chapters).

There were, a few exceptions to this rule. The families of both Isabel de Breteuil and Matilda Beaumont were of considerably higher status than their respective spouses, Ascelin Goël and William Lovell I. The fact that Isabel was illegitimate should not be regarded as lowering her rank considerably. At the time, the illegitimate children of Henry I were marrying into the highest nobility. One illegitimate daughter, Sybilla, was even married to Alexander I, King of Scotland (1107–1124). Ascelin Goël was only able to attain a wife of her status by forcing Isabel's father, William de Breteuil, to give his daughter in marriage to be released from imprisonment in Bréval. It was the strategic importance of the Castle of Ivry that made its castellan William Lovell I important enough for Waleran Beaumont to marry Matilda, one of his sisters.

When medieval noblemen married, one might argue the most important goal all involved parties had in mind was that the women produced an heir that would ensure the family's survival. This was not the only role women were expected to fulfil, as Joanna Laynesmith has pointed out in connection to queens, wives had larger and more complicated roles, but providing an heir was an important one.[6]

In this role as mothers of the future Lords Lovell the Lovell ladies did fulfil their function for a surprisingly long period of time. The family died out in the male line only after 400 years or thirteen generations through a combination of a failure to produce children, in the case of Francis Lovell, and premature death, in the case of his cousin Henry Lovell.

Noble families who succeeded in continuing the family in the male line almost inevitably accumulated land and became more powerful by marrying women who were or became heiresses. The marriages of the Lovells to four heiresses, Maud de Sydenham, Maud Burnell, Maud Holland, and Alice Deincourt, brought considerable estates to the family and were the one of the bases for the Lovells' rise from modest noblemen into the titled peerage at the end of the fifteenth century. Eleanor Morley, wife of William Lovell and heiress of the Morley barony ensured that this younger son was elevated to the parliamentary peerage, and her daughter's son, Henry Parker, became Lord Morley in 1518. Only one of marriage to an heiress did not increase the Lovells' lands, since Isabel du Bois' inheritance went to her daughter Maud and the de la Zouche family (see Chapter 4 and below).

Alice Deincourt is one of the few women whose exact date of birth is known. She was born on 24 February 1404 and her younger sister Margaret was born on 21 September 1405. The dates of their births were noted down so meticulously, since they had become the heiresses of their brother William Deincourt when he died in 1422. To determine who would be gaining control over his large estates after his death, the administration needed to know their exact ages and whether or not they were married. The sisters' status as heiresses also gives us a very narrow window of time when they were married: between receiving her share of her brother's estates in February 1423 and November 1423 when the estates held by her grandmother were divided between Alice, her sister Margaret, and their husbands (see previous chapter).[7]

It is interesting to note that both Alice and her sister Margaret married men who had been campaigning in France with Henry V. Margaret's husband Ralph Cromwell had been appointed to the council governing England during the minority of Henry VI (1422–1461). Alice's husband William Lovell III had not achieved the high positions that Ralph Cromwell held in France, but his considerably higher status, holding the Lovell and Holland baronies, and successfully claiming the Burnell barony probably compensated for this. It is also likely that he had made connections, perhaps with Ralph Cromwell, that now came in useful.[8] Service in war, in the case of William Lovell III and Ralph Cromwell, brought them reward in the form of marriages to two rich co-heiresses.

Marriages were arranged by the fathers of the couple or, if the father died before his son or daughter had achieved majority, by a guardian who often was granted the marriage of the ward as well. However, the marriage of an underage heir could also already have been arranged by his father prior to the father's death. One could speculate that John Lovell V had arranged the marriage of his son and heir to Maud, the granddaughter of Robert Holland with whom had campaigned in France. However, as in most marriages too little information has survived to judge who exactly arranged or may have influenced the arrangement of this marriage.

Six Lords Lovell, John Lovell I, John Lovell V, John Lovell VII, William Lovell III, Francis Lovell, and Henry Lovell, Lord Morley, probably married women chosen by their guardian. It is often assumed that the guardian would marry an heir whose wardship and marriage he received to a daughter or a close relative. However, in the history of the Lovell family this rarely happened. Only one guardian, Alan Basset, married his ward John Lovell I to his daughter Katherine. Another guardian, Richard Neville, Earl of Warwick married his ward Francis Lovell to his niece Anne FitzHugh, the daughter of his sister Alice, even though he had two unmarried daughters of appropriate age. As the heir of several baronies Francis Lovell was no mean catch, but Richard Neville obviously did not think he was a good enough candidate for his own daughters and heiresses and hoped to find better spouses.

The great fear of many noble families was that under-aged heirs would be married to unsuitable, that is lower ranking spouses, was never realised in the Lovell family. Marriages arranged by the Lovell family themselves did not differ from those most probably arranged by a guardian.

Guardians, after all, were often themselves members of the nobility and their interests frequently coincided with the wards' own families. In fact the Lovells profited from most of the marriages arranged by guardians. The marriage of John Lovell I created useful links to the influential Basset family which helped John Lovell II to enter royal service. Maud Holland's inheritance was at least as large as the Lovell holdings at the time and this marriage was a big leap in status for John Lovell VII. Unless, as speculated above John Lovell V and Robert Holland had arranged the marriage of their offspring prior to their deaths, whoever did arrange John Lovell VII's marriage certainly had his best interests at heart.

Marriages also established connections between baronial families or reinforced ties that already existed. The marriages of John Lovell V and John Lovell VIII to Isabel and Eleanor de la Zouche show how important ties between these neighbouring families were. The nobility was closely connected through these marriages, but this did neither dictate people's action, nor were they a sure way to avoid conflict. Then as now, families quarrelled, particularly about money and inheritance.

Though it would be exaggerated to say that parents or guardians did not give their children or wards any say in the arrangement of their marriages, they made the final decision and made the arrangements. However, when the women outlived their first husbands, which they often did, they could and did decide for themselves whether they wanted to re-marry and if so whom, as will be discussed below.

During the arrangement of a marriage between noble families, provisions were made to ensure the bride had a sufficient income to live comfortably if she should outlive her husband. From the fourteenth century on, heiresses were also granted lands in the form of jointures in addition to their dower. This phenomenon has been often criticised. It was argued that by outliving their husbands and taking control of parts, sometimes large parts of the family's estates the dowagers reduced the status and possibilities of their heirs.[9]

Dower and jointure were not concessions noble families were forced to make during marriage negotiations, but were considered necessary to ensure that the women were well provided for. Widows were as interested in the prosperity of the family as their husbands. Mothers or grandmothers holding the family estates could generally be expected to preserve the land better than outsiders, who often exploited the wards' lands to gain maximum profit. Guardians had sometimes paid considerable sums for the wardship after all and wanted to recoup the money as quickly as possible. They were accused of letting buildings decay and exploiting quick income sources like woods. Women like Alice Deincourt or Maud Holland did not have to regain any outlay of money. It was in their own interest to carefully administer these estates, if they wanted to continue profiting from the income of the lands as well as to ensure the prosperity of their offspring.[10]

Conflicts between dowagers and heirs did occur, sometimes between mothers and sons but more often with stepsons or more distant relatives of their deceased husbands. This was however not the norm. It is also not surprising that sometimes conflicts broke out in an era when land was the foundation of power and quarrels about land between families as well as inside families were frequent.

Records about the provisions the Lovells made for their wives only survive from the fourteenth century onward. Joan de Ros, widow of John Lovell III, held the manors of Elcombe and Blunsdon Gay (Wiltshire).[11] As the Lovells became richer, the share of the lands given to their wives in dower and jointure became greater as well. As a great heiress Maud Holland held a substantial part of the Lovell estates after her husband's death, almost twenty manors in eight counties as well as property in London, advowsons, other lands, woods, services, and rents. Among the manors that Maud Holland and John Lovell VII held jointly were Minster Lovell and Wardour.[12] The manors and lands put in jointure on Alice Deincourt and William Lovell III lay in seven counties, and again included the central manors of Minster Lovell and Wardour.[13] Joan Beaumont also held an impressive number of manors, though they did not include the central manors like Minster Lovell or Titchmarsh, since they were still in the hands of her mother-in-law Alice Deincourt.[14]

While widows of attainted rebels were not punished for their husband's crimes and were usually granted their jointure, the situation was different if the husband was still alive. Cecily Neville did not receive any of her dower lands after Richard, Duke of York was attained.[15] Francis Lovell's wife, Anne FitzHugh, was in the same position after the attainder of her husband. She received no dower, instead several of the manors Francis Lovell had settled on his wife were granted to other men by Henry VII

(1485–1509).[16] With Francis Lovell's disappearance after the Battle of Stoke his wife was left in a legal limbo, neither wife nor widow.

Though Anne FitzHugh was later exempted from her husband's attainder, the government was obviously not feeling charitable towards the wife of a prominent rebel and there was no one able or willing to fight for her rights.[17] All Anne FitzHugh received was a grant of an annuity of £20 by Henry VII in 1489. This was not a large sum. By comparison Frideswide Lovell was granted an annuity of 100 marks (c. £66) after her father-in-law participated in rebellion by the duke of Buckingham, and a pittance compared to the dower of approximately £600 she would have received as widow of Francis Lovell.[18]

Though provisions for spouses are mostly talked about in connection with dower and dowagers, men also profited from the estates of their wives if they outlived them. There were two ways for a man who married a rich widow or heiresses to continue holding the lands of his wife after her death: enfeoffments to use and what was referred to as 'courtesy of England'. Courtesy of England allowed a widower to keep possession of his wife's estates after her death, if he and his wife had any children, even if these children had died. A prominent example is John of Gaunt, who retained control of the lands of his wife, Blanche, after her death.

Only one of the Lords Lovell, John Lovell III, outlived his wife, Isabel du Bois. He continued to hold some of her land until his death when it passed to his daughter Maud and her husband William de la Zouche. After Maud Burnell's death in 1341, her widower John Haudlo retained parts of her estates by courtesy of England. John Lovell V inherited the part that was not entailed after the death of John Haudlo in 1346.

In the absence of personal documents, only a few records allow an assessment of the relationship between the Lords and Ladies Lovell. Among them are last wills and testaments.

William Lovell III made his wife Alice Deincourt surveyor of his will and put his 'special faith and trust' in her. Alongside the executors and feoffees Alice Deincourt was charged to decide how much of the 200 marks William Lovell III bequeathed to Greyfriars, Oxford, was to be in cash and which part in ornaments. She was to oversee the deposition of his movable and immovable goods as well.[19] The scope of duties and the freedom William Lovell III gave his wife in the execution shows clearly how much he trusted her.

Two generations earlier, John Lovell VII had appointed Maud Holland as executrix of his testament along with his eldest son John Lovell VIII.[20] Making her one of the executors of his will also showed that he trusted her to fulfil his final wishes and have the business acumen to do so. John Lovell VII felt so closely associated with the family of his wife that he decided to be buried in the Holland family mausoleum in the Hospital of St. James and St. John near Brackley (see Chapter 5).

It was here that John Lovell VII had wished to found a house of Dominican friars. Maud Holland gave the manors of Bagworth and Thornton (Leicestershire) to Thomas Langley, Bishop of Durham for this foundation in 1420. The royal license for the foundation specifies that within ten years a house of thirteen friars should be created. The project was beset by difficulties before it was properly started. In 1411, the archdeacon of Taunton in Wells was ordered by papal mandate to improve and clarify the statutes of the hospital.[21]

Maud Holland efforts were, however, half-hearted at best. No significant progress was made before her death in 1423. The hospital's warden John Brockhampton died in the same year, and an inquisition discovered that there were no brethren resident at the Hospital and its funds had been grossly misused.[22] The fact that Maud Holland's son John Lovell VIII had predeceased her and her grandson William III was a minor no doubt were part of the reasons why the project to establish the friary was never realised. However, in the fifteen years she outlived her husband this pious work to improve the church in which her family and her husband were buried and thereby help their souls in the afterlife seems to have not been a priority for her. It had taken her twelve years alone to obtain a license to provide the land needed for the foundation. Maud Holland's failure to establish the friary should not be regarded as a sign that she neglected her husband's wishes and memory. Though most widows had fulfilled their husbands' wishes by the time they themselves died, there were numerous widows who had not and who in turn asked their heirs to establish the religious foundations their husbands had envisioned.[23] Maud Holland did take a vow of chastity, a sign of both her person piety and her continued loyalty to her late husband.[24]

Maud Holland was not alone in neglecting the project to transform the hospital in Brackley. Her grandson William Lovell III did not fulfilled the wish of John Lovell VII to found a Dominican friary as he had envisioned it either. The hospital was returned to the Lovells and, in 1425, it was re-established on a smaller scale.[25] Eventually it was dissolved, and in 1484 Francis Lovell sold it to William Waynflete, Bishop Winchester who used it as part of his endowment of Magdalen College. Interestingly, the arrangement made between Francis Lovell and William Waynflete only stipulates that obsequies were to be held for Francis Lovell and his wife. Usually parents or ancestors generally were included in such bequests. The fact that Francis Lovell did not sheds an interesting light on his relationship to his natal family, particularly considering that some of his ancestors were buried in Brackley.[26]

Another indication for good relations between husbands and wives are the occasion when the wives accompanied their husbands on their travels or even military campaigns and endure the hardships this brought. Joan de Ros was with her husband John Lovell III in Scotland in 1303, Maud Burnell went with her second husband, John Haudlo, on pilgrimage to Santiago de Compostella, and Alice Deincourt may have accompanied her husband William Lovell III to France.[27] Only on rare occasions records exist that prove women travelled with their husbands, it is likely that they did so more often but without leaving any trace in the records.

A poignant testimony of the relationship between Anne FitzHugh and her husband Francis Lovell can be found in the Paston letters. Anne FitzHugh's mother cancelled a business meeting with John Paston III, because she did not wish to leave her daughter alone in her distressed state. 'My daughter Lovell is very distressed about her husband, my son[-in-law]. Sir Edward Franke has been in the north to inquire about him. He has come back and cannot understand where he is. [Also my doghtyr Louell makith great sute and labour for my sone hir husbonde. Sir Edwarde Franke hath been in the north to inquire for hym. He is comyn agayne, and cane noght vnderstonde wher he is.]'[28] Anne FitzHugh's distress about the disappearance of her husband after the Battle of Stoke surely is a sign that their relationship was affectionate. No doubt her distress was increased by the financial uncertainties Francis Lovell's disappearance meant for her (see above). It would, however, be a very cynical reading to see those problems as the only reason for Anne FitzHugh's grief.

In this rare private letter we can glimpse the close relationship between a mother, Alice Neville, and her daughter, Anne FitzHugh. Unfortunately the relationship between the Lords Lovell and their mothers remain largely untraceable. Only one letter survives in which a mother is mentioned, that of John Lovell IX to his father-in-law John Beaumont. It contains no more than polite phrases. John Lovell IX relates to John Beaumont that his mother Alice Deincourt wants to be recommended to him and that she wishes he acted as her good brother since she has taken him as her chief counsellor.[29] The only definite fact the letter reveals is that Alice Deincourt and her eldest son spent some time together at Rotherfield Greys.

While married women rarely had a 'career' outside their marriages, two of the women of the Lovell family gained positions at the royal court. After her husband's death Alice Deincourt became governess to Prince Edward, the long and eagerly awaited heir of Henry VI and Margaret of Anjou. Jane Parker was a lady-in-waiting of several of Henry VIII's (1509–1447) queens (see Chapter 9).

Unfortunately, no record exists about Alice Deincourt's appointment as governess or how she fulfilled this role. The only source that refers to Alice Deincourt holding this position is the letter patent recording her retirement on 23 March 1460: 'Commission to Alesia, lady Lovell, reciting her service to Edward, prince of Wales, in his tender days, and discharging her from attendance about his person, because he is now so grown as to be committed to the rules and teachings of men wise and strenuous, to understand the acts and manners of a man befitting such a prince, rather than to stay further under the keeping and governance of women; and because she is oppressed with grave infirmities in body and sight, as her petition has shewn.'[30] No further records exist about Alice Deincourt's time as governess.

Even though a considerable number of books were written about education in the late Middle Ages, almost all of these passed over the very first years of a child's upbringing, even if the child in question was a prince. Nonetheless, the role of governess or lady mistress was an important and prestigious one. Unlike the nurse, this position was held by an aristocratic lady of mature age, who over a number of years looked after the royal nursery and its inhabitants, the prince himself and a number of young noblemen who were schooled with him. The mistress was overseeing the prince's early education particularly in matters of courtesy.[31]

A generation earlier, Alice Beauchamp, Lady Butler, was appointed to this position for the young Henry VI. She is described as 'a suitable wise and expert person in matters of "courtesy and nurture"'. The description of the role of governess Alice Beauchamp was vague but she was to instruct the young king in good manners, letters, languages, nurture and courtesy. If necessary she also had the right to chastise her charge without fear of consequences.[32]

As governess Alice Deincourt had to fulfil the same role in the upbringing of Prince Edward. She would have been appointed when he was about 2 years old, towards the end of 1455. It is therefore likely Alice Deincourt's appointment as governess followed not long after the death of William Lovell III. She was holding the position almost certainly by April 1457 when she received a pardon for all fines and amercements stemming from entering her inheritance without the necessary formalities.[33] She must have spent considerable time at the court and have become a known and respected figure to be given this important position.

Alice Beauchamp was rewarded with two annuities for her services as governess to Henry VI.[34] If he had remained king and his son had eventually become Edward V Alice Deincourt would have probably been rewarded in a similar way.

The transition from a predominately female to a male environment for sons and particularly heirs was gradual, and already in 1457 tutors appointed for Prince Edward.[35] In March of 1460, Edward was 6 1/2 years old, old enough to be under the supervision of male tutors, as stated in the letter patent releasing Alice Deincourt from her duties. The political instability of this period also made it advisable to publicly show that the prince already had reached an age of greater responsibility.

It would be interesting to know how much truth was in the claim that Alice Deincourt herself had asked for her dismissal due to her age and serious health problems. The explanation rings a bit hollow considering that not only did she marry again, she also lived for another fourteen years. Perhaps this explanation for her dismissal was more politically motivated than a factual statement.

The death of a husband was an 'unavoidable break in continuity and a degree of instability' for a noble wife.[36] Apart from the emotional distress that losing a partner, often a partner of many years, brought, becoming a widow fundamentally changed the position of the women within the family. Various factors influenced the place the new widows found themselves in, ranging from their own age to the absence or presence of children. Some developments were, however, the same for all widows. All came into the full possession of their dower and jointure. Legally they became individuals. They stepped, willingly or unwillingly, out of the shadow of their husbands and, as rich landholders, became powerful nobles in their own right. Holding their dower and often also a considerable jointure, noble widows were also attractive marriage partners. But not all widows were keen to marry again. Some enjoyed their new independent position while others wished to stay faithful to their husbands, sometimes taking a vow of chastity as Maud Holland did.

Almost all women marrying into the Lovell family outlived their husbands. However, so little information has survived about them that their lives as widows remain almost impenetrable. For many not even the time of their death is known. In the twelfth and thirteenth century, when no *inquisitions post mortem* were made, the exact time of death is generally not known for both women and men of the lower ranking nobility. Even in the fifteenth century, when more records were kept and the Lovell family had reached the higher echelons of the nobility, it is not known when Eleanor de la Zouche, widow of John Lovell VIII, and Anne FitzHugh, wife of Francis Lovell, died.

Some of the Lovell widows outlived their husbands only for a short time, like Isabel de la Zouche and Joan Beaumont, who both died within two years of their spouses. Others died many years after their husbands' death. Katherine Basset, wife of John Lovell I, survived her husband by at least sixteen years. She died after 1268, when she is last mentioned in the records.[37] Maud Holland outlived her husband and her son. Joan de Ros died thirty-eight years after John Lovell III outliving both her son John Lovell IV and grandson John Lovell V.

Whether a widow remarried did not depend on the length of widowhood. Joan Beaumont, who died a year and just under seven months after John Lovell IX, was already married again to Sir William Stanley. Though large parts of the Lovell estates were in the hands of her mother-in-law, she held a considerable dower. Additionally, she was the heiress apparent of her brother William, Viscount Beaumont. It is more than likely that she was at least strongly encouraged to marry again. Another widow who remarried quickly was Maud Burnell, who had become a very attractive match after the death of her brother. The marriage seems to have been her own choice (see Chapter 4). Some of the longest living dowagers, including Katherine Basset and Joan de Ros, did not marry again.

Widowed at the age of 51, Alice Deincourt's dower was assigned on 21 October 1455. When she inherited the second half of the Deincourt and Grey of Rotherfield estates that her sister Margaret had inherited after the death of her brother-in-law Ralph Cromwell, Alice Deincourt became very wealthy indeed.[38]

As governess of Edward, Prince of Wales, Alice Deincourt was in no hurry to marry again. Eight years into her widowhood and three years after her dismissal as governess, in 1463, she married her second husband Ralph Butler, Lord Sudeley.[39] A stained-glass window in Chilton (now part of Sudbury, Suffolk) commemorated both Alice Deincourt and Ralph Butler.[40]

There is no doubt that Alice Deincourt's second marriage to Ralph Butler was her own choice. If she had suffered from serious health problems, as her dismissal as governess states, Alice Deincourt must have recovered. At the time of her second marriage Alice was almost sixty and her second husband Ralph Butler, Lord Sudeley was already well into his seventies.

Alice Deincourt and Ralph Butler were well acquainted from the time both spent at the Lancastrian court. His mother Alice Beauchamp, Lady Sudeley had been the governess of Henry VI. Like Alice Deincourt's sons John Lovell IX and William Lovell, Ralph Butler was a firm supporter of Henry VI. He was at the Battle of St Albans but, probably due to his advanced age, did not participate in the other battles of this first phase of the Wars of the Roses. He made his peace with Edward IV, as did John Lovell IX. In the first years of his reign, Edward IV treated Ralph Butler leniently, but later his attitude changed. In November 1469 Edward IV 'forcibly extracted' from Ralph Butler the castle and lordship of Sudeley, which was the central manor of Butler's estates, to endow his younger brother Richard with it.[41]

Ralph Butler's daughter-in-law, Eleanor Talbot, was the woman at the centre of Richard's claim to the throne. It was the precontract to marry between her and Edward IV that, according to the *Titulus Regius,* made Edward IV's marriage to Elizabeth Woodville invalid, their children illegitimate, and Edward's younger brother Richard the rightful heir to the throne. (The argument that children were regarded as legitimate if their parents were not aware that their marriage was invalid does not apply in this case, as Edward IV would have been well aware of the situation.)

Since Alice Deincourt was Francis Lovell's grandmother, her second marriage to Ralph Butler created a link between Eleanor Talbot, Ralph Butler's daughter-in-law and the immediate circle around Richard, Duke of Gloucester. A fact that has been pointed out by defenders of Richard III.[42] If the claim of the marriage between Edward IV and Eleanor Talbot was true – and this is, of course, one of the most hotly debated aspects of Richard III's reign – Richard may well have heard about it from Francis Lovell, who was one of his closest friends and companions. Francis Lovell in turn could have heard about the scandalous secret marriage from his grandmother who was, after all, married to Eleanor Talbot's father-in-law. Francis Lovell himself would have been a child when his grandmother told him. He was not the only person who could have told Richard about the secret marriage. William Catesby was also close to Richard III and Eleanor Talbot, but Francis Lovell was certainly a closer personal friend of Richard.[43]

Widows who married again have sometimes been described as hapless victims of their inexperience. McFarlane for example writes about often finding a dowager who 'choose to throw herself away upon a social inferior'.[44] It is certainly an interesting phenomenon that the second husbands of many widows' were of lower rank than the widows themselves. Among the most prominent is Joan of Acre, daughter of Edward I, who married Ralph de Monthermer after the death of her first husband Gilbert de Clare, Earl of Gloucester. Famously she is reported to have told her enraged father, 'It is not ignominious or shameful for a great and powerful earl to marry a poor and weak woman; in the reverse case it is neither reprehensible or difficult for a countess to promote a vigorous young man.'[45] Other examples are Katherine of Valois, the widow of Henry V, who married Owen Tudor, and Jacquetta of Luxembourg, widow of John, Duke of Bedford, who married Sir Richard Woodville.

The reasons widows married men of lower status no doubt varied. Often they were men they knew. Ralph de Menthermer for example had been in the entourage of Joan of Acre's first husband. Maud Burnell knew her second husband as a member of the Despenser household through her sister-in-law Alina Despenser. Their second husbands were men they trusted and liked. In addition, by marrying men who were their social inferiors, some widows may have hoped to retain more independence.

The great fear of disparagement that was often expressed when heiresses or heirs were minor, was obviously not shared by these women, who often defied their families to marry whom they wished or did so without the necessary permission by the king.

But not all widows married men below their ranks. Maud Burnell is the only Lovell dowager whose second husband was of lower rank. Both Alice Deincourt's and Joan Beaumont's second husbands were of baronial rank. Alice Deincourt definitely cannot be accused of falling for one of the 'adventurers with pretty faces' that McFarlane sees pursuing rich dowagers.[46] Her husband was in his seventies when they married. It seems hardly necessary to point out that most of these widows were mature women, Alice Deincourt was almost sixty at the time of her second marriage. They had experience in the world of noble landholding and could very well make up their own mind.

Were these 'tough, dower-clutching widows', in particular those who remarried again, responsible not only for the reduction of their heirs' income but also for his reduced status and lower chances to fulfil his potential?

The Lords Lovell whose mothers and/or grandmothers were holding large parts of the family estates certainly were less prominent men than their fathers. However, they all died young. John Lovell IV died only four years after his father, John Lovell VIII six years after his father John Lovell VII, and John Lovell IX ten years after William Lovell III. John Lovell IX's position within the nobility had no doubt also suffered from his support for Henry VI during the Wars of the Roses. The relatively lower status of these three men was therefore not caused by their mothers' longevity but by their own short lives.

Alice Deincourt was past her child-bearing years at the time of her second marriage to Ralph Butler. Her age meant neither could her inheritance be diverted to another family, nor could her second husband have been able to keep her estates 'by courtesy of England' even if he had outlived her. In due course, all the lands she held in dower and in jointure did pass to her grandson Francis Lovell after her death in 1474. The fact that Alice Deincourt was holding a large part of the Lovell estates prevented them from falling into the hands of Francis Lovell's guardian.

Maud Burnell's second marriage did negatively influence the fortunes of the Lovell family. The Burnell estates that she inherited from her brother Edward did not pass to John Lovell V, Maud Burnell's son from her first marriage to John Lovell IV, but to Nicholas Burnell, her son from her second marriage to John Haudlo. John Lovell V did only receive a small part of the Burnell estates, including the manor of Sparkford and the hamlet of Upton (Somerset). The Lovells eventually reaped the benefits from John Lovell IV's marriage to Maud Burnell when her grandson Hugh Burnell died without male heirs. The diversion of most of the Burnell estates to her second family was no doubt disappointing for John Lovell V, but Maud Burnell had not been expected to inherit her brother's estates when she became the wife of John Lovell IV. She did not renege on an arrangement made at their marriage. Maud Burnell simply exercised her right to pass the land to whom she wished to leave it. The same right men exercised when they diverted parts, sometimes significant parts, of their estates to younger sons.

Joan Beaumont's marriage to Sir William Stanley was so brief that it had no impact on the family's fortunes. Particularly since large parts of the Lovell estates were held by another dowager, Alice Deincourt.

As already mentioned, earlier daughters are almost impossible to trace as they so often did not exist as a legal person under the laws of the time. In most cases their existence, their names, and the names of their husbands only comes to light when they inherited or were granted some land, as landownership and its descent was carefully recorded. It is therefore unsurprising that the first known daughter of the Lovell family is Maud Lovell, who inherited the du Bois lands of her mother Isabel du Bois. Similarly Joan Lovell, daughter of John Lovell IV and Maud Burnell, was her father's heir when he died in 1314. After the birth of her brother John Lovell V a few months later, who replaced her as heir to the Lovell lands, Joan vanishes from the records without a trace.

After the Lovells of Titchwell, the cadet branch of the Lovells of Titchmarsh, died out in the male line in 1415, a lawsuit about the right owner of their lands began between Sir John Fastolf, who had bought them, and the Lovells of Clevedon who claimed they were the legal heirs. During his investigation to discover the veracity of their claim, William Worcester included a list of the sons and daughters of John Lovell VII and Maud Holland. Next to the heir John Lovell VIII and Robert Lovell, they had two more sons, Ralph, who became a canon at Salisbury Cathedral, and Thomas, who was married to Alice, but about whom not much more is known. They also had three daughters but only one of them married. Philippa first became the wife of Sir John Dinham and secondly of Nicholas Broughton. The other two daughters were both in religious orders. Maud became abbess of Romsey Abbey, and an unnamed daughter joined the minoresses in London.[47]

William Lovell III's will reveals that he and Alice Deincourt had a daughter as well as four sons. He left £200 for the marriage of his granddaughter, Anne Ogard, 'if she be married worshipfully and to such as is or shal be a lorde of name'.[48] Nothing else is known about Anne Ogard as she completely disappears from the records.

Since Ogard was a very unusual name it is almost certain that William Lovell III's unnamed daughter was married Sir Andrew Ogard, a Danish knight and a member of the council of the Duchy of York from the 1440s onwards. Though Andrew Ogard was not a baron, he was certainly wealthy. He had served in Normandy and had been granted land worth £1,000 per annum.[49] William Lovell III's unnamed daughter must have died young, since Andrew Ogard married again. His second wife was Alice, daughter of John Clifton. Andrew Ogard moved from the household of Richard, Duke of York to that of Queen Margaret's. After his death in 1454 she looked after the son he had with his second wife. His first wife, William Lovell III's unnamed daughter, therefore must have died several years earlier, and when William Lovell III made his will his granddaughter Anne Ogard was an orphan and in particular need of support for finding a suitable husband.[50]

The Lovell daughters whose marriages we can trace were almost exclusively married to men of gentry rank, and though the family became richer, this did not change. Elizabeth, daughter of John Lovell V and his wife Isabel, married Sir Robert of London in the late fourteenth century. Joan and Frideswide, daughters of John Lovell IX and Joan Beaumont, married Sir Brian Stapleton and Sir Edward Norris respectively, one hundred years later. Only Maud Lovell, daughter of John Lovell III and

Isabel du Bois, married a married into a family of equal rank as her own. Since her uncle John du Bois had died childless in 1290 and her other uncle William du Bois was a cleric, it was certain that Maud Lovell would inherit the du Bois estates after his death. As an heiress she was an attractive bride for a baron, William de la Zouche.

Another exceptionally good marriage was that of Jane Parker, daughter of Henry Parker, Lord Morley. She married George Boleyn, son of Thomas Boleyn and brother of Anne Boleyn. The Boleyn family had already forged marriage links to several of the greatest noble families, including the Howard Dukes of Norfolk. However, their meteoric rise as well as their fall was due to Henry VIII's infatuation with Anne Boleyn. The three families, the Parkers, Boleyns, and Howards, were neighbouring landholders and multiple ties existed between the families. The second husband of Alice Lovell, Jane Parker's grandmother, was Edward Howard, whose sister was George Boleyn's mother. Thomas Boleyn was an executor of the will of Henry Lovell, Jane Parker's uncle (see Chapter 9).

By marrying their daughters to neighbouring aristocratic families created more ties or reinforced existing links which held the aristocracy together. The gentry from which most of the daughters' husbands came were still part of the ruling, landholding class. The difference in status between barons like the Lovells and the gentry was often more apparent than real. Not only were the younger sons of a baronial families themselves part of the gentry, the families the Lovell daughters married into were from the richer gentry whose interests coincided mostly with those of the peerage.

Even though little is known about the lives of the women of the Lovell family, they were integral parts of the family. They were mothers to the next generation of the family, ensuring the survival of the Lovells for almost five hundred years. The lands that the heiresses brought to the Lovells was, alongside the service the Lords Lovell rendered, the main reason for the family's rise within the nobility. Their role in the family fortunes was acknowledged and proudly displayed when the Lords Lovell adding their wives' families' titles and coats of arms to their own.

As far as evidence allows any judgement, the relationship between the Lords Lovell and their respective wives was amicable. John Lovell VII and William Lovell III both gave their wives a prime role in the execution of their wills. Some women, like Joan de Ros and Alice Deincourt, did accompany their husbands to war. Maud Holland took a vow of chastity after the death of her husband.

The often maligned long-lived dowagers were not responsible for their sons' misfortune. Rather it was their sons' short lives that was the reason why they did not achieve the same prominence as their father. Mothers and sons saw themselves not as rivals but as partners who wished to retain the family's status and keep the estate profitable and well maintained. Rather than wishing 'their mothers to an early grave', their sons appreciated their experience and expertise. Moreover, mothers of minor heirs managed the family lands they held more responsibly than guardians did.[51]

The marriages of the Lords Lovell and their wives, as well as the marriages of their daughters and sons, created and reconfirmed the ties that held the nobility together. But these ties were not unbreakable and friction between and within families, often about lands, but also about influence, were common. During the reign of Henry VI, his inability to act as an arbiter of conflicts led to an escalation of conflicts that eventually turned into a civil war.

1. The ruins of the castle of Ivry-la-Bataille. Once a formidable border fortress, it was the focus of ambition of Ascelin Goël and his sons. (*I, Nitot; https://commons.wikimedia.org/wiki/*)

2. Location of the vanished Castle at Titchmarsh. Only a ditch and the so-called Chapel Hill are still visible. (*Author*)

3. Miniature of the Resurrection of Christ, with marginal praying figures of Lord Lovell and his wife Maud Holland. (*Harley, 7026, fol. 9 v, © British Library*)

4. The seals of Maud Holland her three sons, John Lovell VIII, Robert Lovell, and Ralph Lovell. (© *The National Archives TNA E42/278*)

5. The coats of arms used by the Lovell family. Top row, left to right: Lovell of Titchmarsh, Burnell, Holland. Bottom row, left to right: Deincourt, Grey of Rotherfield. The Burnell coat of arms is differenced with a bordure azure and missing the sword the lion is often depicted as holding. (© *Gill Smith*)

6. Old Wardour Castle, an eccentric, hexagonal tower house, was built by John Lovell VII. (*Author*)

7. Old Wardour was severely damaged during the Civil War, when a mine accidentally exploded during the siege of the castle. (*Author*)

8. The ruins of Wardour Castle were later integrated into the park of New Wardour House. (*Author*)

9. The ruins of the hall at Minster Lovell. (© *The National Archives SC 1/46/102*)

10. Some of the elaborate window tracings of the Hall still remain. (*Author*)

11. The tomb of John Lovell IX in St Kenelm's Church, Minster Lovell. The heraldic decorations are (left to right): 1) Quarterly: Lovell, Sydenham, Grey of Rotherfield, Zouche; 2) and 3) quarterly of six: Lovell, Deincourt, Holland, Grey of Rotherfield, Burnell, divided per fess in chief Sydenham, in base Zouche; 4) Sydenham. (© *Tim Sutton*)

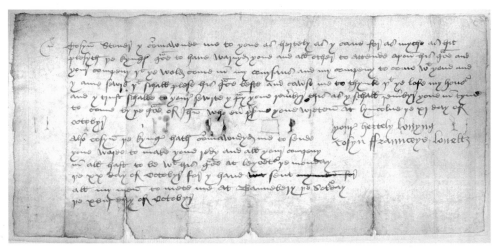

12. Francis Lovell's letters to his 'cousin' Stonor. (*C47/37, National Archives*)

13. Francis Lovell's garter stall plate in St George's Chapel, Windsor Castle, a combination of the coat of arms of the five baronies he held. The shield is divided quarterly, 1) Lovell, 2) Deincourt, 3) Holland and 4) Grey of Rotherfield with a scutcheon of pretence of Burnell. (*Public Domain, digitized by Google*)

14. Albrecht Dürer's portrait of Henry Parker, Lord Morley. (© *The Trustees of the British Museum*)

Chapter 8

The Wars of the Roses

The first Battle of St Albans on 22 May 1455 is usually seen as the point when the political conflict between different factions at court turned into the war we know as the Wars of the Roses. However, at the time no one could have foreseen that it was the start of a series of different but interdependent conflicts that lasted for more than thirty years. The Wars of the Roses had a profound impact on the lives of Alice Deincourt, her two sons John Lovell IX and William Lovell, Lord Morley, and her grandson Francis Lovell.

As governess of the young Prince Edward, Alice Deincourt spent the last years of the 1450s mostly at court and close to Henry VI and Margaret of Anjou. Both her sons, John Lovell IX and William Lovell, as well as her second husband Ralph Butler were firm supporters of the king and queen. John Lovell IX was also married to Joan Beaumont whose father John, Viscount Beaumont, was regarded by the Yorkist side as one of their principle 'mortal and extreme' enemies by 1460.[1]

John Lovell IX and his wife Joan had three children, one son and two daughters. In a surprising break from family tradition, their son was named Francis. Why they choose this unusual name is unclear. Possibly, he was named after his godfather, which was often the case and could explain the introduction of the name.[2] However, Francis was an extremely unusual name at the time. It also was not used either by the Beaumont or by the Deincourt family. It was more popular in France, where several dukes of Brittany were called Francis and it became increasingly popular in England in the sixteenth century with Francis Drake and Francis Bacon just the most famous men bearing this name. Joan Beaumont and her husband were most likely simply preferring unusual names for their children. While one of their daughters was given the more traditional name Joan, their other daughter was named Frideswide after Saint Frideswide, whose shrine was located in the Priory of St Frideswide in Oxford (now Christ Church Cathedral).

Through his father-in-law John Beaumont and his mother as governess of Prince Edward, John Lovell IX had close ties to the Lancastrian court. It is possible, if only a speculation, that his son Francis spent some years at court as a young child as companion to the prince of Wales. Young noblemen were often sent to court to keep company of young princes.[3] Francis Lovell was about the same age as Edward and would have been an appropriate companion to the young prince. As companion Francis would have had the opportunity to create a friendship or at least companionship with the prince of Wales, which, had the Wars of the Roses not happened, would have been useful for the future.

In the years following the death of William Lovell III, his son John Lovell IX was appointed to very few commissions in the localities, which is surprising for a man of his wealth and status. The commissions John Lovell IX was appointed to were not concerned with regular administrative work, like commissions of oyer and terminer or to inquire about land holdings. In 1457, John Lovell IX was appointed to a posse against rebels and a commission of array in Oxfordshire. Perhaps he also spent a large of part his time at court like his mother and father-in-law. He was also appointed to only three commissions of the peace, in Berkshire, Northamptonshire, and Oxfordshire, while his father had been on seven.[4] He attended the only parliament that was held between the death of William Lovell III in 1455 and the outbreak of open hostilities in 1459 and was appointed as trier of petitions for England, Ireland, Wales, and Scotland.[5]

When repeated attempts to find a peaceful solution to their differences failed the conflict between Henry VI and his court on the one side and Richard, Duke of York, Richard, Earl of Salisbury, his son, Richard, Earl of Warwick, and their followers escalated further. The three Yorkist lords assembled their army in Ludlow, where Henry VI confronted them with his own forces. John Lovell IX was present alongside his father-in-law at what is known the 'Battle of Ludford Bridge' (12 October 1459).[6] Henry VI and his forces prevailed and later in the same year, John Lovell IX was granted the office of master forester in Wychwood, expressly as a reward for his good service against the duke of York, the earl of Salisbury, and the earl of Warwick.[7]

The leaders of the uprising were attainted, and the conflict became a dynastic struggle when the duke of York unsuccessfully claimed the throne for himself. As a loyal supporter of the Crown, John Lovell IX was appointed to commissions to arrest all followers of the rebellious Yorkist lords in Oxfordshire, Berkshire, Hampshire, and Wiltshire and to call together all available men in Oxfordshire and Berkshire to resist them if they should return from their exile abroad.[8]

When the Yorkist leaders returned in the spring of 1460, the earls of Warwick and March were able to gain control of London with the support of the citizens. They failed, however, to take the Tower of London, which was held by troops under the command of the constable of the Tower Henry, Duke of Exeter. Other high-ranking defenders were Thomas, Lord Scales, Robert, Lord Hungerford, Richard de la Warre, who was married to Robert Hungerford's sister Katherine, and John Lovell IX. When the citizens of London cut off the Tower and food was running low, the besieged turned the guns of the Tower on the surrounding city.

While the siege continued, Henry VI's army was defeated at the Battle of Northampton on 10 July 1460. Henry VI was captured and John Lovell IX's father-in-law Viscount Beaumont was killed. After this devastating defeat the garrison of the Tower surrendered. Several of the Tower's defenders were killed by an angry London mob as a revenge for pointing the cannons at the town. Rank was no protection: Thomas, Lord Scales was one of those lynched, and his naked body thrown into the cemetery of St Mary Ovary (now Southwark Cathedral). Other defenders were executed at Tyburn.[9] John Lovell IX was lucky to escape with his life.

Despite this harrowing experience, John Lovell IX remained a steadfast supporter of Henry VI. In the final decisive battle of this phase of the Wars of the Roses, the Battle of Towton on 29 March 1461, John Lovell IX fought for Henry VI. After the triumph of the Yorkist side, John Lovell IX's lands in Cambridgeshire, Shropshire, and Essex as well as his estates in Northamptonshire and Rutland were seized by the Crown. The lands held by his mother Alice Deincourt in Northamptonshire and Rutland were also confiscated. She was the only woman amongst a number of noblemen who was deprived of her lands. This shows that she was not only a great landholder but also that she was considered a threat to the new king.[10]

John Lovell IX was summoned to Edward IV's first parliament, the writs for which were sent out on 23 May 1461. As the list of noblemen summoned is almost identical to that of the previous parliament this is no indication of him being recognised as a supporter of the new king. However, he eventually made his peace with Edward IV and by 27 December 1461 his possession in fee tail were confirmed.[11]

As a consequence of the confiscation of his estates John Lovell IX's financial position was strained. Shortly after the Battle of Towton, on 4 March 1461, John Lovell expelled James Butler, Earl of Wiltshire and Ormond from Ashby-de-la-Zouche. This manor was part of the Beaumont lands, and John Lovell IX's attack on the current owner was probably an attempt to claim the Beaumont estates after the death of his father-in-law in the Battle of Northampton in 1460.[12] Acquiring this property would have improved his income. The attempt failed, since Ashby-de-la Zouche was later in the hands of William Hastings. In 1462 John Lovell IX recognized a debt of 1,000 marks to Richard Quartermayns and sold the manors of Pitchford, Rowton and Amaston.[13] To gain the trust of the new government John Lovell IX was one of the people who 'rushed to bestow estate offices upon [William] Hastings, the new chamberlain', making him steward for life of his manors of Bagworth and Thornton (Leics.) and master of the game in Bagworth for life in 1461.[14]

It took close to three years until John Lovell IX was again appointed to commissions concerning local government or to the commissions of the peace in the counties in which he held considerable estates. In 1464 his name first appears in a commission of oyer and terminer in Oxfordshire and Berkshire.[15]

John Lovell IX died not even a year later, on 9 January 1465. He was buried in St Kenelm's Church in Minster Lovell, where his tomb can still be visited today (see plate 11 and Chapter 6).[16] Soon after his death, his widow Joan Beaumont married Sir William Stanley. The marriage was a short-lived one, as Joan Beaumont died a year and a seven months after her first husband, on 5 August 1466.[17]

At the time of John Lovell IX's death, his son and heir, Francis Lovell, was 7 years old.[18] Francis's two sisters, Joan and Frideswide, were likely of similar age. Though Francis Lovell's wardship and marriage was granted to Richard Neville, Earl of Warwick only on 19 November 1467, he was already married to Anne FitzHugh. John Wykes reported on 17 February 1466 in a letter by to John Paston II that 'the Lord Lovell ys son hath weddyd my Lady Fytzhugh ys doghtere'.[19] It is interesting to note that it was Anne's mother, Alice Neville, Lady FitzHugh, rather than her father Henry, Lord FitzHugh, whom John Wykes choose to identify Francis Lovell's bride. Alice was the sister of the earl of Warwick and her daughter Anne was Warwick's niece. It seems therefore likely that Francis Lovell had already been under informal guardianship of Richard Neville, when the marriage was arranged.

The timing of the grant is also interesting, since at the time Edward IV and the earl of Warwick were at odds about foreign policy and Edward IV's decision to marry his sister Margaret to the widowed Charles the Bold, Duke of Burgundy. With the wardship of Francis Lovell Warwick received the control of substantial lands, though a considerable part of the estates was still held by Francis's grandmother Alice Deincourt. Alice Deincourt was well into her 60s at the time and it was almost certain she would die before her grandson came of age. Francis Lovell's relocation from southern England, where the centre of Lovell estates lay, to the north was to shape his life.

It is often assumed that Francis Lovell spent several years in Middleham with Richard, Duke of Gloucester.[20] This is possible, if Francis Lovell had already been in the custody of Richard Neville before his wardship was granted to him. There is, however, no evidence where Francis Lovell was living during this time. He may have stayed at the royal court or lived with his parents-in-law at Ravensworth as he did a few years later. How long Richard, Duke of Gloucester, stayed at the earl of Warwick's castle is also not certain. Different historians have come to widely different conclusions. If Richard already left the earl of Warwick's care in 1464, as Paul Murray Kendall thinks, he and Francis Lovell would have spent only a short time together in Middleham. If he stayed until 1468 or even into 1469, as Charles Ross concludes, they would have been companions for several years.[21]

In the end the exact time and circumstances of how Francis Lovell and Richard, Duke of Gloucester met are not important. What we do know is that a close companionship and friendship developed between the two, which eventually propelled Francis Lovell to the centre of power and made him the most famous of all Lovells.

It is tempting to imagine that Francis Lovell was present in Middleham after the renewed outbreak of civil war in 1469, when the earl of Warwick brought Edward IV there, a prisoner in all but name. A year later, when the fortunes of war had turned again, and Warwick had fled to France, his brother-in-law, Henry FitzHugh started a revolt that considerably disturbed the re-established rule of Edward IV. However, the revolt broke out prematurely and was easily supressed. Francis Lovell, his wife Anna FitzHugh, and his two sisters, Frideswide and Joan, were living with Lord FitzHugh at the time. They were included in the pardon the rebels received.[22]

William Lovell, Francis Lovell's uncle, was another supporter of the earl of Warwick's rebellion. Though he had married Eleanor Morley, the heiress of the Morley and Marshal baronies he had not received summonses to parliament as Lord Morley. At this time, husbands were still not automatically summoned to parliament if they were holding a barony in the right of their wives but depended on the goodwill of the king. It seems that Edward IV considered William Lovell as not reliable enough to merit being invited to the House of Lords. In contrast, William Lovell was summoned to the parliament scheduled to take place in York at the time in when Edward IV was a virtual prisoner of the earl of Warwick.[23] He was again summoned as William Lovell, Lord Morley for the one parliament held during Henry VI's restoration to the throne in 1470.[24] Due to his partisanship for Henry VI, William Lovell was not summoned again to parliament when Edward IV had regained the crown.

Another relative, Ralph Butler, Alice Deincourt's second husband and Francis Lovell's step-grandfather, also supported Henry VI during his short return to the throne. Ralph Butler carried the sword of state before Henry VI in what Ashdown-Hill describes as 'the sad little procession' through London.[25] Unlike William Lovell, Ralph Butler, was not struck from the list of peers who received summonses for the only parliament held between Edward IV's return and his own death in 1473.[26]

At the Battles of Barnet and Tewkesbury in 1471, Edward IV successfully defeated both Warwick's and Henry VI's forces. After the death of his guardian at the Battle of Barnet, Francis Lovell's wardship, together with some of his lands, were granted to the king's sister Elizabeth and her husband John de la Pole, Duke of Suffolk. Elizabeth and John de la Pole did not receive the entire Lovell estates as parts were given to other aristocrats including Ralph Hastings and Humphrey Blount.[27] Francis Lovell may have lived with the de la Poles for the next few years, but he continued to have close contact with his wife's mother, Alice

Neville. In 1473, the year after her husband died, Alice Neville, her two daughters Anne and Elizabeth, and her son-in-law Francis Lovell joined the Corpus Christi Guild at York.[28]

When his grandmother, Alice Deincourt, died in 1474, custody of her land was given as a payment for outstanding debts of the Crown.[29] In November 1477 Francis Lovell reached full age and was given permission to enter his estates.[30]

There is astoundingly little we know about Francis Lovell's life over the next years. For three years he disappears completely from the records. In 1480 he was appointed to commission of array in the North Riding of Yorkshire. He also accompanied the duke of Gloucester on his campaign into Scotland, where he knighted Francis Lovell. In 1482 he was appointed to a commission of oyer and terminer in the three ridings of Yorkshire.[31] Though the evidence is thin, it seems that he spend most of his time in the north and in the service of Richard, Duke of Gloucester, far away from the regions in the south where most of his estates were situated. Despite his distance from the court in London, Francis Lovell actively participated in parliamentary business and was appointed trier of petitions for England, Ireland, Wales and Scotland in the parliaments of 1483 and 1484.[32]

Francis Lovell was one of the richest barons of his time. He held five baronies and his estates were spread over a large part of England. How Francis Lovell administered his large estates is one of the many aspects of his life that eludes us, as no records have survived. It is clear, however, that he and the men working for him, were carefully monitoring estates that he had a right to. In 1481, Francis Lovell sent his men to enter the manor of Bridgeford, held by William Wainfleet, and to claim it in his name. The manor was part of the Deincourt inheritance and had been given by Ralph Cromwell to his niece Joan Stanhope. She had died childless earlier in 1481 and since the manor had been entailed, Francis Lovell was the rightful owner.[33]

On 4 January 1483, Edward IV created Francis Lovell Viscount. Without a doubt, his elevation into the titled peerage was made possible by his close association with Richard, Duke of Gloucester.

A description of the ceremony of Francis Lovell's creation to viscount has been preserved in a British Library manuscript.[34] The description wrongly identifies the king as Richard III and therefore must have been written some time after the event. According to the report, Francis Lovell was not accompanied by two viscounts as was the tradition, but by two relatives: his brother-in-law, Richard FitzHugh, and his young cousin, Henry Lovell, Lord Morley. It is possible that the ceremony had to be changed, as there was only one viscount, William, Viscount Berkeley, available. The other viscount, Francis Lovell's maternal uncle William, second Viscount Beaumont, was imprisoned.[35] Francis Lovell's full title was now Viscount Lovell, Lord Holland, Burnell, Deincourt, and Grey of Rotherfield.

The unexpected death of Edward IV on 9 April 1483 threw the kingdom in turmoil and brought Francis Lovell to the centre of the rapidly changing situation. It is not known whether Francis Lovell was in the company of Richard, Duke of Gloucester or joined him in the capital shortly after the duke and the new king Edward V (1483) arrived there. Richard, Duke of Gloucester was soon made Lord Protector, and Francis Lovell was promoted to influential posts. He was appointed Chief Butler as well as constable of Wallingford Castle.[36]

At the end of June 1483, in what must have been a truly shocking development for the contemporaries, Edward IV's children with his queen, Elizabeth Woodville, were declared illegitimate, and Richard, Duke of Gloucester was asked to become king in the place of the young Edward since as a bastard he had not right to the throne.

Obviously, this is not the place to discuss the details of whether Richard III's claim to the throne was valid or not or the fate of Edward IV's sons. Academic studies and popular discussions have examined all available information from different perspectives and come to widely different conclusions. These mysteries and debates have made Richard III one of the most famous or infamous kings in English history, depending on one's point of view. It is, however, not possible to completely ignore these questions when writing about Francis Lovell. Depending on whether Richard III is seen as ruthless usurper or rightful king, Francis Lovell as his close friend will be viewed either as an equally ruthless villain or the friend and faithful servant of a legitimate king.

The precontract between Edward IV and Eleanor Talbot has already been touched upon in the previous chapter. Different researchers have drawn opposing conclusions from the existing evidence. Nigel Saul, for example, categorically states that 'There can be little doubt that the charge was a fiction'[37] while John Ashdown-Hill, quoting James Gairdner, states 'that there were no grounds for dismissing this marriage as "mere political invention". The marriage remains entirely credible.'[38] Both sides claim that there is no evidence that proves their opponents' allegations. There is no chance that this question will ever be conclusively answered.

Another fiercely discussed question that has to be at least briefly addressed is that of the fate of Edward IV's sons, since if Richard III did kill his nephews, Francis Lovell supported a ruthless usurper and murderer of innocent children. Once more, this question cannot be answered. While it is certain they disappeared, what happened to them is not. Richard III is not the only suspected murderer of Edward V and Richard, Duke of York. The range of alternative suspects include the duke of Buckingham and Henry VII. It has also been argued that the boys, or at least Edward V, died of natural causes. The argument continues and, just like the one about the validity of Richard III's claim to the throne, there is little chance that it will be solved one way or the other. Even if the bones resting in Westminster Abbey and said to be those of the two murdered princes were examined and it could be proven beyond reasonable doubt that they are those of the princes, and it could also be established (which is highly unlikely) that they were murdered, the identity of the person who ordered them killed would still not be settled.

As is well known, after the princes' disappearance rumours persisted that one or both princes survived and were spirited away. A less well known tale involves Francis Lovell directly. A legend in Cheshire claims that the two 'Princes in the Tower' were not murdered but secretly moved by Francis Lovell from the Tower to Longdendale, one of his properties in Cheshire.[39] However, while the story is interesting it raises too many questions. Whom was Francis Lovell hiding the princes from and why would this be necessary? As one of the most loyal supporters of Richard III, he would hardly hide them from their uncle. If they were simply removed from London, to be out of the focus of attention, the obvious place to take them would be to Sheriff Hutton in North Yorkshire where other royal children, including their cousins Edward, Earl of Warwick and John de la Pole, were staying. After the Battle of Bosworth, Francis Lovell would not have had the opportunity to sneak them out of the

Tower, even if he had feared that the new king Henry VII would be a threat to their safety.[40]

Both questions, the existence of Edward IV's marriage with Eleanor Talbot and, as a consequence of it, Richard III's right to the Crown, and the fate of Edward V and his younger brother Richard are closely and inextricably linked. Since neither can be answered conclusively, the question whether Francis Lovell was the henchman of an evil monarch or the close friend and supporter of a righteous king can also not be answered.

On 28 June 1483, in the run-up to Richard III's coronation Francis Lovell was appointed lord chamberlain of the royal household as successor of William Hastings.[41] The lord chamberlain was in constant attendance on the king and was therefore always a person the king implicitly trusted. Just as his predecessor William Hastings had been a very close friend of Edward IV, Francis Lovell was the closest friend of Richard III.

The close and constant contact with the monarch and his responsibilities, including the control of both written and personal access to the king, gave the chamberlain a position of power reached by few if any other member of the royal household with the exception of the queen. The chamberlain was also in charge of the treasure and jewels stored in the king's chamber, and several of the other members of the household had to submit their accounts to him. He also oversaw the proper equipment of the king's chamber. Should the chamberlain be absent from court, he was supposed to appoint a deputy who would perform his duties. Unfortunately, no records survive that would allow us to judge whether Francis Lovell appointed deputies and who they were if he did.[42]

The chamberlain's influence meant that he often attracted the envy and hostility of other members of the court, and critics of the king's government and policies frequently complained that the chamberlain abused his position to gain undue influence over the king. William Latimer, Edward III's chamberlain, was impeached, and Simon Burley and William Scrope, Earl of Wiltshire, both chamberlains of Richard II, were executed.[43]

The records of the coronation of Richard III throws a revealing light on how close Francis Lovell had become to the King, and how important his family had become as a result. A large number of his relatives were present: his wife, Anna FitzHugh, his mother-in-law, Alice Neville, and her daughter-in-law, Elizabeth Borough, were three of the twelve noblewomen of the queen. Henry Lovell, Lord Morley, Francis Lovell's cousin, was the highest ranking of the king's henchmen. Francis Lovell himself carried the third sword during the ceremony. At first Francis Lovell's role was to be to carry the queen's sceptre, but he exchanged functions with the earl of Huntingdon. Perhaps Francis was given this task 'as a friend of the King'. Next to his (unfortunately unspecified) duties as chamberlain of the household, Francis Lovell stood before the king during the coronation banquet. Another, probably informal, function Francis Lovell fulfilled for the coronation was the purchase of the queen's ring. Francis Lovell's duties were not those that were traditionally performed by the chamberlain and chief butler. His close personal connection to the king allowed him to take a prominent role in the proceedings, and probably had an influence on the parts his family were given in the ceremonies.[44]

Even though Francis had already been appointed chief butler during the reign of Edward V, he was now re-appointed on account of the death of Anthony Woodville, Lord Rivers.[45] The chief butler collected the so-called 'butlerage', a custom fine on imported wine. He was also responsible for supplying the royal household with wine, purchasing the amount of wine necessary, and ensuring that it was stored where it would be consumed. He also had to buy the wine that was to be given as alms to individual recipients and religious houses.[46]

Francis Lovell did not fulfil all the daily routine work of chief butler. As chamberlain he had to be in constant attendance on the king and could not possibly have 'travelled largely independently of the household', as the duties of chief butler demanded.[47] The collection of butlerage was deputised and some of Francis Lovell's appointments in various ports are known from the Patent Rolls. Most of the deputies had no known previous connections with Francis Lovell. Only two men, Geoffrey Frank in Newcastle-upon-Tyne and William Catesby for Bristol, Exeter and Dartmouth, had established links to Francis Lovell.[48]

Francis Lovell's closeness to the king also ensured he received rich rewards. He was re-appointed as constable of Wallingford Castle and was granted the honour of Wallingford St. Valery, and four and a half Chiltern hundreds including fees and wages.[49]

Probably still in 1483 Francis Lovell was elected to the prestigious Order of the Garter, an honour that had already been bestowed on his great-great-grandfather John Lovell VII.[50] Commemorating Francis Lovell's membership in this most exclusive of all knightly orders is a plate of his coat of arms in St George's Chapel, Windsor. The shield is divided quarterly, 1) Lovell, 2) Deincourt, 3) Holland, and 4) Grey of Rotherfield with a scutcheon of pretence of Burnell. The coat of arms is enclosed by a garter on which the motto of the order is inscribed. Above shield and garter is a helmet, surrounded by mantling powdered with padlocks, the arms of the Sydenham family. On top of the helmet sits a dog or perhaps wolf, a play on the origin of the name 'Lovell' (see plate 13). The representative nature of the arms, each standing for a barony, is reinforced by the fact that Francis Lovell also listed all five titles on the stall plate. Considering the importance of heraldry at this time and the highly significant place this particular plate was installed, it is not merely decoration but allows us a fascinating glimpse on how Francis Lovell wanted to present himself to his contemporaries and to posterity: as the head of a family that had accumulated both titles and riches.

Only a few months after Richard III's accession to the throne, a series of rebellions against him broke out across southern England. The best known rebel was Henry Stafford, Duke of Buckingham, who up to that point had been one of the most vociferous supporters of Richard III. The rebellion brought together a disparate group of people, some had been close supporters of Edward IV, others were die-hard Lancastrians who supported the exiled Henry Tudor.

Francis Lovell was appointed to the general commission of array for the resistance against Henry, Duke of Buckingham, and to the commission to arrest and imprison the rebellious duke.[51] Though his family's centre of power was in the south and the midlands, with a particular concentration of estates in Oxfordshire and Berkshire, Francis Lovell had become detached from this area during his long stay in the north. How ignorant he was about the feelings of the nobility of the area where he should have had his greatest influence is clearly demonstrated by a letter he wrote to his neighbour in Berkshire, Sir William Stonor. On 11 October 1483 Francis Lovell wrote to his 'cousin' William Stonor, commanding him to array men against the duke of Buckingham and meet with the king on 20

October in Leicester. Francis Lovell also assured to remember Stonor in the future, a hardly concealed promise to wield some of his influence at court in his favour and concludes with 'your heartily loving cousin Francis Lovell'. A more obvious statement of his ignorance of William Stonor's actual political leanings is hardly imaginable.[52] By this time William Stonor had already joined the duke of Buckingham (see plate 12).

The premature beginning of the rebellion in Kent and the swift action of John Howard, Duke of Norfolk, ensured the suppression of this uprising. The duke of Buckingham failed to raise enough support in Wales. Even the weather seemed to conspire against the duke, swollen rivers prevented his escape, a storm scattered the small fleet of Henry Tudor who had intended to cross from Brittany to claim the English Crown.

In the aftermath of the rebellion Francis Lovell received considerable grants of land to reward him for his services. He was granted the Berkshire estates forfeited by Sir William Norris, father-in-law of his sister Frideswide, who had participated in the rebellion and fled abroad after the collapse of the uprising.[53] Francis Lovell probably also used his position at court to procure an annuity of 100 marks for his sister Frideswide in 1484.

Francis Lovell was given the constableship of the Castle of Rockingham together with William Catesby. Francis Lovell was also granted the manors and lordships of Cookham and Bray (Berkshire). He was made master forester of Wychwood, a position that had already been held by his father and grandfather. The list of lands, lordships, and manors granted to Francis Lovell, is impressive. Richard III also recommended Francis to his mother Cecily Neville as officer for her estates in Wiltshire.[54]

Francis Lovell, who previously had been only appointed to the commission of the peace in Oxfordshire, was now appointed to another eight commissions: in Bedfordshire, Berkshire, Buckinghamshire, Essex, Northamptonshire, the town of Oxford, Wiltshire, and the East and North Riding of Yorkshire.[55] After the rebellion of 1483, Richard III was promoting many of his servants and associates from the north to positions in the southern counties and to the commissions of the peace. Francis Lovell was to some extent part of this relocation, but he held considerable estates in all the counties in which he was added to the commission of the peace. His grandfather had been appointed to most of the commissions of the peace that Francis Lovell now joined. As one of the most influential men in the country and a close friend to the king, the appointments reflect both the status Francis Lovell held in these localities and his importance as a vital link between the court and these counties.

However, Francis Lovell was never able to use these new estates for political influence.[56] His position as chamberlain required that he remained in attendance of the king at court, the turbulent political developments, as well as the shortness of Richard III's reign meant that Francis Lovell was not able to establish a position of influence and power.

While Francis Lovell held several high and prestigious positions in the government of Richard III, it is impossible to evaluate how much Francis Lovell actually influenced Richard III's decisions. He was a person of great importance, but unlike other nobles who achieved a position of power and influence close to the monarch, Francis Lovell did not provoke open hostility from Richard's opponents. The only indication of animosity is the famous doggerel of William Collingbourne, quoted in the introduction. This is remarkable since Richard III's reign never lacked critics both during his reign and afterwards. As an interesting aside, Francis Lovell was a member of the commission to investigate the treasonous activities of William Collingbourne, the author of the famous doggerel.[57]

The fact that Francis Lovell filled his positions in such an unobtrusive manner has the negative effect, from the present perspective, that few chronicles mention him at all. Neither Mancini in his *Usurpation of Richard III* nor Thomas More in his *History of Richard III* mention him. He remains a 'shadowy presence' for the modern historian.[58] Only after Richard III's death Francis Lovell becomes more prominent in the chronicles.[59]

Like his ancestors and his peers, Francis Lovell was involved in a number of lawsuits over land. During the reign of Edward IV he lost both his quarrel with Sir Richard Grey, the king's stepson, and with William Hastings, the king's chamberlain. William had been granted parts of the Beaumont inheritance after they were forfeited by John Beaumont, Francis Lovell's grandfather. These lands included Ashby-de-la-Zouche, which John Lovell IX had already tried to claim in 1461. Francis Lovell now received a third of the Beaumont lands during the minority of William Hasting's heir. William Hastings' widow Katherine made an indenture with Francis Lovell, accepting him as her 'good lord and cousin', and paying 200 marks for the privilege, a transaction that Colin Richmond described as a clear case of bullying. In 1484, Richard III also granted Francis Lovell the possession of the estates which Edward IV had previously granted to his step-son Sir Richard Grey.[60]

Francis Lovell also quarrelled with his young cousin Henry Lovell, Lord Morley about the possession of the manor and lordship of Clayton (Buckinghamshire). Disputes over the possession of estates between noblemen were common as were arguments about land within a family. These conflicts did not necessarily mean that the contenders were hostile to each other. In fact, often they were a means to clarify the legal status of a property. Interestingly, in the dispute between Francis Lovell and Henry Lovell, Lord Morley, Richard III instructed the men running the manor of Clayton that *neither* of the contenders should get any income from the manor and lordship.[61]

In the summer of 1485, Henry Tudor, the Lancastrian contender for the Crown, prepared to invade England again, this time with the support of the French government. After news of this threat reached Richard III, he put the country on alert. According to the Croyland Chronicle, Francis Lovell was sent to Southampton to refit the fleet and prepare the defence of the coast. The Patent Rolls only record a commission to Francis Lovell, William Catesby, the mayor of Southampton and others. On 26 June 1485 and at any convenient place near Southampton they were to take muster of John Grey of Powys and 1,000 archers that were be sent to Brittany. The Croyland chronicler is considered a reliable, if biased, source. It is possible that Francis Lovell was sent to Southampton twice within a short period. How long he remained there, however, is not known.[62]

In these uncertain times, Francis Lovell also took steps to ensure his wife, Anne FitzHugh would retain a suitable income. He settled several manors, including Titchmarsh and Brackley on her in fee, which meant that these estates would be hers and she could pass them to her children of a second marriage.[63]

On 7 August 1485 Henry Tudor accompanied by troops provided by the French Crown, landed in Milford Haven near Swansea. Gathering supporters both from Wales and England, he marched into England.

Two weeks later, on 22 August 1485, the forces of Richard III and of his challenger met in the Battle of Bosworth. Richard III was killed and Henry Tudor became king Henry VII.

Since Francis Lovell had been sent to prepare the defence the south coast before Henry Tudor's landing, the question has been raised, whether he was present at the Battle of Bosworth.[64] Two sources written immediately after the battle, Henry Tudor's proclamation written on the eve of the battle and the York Memorandum from 23 August 1485 or the next day, lists Francis Viscount Lovell as among the dead.

While it is impossible to be certain, it seems likely that Francis Lovell was at Bosworth. As Richard III's chamberlain he had to be at the side of the king all the time. The report of the Croyland chronicler does not specify when Francis Lovell had been sent to the coast and the commission of array mentioned in the Patent Rolls dates almost two months prior to the battle allowing sufficient time for Francis to return to Bosworth in time to participate in the battle .[65]

The list of the dead in the new king's proclamation includes both men who had been killed, like John Howard, Duke of Norfolk, and Richard Ratcliffe, and men who had survived like Thomas Howard, Earl of Surrey, John de la Pole, Earl of Lincoln, and Francis Lovell. That the three men whose death was wrongly proclaimed by Henry Tudor after the battle were the highest ranking survivors who had fought on Richard's side is an interesting aspect. It is tempting to assume that by declaring them dead, Henry VII tried to discourage opposition to his reign. However, it is more likely, that in the confusion immediately after the battle when the true death toll was not yet know, the proclamation simply included the highest ranking men of the vanquished side. Richard Ratcliffe was first correctly included in the list of the fallen, but the following day, Henry VII ordered his arrest.

Henry VII, like all new kings, had to make his peace with as many of his dead opponent's supporters as possible. He needed these men for the government to function and would push them to continue fighting him if he was not prepared to accept their support (real or pretended as it may be). By dating the start of the reign to the day prior to the Battle of Bosworth Henry VII created the legal fiction that all men who fought for Richard III were traitors. However, Henry VII accepted many back into his grace, even close relatives of Richard III, including his nephew John de la Pole, Earl of Lincoln, and Richard's illegitimate son, John. Francis Lovell's brothers-in-law, Richard FitzHugh and Brian Stapleton, also joined the new king, and his young cousin Henry Lovell, Lord Morley, remained at court (see next chapter). For many of them, fighting against the new king must have seemed like a futile exercise.

With so many relatives who made their peace with the new king, it seems likely that Francis Lovell could have made his peace with Henry VII. Instead he chose to flee to sanctuary in Colchester, refused to seek a pardon, and fought on with stubborn determination. The attainder of Francis Lovell was passed in the first parliament of Henry VII, on 7 November 1485. Around this time he was also degraded from being Knight of the Garter.[66]

The lands that Francis Lovell had held were declared forfeit and distributed to Henry VII's supporters. Henry VII's uncle Jasper Tudor was granted a number of Lovell estates including Minster Lovell and Rotherfield Greys. John de Vere, Earl of Oxford, was also generously rewarded, partly with estates in Essex forfeited by Francis Lovell. Thomas Lovell of Barton Bendish, no relation to Francis Lovell, was granted the lordship of Didlington (Oxfordshire).[67] Other recipients of grants of Francis Lovell's estates over the next years included Charles de Somerset, illegitimate son of Henry, Duke of Somerset, John Mortimer, knight of the king's body, John, Viscount Welles, William Stanley, and John Dudley.[68]

After spending several months in hiding, Francis Lovell tried to kidnap Henry VII at York in April 1486. At the same time Humphrey Stafford of Grafton stirred up trouble in Worcestershire, and John Sante, Abbot of Abingdon, had the task of freeing the young Edward, Earl of Warwick, son of George, Duke of Clarence. The attempts all failed miserably. Francis Lovell probably fled to Furness Fells (Lancashire, now Cumbria), where other rebels had hidden. He was then reported as being in Ely on 19 May 1486. It is possible that Francis also received help from his mother-in-law, Alice Neville, Lady FitzHugh and her associate John Paston III. John Paston III certainly does not seem to have over-extended himself in his attempts to capture Francis as both a letter from John de Vere, Earl of Oxford and one from Sir Edmund Bedingfield show.[69]

Eventually Francis Lovell fled to the court of the dowager duchess of Burgundy, Margaret, a sister of Richard III and Edward IV. Another guest of Margaret of York was a boy who claimed to be Edward, Earl of Warwick, son of George, Duke of Clarence. They were later joined by John de la Pole, Earl of Lincoln, who arrived in the spring of 1487.

John de la Pole and Francis Lovell were the most prominent noblemen supporting the young man, who as Richard III's nephew, claimed to be the rightful king. It is generally accepted as fact that the boy was an impostor called Lambert Simnel, who was trained by a priest, and then coached by his supporters to pretend to be Edward, Earl of Warwick, who was in fact a prisoner of Henry VII at the time. But, like many aspects of Richard III's reign and its aftermath, doubt has been thrown on this. John Ashdown-Hill discusses various possibilities who 'Lambert Simnel' could have been, including the theory that George, Duke of Clarence had smuggled his infant son out of the country to Ireland and that 'Lambert Simnel' really was his son Edward, and that the boy held in the Tower was the substitute. Though the theory sounds rather farfetched, it would explain why John de la Pole and Francis Lovell, Richard III's nephew and best friend respectively, supported the boy.[70]

In the spring of 1487, the boy who claimed to be Edward, Earl of Warwick, accompanied by John de la Pole, Francis Lovell, and mercenaries under the command of Martin Schwartz sailed to Ireland. On 24 May the boy was crowned king of England in Dublin. In June, the newly crowned 'Edward VI' and his supporters crossed to England and tried but failed to raise the country against Henry VII. At the Battle of Stoke, on 16 June 1487, the rebels were soundly defeated by the troops of Henry VII under the command of the earl of Oxford. John de la Pole and Martin Schwartz were killed, and the boy king was taken prisoner. Francis Lovell survived the battle itself but disappeared afterwards, his fate uncertain.[71]

What happened to Francis Lovell after the Battle of Stoke remains shrouded in mystery. One thing seems certain, his wife and her mother were just as much in the dark about his whereabouts after the battle as we are. Their efforts in the spring of 1488 to find out what happened to him were not successful, as the letter from Alice Neville, Lady FitzHugh to John Paston III, already mentioned in the last chapter, makes clear.

There are different stories about what happened to Francis Lovell after his disappearance. Most likely he made his was to Scotland with Sir

Thomas Broughton, Sir Roger Hartlington, and others. A safe conduct was granted to them by James IV of Scotland (1488–1513) on 19 June 1488. But after this date Francis Lovell disappears from records. In a later retracted statement by a 'simple and poor person' from York the man claimed he had spoken to both Francis Lovell and Thomas Broughton at some time. This seems to be the last reference to Francis Lovell.[72]

According to a well-known story Francis Lovell returned to his ancestral home in Minster Lovell, where he lived secretly in a vault under Minster Lovell Hall, a trusted servant providing him with food and other necessaries. A report describes that a body was discovered on 6 May 1728 in a basement of Minster Lovell Hall 'as having been sitting at a table, which was before him, with a book, paper, pen, etc., etc.; in another part of the room lay a cap; all much mouldred and decayed. Which the family and others judged to be this Lord Lovel, whose exit hath hitherto been so uncertain.' It was assumed that at some point after Francis Lovell went into hiding in the secret chamber, the servant on whose services he relied for survival, was prevented from coming to him, and he died of starvation and thirst. The body is said to have turned to dust after exposure to the outside air.[73]

Romantic as the notion may be, it is simply impossible. For one, no cellar was ever rediscovered at Minster Lovell. Secondly, Minster Lovell was granted to none other than Henry VII's uncle Jasper Tudor after the forfeiture of Francis Lovell's lands in 1485. As Francis Lovell had spent little time at Minster Lovell it was highly unlikely that he knew a servant working there well enough to trust him with his life. Last but not least, on a very mundane level, bodies do not crumble to dust even if they had been in a tightly locked room for centuries. Without any efforts at conservation the tissue of a mummified body would rapidly start to decay, but instant transformations of human remains to dust only happen in legends, films, or on TV.

In the end, we simply do not know what happened to Francis Lovell and his fate will remain a mystery.

His wife, Anne FitzHugh, was left in a very difficult position. Her husband had been declared a traitor, all his estates were confiscated, and no exception was made for her dower in the attainder. Only in the second attainder of Francis Lovell in 1495, Anne FitzHugh's interests were protected, but there is no evidence that any lands were granted to her. The purpose of the second attainder was more likely one of tying up loose ends and reconfirming the new holders' possession of former Lovell property rather than a sign that Francis Lovell was still alive and dangerous at the time.[74]

Anne FitzHugh's position was particularly insecure. It was unclear whether she was the wife or the widow of a declared traitor. Her financial situation was precarious as the annuity of £20 Henry VII granted her in 1489 was insignificant compared to the income she would have had if her full dower to a third of Francis Lovell's estates had been assigned to her (see Chapter 7).[75] Anne FitzHugh was still living in 1495; the date of her death is not known.[76]

The Wars of the Roses threw a long shadow over the Lovell family. The lives of both John Lovell IX and his son Francis Lovell were profoundly affected by it. The relatively short time they were head of the family coincided largely with particular turbulent periods. When Edward IV emerged victorious from the conflict John Lovell IX's engagement on the side of Henry VI caused him both political and economic problems. His son's unswerving support of Richard III first elevated Francis Lovell to one of the highest positions in the government and then turned him into an attainted fugitive.

The fact that John Lovell IX fought on the side of the 'Lancastrians' and his son on that of the 'Yorkists' is a difference more of appearance than substance. Both father and son fought on the side of the ruling monarch. However, John Lovell IX made his peace with the new king and there is no reason to doubt that eventually he would have regained more influence and power. If had he lived longer he, like his brother William Lovell, Lord Morley may have supported the readaptation of Henry VI, but that is pure speculation. Francis Lovell, by contrast, did not make any attempt to make peace with the new dynasty. On the contrary, he first tried to kidnap the new king and later supported the pretender who claimed to be Edward, Earl of Warwick, the son of George, Duke of Clarence. This unbending opposition, refusing to accept the changed political landscape is at the same time admirable and deplorable. Admirable because Francis Lovell stayed faithful to his friend and monarch, Richard III, but also deplorable because it was one of the reasons that brought the long and successful history of the Lovells of Titchmarsh to an end. The second, but equally important reason was that Francis Lovell and Anne FitzHugh did not have any children, despite having been married for many years when he became a fugitive. Francis Lovell did not die as a youth who had not time to father children; he disappeared at the age of roughly 30.

An interesting aspect of Francis Lovell's life is that though he is the most famous Lovell, there is remarkably little information about him. Compared to his predecessor as chamberlain, William Hastings, he remains a 'shadowy figure' to use Joanna Williams's fitting words again. The life of another contemporary, John Howard, Duke of Norfolk, is much better documented thanks to a number of private papers that have survived, while only two private letters of Francis Lovell to the Stonors have survived.[77]

Francis Lovell's fame is therefore not so much based on what we know about him, or his closeness to Richard III. It is rather based on the fact that Richard III's reign remains an exceptionally controversial one that has attracted more attention than many much longer reigns, and still causes passionate debates today.

The Wars of the Roses brought fortune and disaster to the Lovells of Titchmarsh and the end of this branch of the family is inextricably intertwined with it. However, their lack of male heirs was as much responsible for their extinction as the violence of the wars.

Chapter 9

Beyond the Lovells of Titchmarsh

Had Francis Lovell simply died without children, the Lovell estates would have been inherited by his sisters and his cousin. The lands held in fee tail would have been split between his sisters Frideswide and Joan. His cousin Henry Lovell, Lord Morley would have inherited the lands held in tail male. However, as he had been attainted before his disappearance, the lands were confiscated by the Crown and both his sisters and his cousin received nothing.

Henry Lovell, Francis Lovell's cousin, was the son of William Lovell and Eleanor Morley. It is possible that his parents chose the name Henry, a name that only rarely been used in either family, in honour of his uncle Henry Lovell, the youngest son of William Lovell III and Alice Deincourt. Another is that he was named after King Henry VI. William Lovell supported the readaptation of Henry VI (see previous chapter) and it was only during this period that he was summoned to parliament as Lord Morley.

Henry Lovell was born around 1466. When his parents both died within a months of each other in the summer of 1476, the *inquisition post mortem* recorded different ages for him. Some record his age as 9 years, others as 11.[1]

As a minor heir of a great barony, Henry Lovell became a ward of King Edward IV. Shortly after the death of his father, Edward IV distributed the Morley lands to several noblemen, including Thomas Howard, and appointed John Russell receiver general of the Morley estates. In 1477, Edward IV granted all lands, castles and further possessions as well as Henry Lovell's marriage to Richard Beauchamp, Bishop of Salisbury and Peter Courtenay.[2] Some of the Morley lands seem to have remained in the king's hands or had returned to it.

While there is no clear evidence where the orphaned Henry Lovell spent his childhood, it is possible that he stayed at court. He may have acted as companion to Richard, Duke of York. The prince was several years younger than Henry Lovell, but the young noblemen that were chosen as companions for the royal princes were often of a significantly different age than the prince himself.[3] In 1483, Henry Lovell was one of Edward IV's 'henchmen', the young men who received their education at court.[4] Henry Lovell also escorted his cousin Francis Lovell during his investiture as viscount and he was present at the funeral of Edward IV in 1483.[5]

At the coronation of Richard III on 6 July 1483, Henry Lovell was the highest ranking of the king's henchmen.[6] Though Henry Lovell was still underage he was regularly referred to as Lord Morley, as for example in the dispute with his cousin Francis Lovell about the income of Clayton (Buckinghamshire) in December 1483. By 1484, Henry Lovell had become a member of the extended royal family, as he married Elizabeth de la Pole, the daughter of John de la Pole, Duke of Suffolk and Elizabeth, sister of Edward IV and Richard III. This was the first marriage of a member of the Lovell family with a royal relative and shows that the family had become noble and affluent enough for this honour.[7]

When Richard III set up his nephew John de la Pole, Earl of Lincoln as the nominal head of the Council of the North in the summer 1484, Henry Lovell was sent to the North as well.[8] As brother-in-law of John de la Pole Henry Lovell must have seemed to be the natural choice for this position.

Unlike his cousin Francis Lovell and his brother-in-law John de la Pole, Henry Lovell seems to have not harboured any rebellious intentions against Henry VII after the Battle of Bosworth. His non-involvement in the various schemes of his cousin and his brother-in-law may be explained by the fact that he was still underage. However, it is also worth remembering that his wife's cousin Elizabeth was now queen and mother to the king's heir, Prince Arthur. Henry Lovell might have well considered that this relationship was more important than continuing to fight for a lost cause. The disappearance of his cousin Francis Lovell and the death of his brother-in-law John de la Pole at the Battle of Stoke certainly would have confirmed this choice.

On 5 February 1489, Henry Lovell had licence to enter his inheritance without proof of age.[9] His future looked bright. In June 1489, Henry Lovell was given command of the troops, 2,000 English archers and 1,000 pikemen, to support Archduke Maximilian against Flemish rebels and their French allies. Only a few days later, on 13 June 1489, Henry Lovell was killed in the battle of Dixmude. When the English troops heard that their commander had been killed, they slaughtered their prisoners. Henry Lovell was by all appearances a popular commander which could explain the soldiers' behaviour, which was as shocking for the chronicler Molinet as it is today.[10]

His young widow, Elizabeth de la Pole, was assigned her dower in December 1489.[11] She did not remarry even though she lived to be 51. It may be tempting to think that Elizabeth de la Pole was discouraged by King Henry VII from remarrying because he viewed all close relatives of the Yorkist royal family as a threat to the security of his reign. However, since three of Henry VII's four sisters-in-law married during his reign, their cousin could certainly have married again had she wished to. Henry VII, like any other king or nobleman, used his wife's sisters' marriages as a means to forge ties with his closest allies.[12] It was not until 1499 and the flight of Edmund de la Pole to Flanders that the relationship between Henry VII and the de la Pole family began to sour. It may be that Elizabeth de la Pole's epitaph is correct when it states that she remained unmarried for the rest of her live, because she had loved her husband Henry Lovell so much that she could never think of remarrying again.[13]

With Henry Lovell's death, the family became extinct in the male line. Noble families continuously died out in the male line mostly by failing to produce male heirs but also through war, treason, and illness. With a four-hundred-year-long history, the Lovells of Titchmarsh were among the most enduring noble families. Though the last two male members of the family died in or as a consequence of battles, the real reason for the family's extinction, as K.B. McFarlane has pointed out, was that that too many of them died childless. Henry Lovell was still very young at the time of his death. Francis Lovell, however, was about 31. He had been married since childhood but still died without fathering any children. Both of their uncles, Henry Lovell and Robert Lovell, also died childless.[14]

However, the family lived on through daughters. Francis Lovell's sisters Frideswide and Joan, and Henry Lovell's sister Alice had children and it is their descendants, in particular those of Alice Lovell, that this chapter is dedicated to. All three women had married men of gentry rank. Francis Lovell's sisters, Joan Lovell and Frideswide Lovell, married Brian

Stapleton and Edward Norris, respectively. Their cousin Alice Lovell married William Parker.

The sons of Joan Lovell and Brian Stapleton and Frideswide Lovell and Edward Norris did not greatly profit from the disappearance of their brother-in-law Francis Lovell. Had he not been attainted, his sisters and their children would have inherited a significant portion of the Lovell estates. Attainders were often reversed, but neither Frideswide nor Joan Lovell nor their husbands had sufficient influence at court to retrieve the Lovell lands from the powerful men they had been granted to. Joan Lovell's situation was certainly worsened by the fact that her husband Brian Stapleton died in 1486 leaving a 9-year-old son, also called, Brian as his heir.[15] Frideswide Lovell's husband Edward Norris and her father-in-law William Norris had fought at the Battle of Stoke on the side of Henry VII and both were knighted afterwards. The Norris family had certainly earned their reputation as loyal to Henry VII, as William Norris had already shared Henry VII's exile.[16] This service was, however, not enough when pitted against men like Jasper Tudor or Chancellor Thomas Lovell.

After William Beaumont, the uncle of Frideswide and Joan Lovell, died without heirs in 1508, their two families received only a small part of the Beaumont estates, though the whole inheritance should have been split between Frideswide's son John Norris and Joan's son Brian Stapleton. Henry VIII sold or granted large parts of the Beaumont estates to his courtiers.[17]

Henry Norris, Henry VIII's Groom of the Stool and one of Anne Boleyn's alleged lovers, was, according to the *Complete Peerage*, the son of Frideswide Lovell and Edward Norris.[18] However, Eric Ives concluded that Henry Norris was the son of Richard Norris and an unidentified mother. Richard Norris was the son of Sir William Norris of Yattendon (d. 1506) and his first wife Jane, daughter of John de Vere, 12th Earl of Oxford. William Norris of Yattendon was Frideswide Lovell's father-in-law and Richard Norris was in turn her brother-in-law and Henry Norris her nephew. The old *Dictionary of National Biography* confuses the family history even more, since according to it, Henry Norris was not only Frideswide Lovell's son, but Frideswide is wrongly identified as the *daughter* of Francis Lovell. The unfortunate Henry Norris, who was executed in 1436, was therefore related to the Lovells by marriage but was no descendant of the Lovells. The fact that he was granted the house and manor of Minster Lovell shortly before his arrest in 1436 should not be regarded as indicating any direct relationship.[19]

The sons of Frideswide and Joan Lovell, like their husbands were members of the gentry. As such, and with first names that were incredibly common, it is very hard to keep track of them and all too easy to confuse relatives. For example, the records do not allow to determine whether William Norris, Frideswide's father-in-law, was succeeded by his son Edward or his grandson John when he died in 1506.[20]

While the sons of Francis Lovell's sister became members of the gentry, the descendants of Henry Lovell's sister Alice remained part of, or to be more precise were restored to the peerage. At the time of Henry Lovell's death his heiress was his sister Alice who was in her early 20s and married to Sir William Parker.[21] Like the husbands of Frideswide and Joan, her husband was a member of the gentry. However unlike Edward Norris and Brian Stapleton, who came from richer gentry, William Parker was from an obscure gentry family.[22] When exactly William Parker and Alice Lovell were married is unclear, but it must have occurred before c. 1481 when their son Henry Parker was born.

William Parker had made his career in the service of Richard, Duke of Gloucester, and was knighted by him in 1482 during the campaign in Scotland. For a man of William Parker's humble background to marry a woman of Alice Lovell's rank was unusual. Particularly since Alice was her brother's heiress apparent at the time. There can be little doubt that this fortunate marriage was a reward for his service, facilitated or arranged by Alice's cousin Francis Lovell and Richard, Duke of Gloucester.

William Parker continued his service to Richard III and was rewarded for his participation in the suppression of the Buckingham Rebellion. At the Battle of Bosworth he was Richard III's standard bearer.[23] After Richard III's death and the accession to the throne of Henry Tudor, William Parker spent some time in prison, at least according to later family tradition.[24] He was plagued by bouts of insanity which may have been the result of a severe head wound he received when fighting for Richard III.[25]

The close links of William Parker to Richard III, could be thought to have seriously damaged the chances of his family to prosper under the new ruler. However, Henry VII did not and could not exclude all men who had fought for Richard III nor their families from his grace. William Parker was also not imprisoned for ever. He attended at least one of Margaret Beaufort's New Year's celebrations, as his son Henry Parker describes in one of his later writing. As his son recalls it, William Parker was on good terms with Margaret Beaufort, mother of Henry VII.

After the death of her brother Henry, Alice Lovell inherited those parts of the Morley estates that were not held in tail male. The parts held in tail male were granted by Henry VII to a number of his supporters. Though the estates Alice Lovell inherited were diminished she still became a very wealthy landholder.[26]

By 1491 at the latest, Henry Parker, William Parker's and Alice Lovell's son, had entered the household of Margaret Beaufort.[27] Henry Parker, who was about 10 years old at the time, became her cup-bearer and personal attendant.

Margaret Beaufort was immensely rich and had significant influence on her son Henry VII. She was also famous for being deeply religious. Henry Parker was devoted to her, as his later writings show, and she was a major influence on his own religious belief. She in turn held Henry Parker in high regard. In the late 1490s Margaret Beaufort arranged his marriage to Alice St John, the granddaughter of her half-brother John St John (see Genealogy 10). Margaret Beaufort was very careful in choosing partners for her extended family and she considered Henry Parker, heir to substantial estates, a suitable husband to her great-niece.

Henry Parker and Alice St John had five children: Henry, Jane, Margaret, Francis, and Elizabeth. Little is known about Francis and Elizabeth, but the elder three married into neighbouring noble families and took their places among their peers. While it is possible that Francis Parker was named for his grandmother's cousin, Francis Lovell, this connection may not be one that Henry Parker and his wife wanted to publicly acknowledge. It is more likely that it was just a change in fashion. Similarly, the name of their daughter Jane became considerably more popular at the time.[28] Margaret was almost certainly named after Margaret Beaufort.

With Margaret Beaufort Henry Parker had acquired a powerful and dedicated patroness and she continued to look after his wife and children when he was absent. Margaret Beaufort also supported him financially, as in 1507 when she paid for him to go to London to see a joust. She was also a patron of education and founder of two colleges in Oxford and obviously infected Henry Parker with her interest in learning and reading. Her love for reading and her continuing close connection to her great-niece is confirmed by a present she gave Alice St John: an English translation of Gower, probably the *Confessio Amantis*. Margaret Beaufort may have paid for Henry Parker's education at Oxford though no records of his attendance can be found.[29]

Whether or not Henry Parker went to university, which at the time was still a highly unusual route for a young nobleman to take, it is clear that he received an excellent education. Apart from the standard Latin, he was fluent in French which had become so rare a skill that those, like Thomas Boleyn, who spoke it well, were sought-after as diplomats. Henry Parker also knew Italian well enough to not only to read Machiavelli or Boccaccio but to translate them into English. In taking up translations he may also have been influenced by Margaret Beaufort, who herself had translated devotional books from French into English.[30]

As her son Henry Parker started his own family, Alice Lovell married a second time. Her first husband William Parker had died around 1504, and she married Sir Edward Howard, the son of Thomas Howard, Duke of Norfolk. Like Alice's first husband, Thomas Howard had fought alongside Richard III at the Battle of Bosworth. Just like the Lovell-Parker family, the Howards had long made their peace with the Tudor regime. As usual with the nobility multiple links existed between the families. The Howards were related to the Boleyn family, Edward Howard's sister Elizabeth was married to Thomas Boleyn. Thomas Boleyn's father William Boleyn had been one of the executors of Henry Lovell's will. Thomas Howard had been a henchman of Edward IV with Alice's brother Henry Lovell.[31]

Alice Lovell was a fortunate match for a younger son like Edward Howard. She was about ten to twelve years older than her second husband, approaching or already passed her fortieth birthday. It would have been clear to both that it was very unlikely that she would bear any children and the couple did indeed remain childless. The relationship between the two was amicable, as his letters to her from shipboard during his campaigns testify. Edward Howard became an admiral in 1512 and after successfully campaigning in France, he was killed at Brest when he lead the charge on the opponent's flagship on 25 April 1513.[32] Alice Lovell, now widowed a second time, did not remarry. She died in 1518 aged about 52. Alice Lovell's will reveals the luxurious items that she left her son, including beds, bowls with her and her first husband's coat of arms, and embroidered wall hangings.[33]

After her death her son Henry Parker was first summoned to parliament as Lord Morley. Effectively, the title had lapsed with the death of his uncle Henry Lovell in 1489. Though Henry Lovell himself had died before he was ever summoned to parliament as Lord Morley, he had been styled 'Lord Morley' in official records. Due to William Parker's closeness to Richard III and his mental instability, he was never summoned to parliament. Henry Parker's summons to parliament was therefore reviving an old title, but it was the decision of the king alone to recreate such titles or not.

Henry Parker did not conform to many of the expectations of how a nobleman of his status should live. He was not interested in participating in either tournaments or war. Both were favourite pursuits of Henry VIII since the start of his reign and were important routes to become close to the young king and make a career. Charles Brandon is the most striking example of a man who took this route. Though he was the son of a mere knight he became duke of Suffolk and married Mary Tudor, the sister of Henry VIII.

Henry Parker's non-involvement in war makes him 'wholly exceptional' for a man of his rank.[34] Since the Tudor aristocracy just like their medieval forbearers were *per se* still a military elite, Henry Parker's non-participation is in itself unusual and it is impossible to find a real explanation for it. It is true that he grew up in a family which only recently had experienced the devastating effects war could have. First Francis Lovell's attainder for treason and disappearance, followed only two years later by the early death of Henry Lovell, Lord Morley, and the death of his mother's second husband Edward Howard at Brest. Henry Parker knew about the dangers of war. However, there was scarcely a noble family who did not suffer similar losses without deterring their relatives or descendants from engaging fully in wars. John Howard had been killed at the Battle of

Bosworth, but his son, Thomas Howard, did not shy away from battle, quite the contrary. It was his steady and successful military service to the new dynasty that enabled him to recover his estates, title, and reputation.

While Henry Parker had little interest in the military duties of his rank, he fulfilled his role in administration and representation diligently. He was 'exceptionally active in civilian life', attending parliaments and trials by peers with unusual regularity.[35] The men and women whose trials he participated in were all acquaintances, friends, or even family. The duke of Buckingham had been a ward of Margaret Beaufort when Henry Parker was in her household and George Boleyn was his son-in-law. He also was present at the trial of his own daughter Jane (see below).[36]

Another role Henry Parker fulfilled just as diligently was that to attend to the king at great ceremonial events. In 1520, he and his wife Alice St John were at the Field of Cloth of Gold, the famous meeting between Henry VIII and King Francis I of France. His daughter, Jane Parker, was in the retinue of Catherine of Aragon.[37]

Henry Parker and his daughter Jane began their very different careers at court around the same time. Henry Parker's new status as Lord Morley gave him an increased role and visibility. His rise into the peerage may have helped his daughter to gain the much sought-after position of one of the ladies of the Queen Catherine of Aragon. Jane was of the right age and must also have had the accomplishments and good looks that were required for this position.

Two years later, in 1522, Jane Parker took a more prominent role in a spectacular pageant staged for the entertainment of the imperial envoys Jacques de Castres and Charles Poupet de Lacheaulx. The pageant featured an artificial castle, the Château Vert, filled with ladies dressed as virtues, a mock fight between boys representing vices, and eight gentlemen led by the king who also bore mottos. The pageant is mostly famous for the participation of another recent arrival at court, Anne Boleyn, who played the role of Perseverance. Among the other ladies of the castle were Henry VIII's sister Mary as Beauty and Jane Parker who was given the role of Constancy. With the exception of the king's sister the ladies who participated in the pageant were not chosen for their family connections. What was important for the success of the pageant was their ability to perform and dance well and look good.[38]

The following year, Cardinal Wolsey sent Henry Parker and the Garter King of Arms to meet with Archduke Ferdinand in Nuremberg and present him with the Order of the Garter. Henry Parker seemed to have enjoyed this visit, and a few letters he wrote during his travels have survived. Henry Parker had the time to have his portrait drawn by the renowned artist Albrecht Dürer (see plate 14).

In the 1520s, Henry Parker arranged marriages for his elder children. In 1523, his son and namesake Henry Parker was married to Grace Newport who was the heiress of her father John Newport and a very good match for the younger Henry Parker.[39] Two of the daughters of Henry Parker and Alice St John married into the extended Boleyn clan. Margaret married Sir John Shelton the younger, the son of Sir Thomas Boleyn's sister Anne and her husband Sir John Shelton the elder, and Jane married George Boleyn, son of Thomas Boleyn, a well-established courtier, and Elizabeth Howard, daughter of Thomas Howard, 2nd Duke of Suffolk (see Genealogy 11).[40]

Jane Parker and her husband George Boleyn knew each other already, both of them had been at court for some years. It is almost certain, that they had no children, although there were rumours that a George Boleyn who died in 1603 was their son.[41] Henry Parker and his son-in-law were both fond of literature and both were translators. In fact, until recently George Boleyn's translation of 'The Pistellis and Gospelles for the LII Sondayes of the Yere' had been attributed to Henry Parker.[42]

In the years following her marriage, Jane Parker profited from the infatuation Henry VIII had developed for her sister-in-law, Anne Boleyn. Her husband, George became a Squire of the Chamber and received a number of grants, some with considerable salaries. After his father had become earl of Wiltshire, George Boleyn received the courtesy title of Viscount and his wife Jane became a Viscountess.

Both Jane and her husband were part of the royal court and spent most of their time there, participating in the rituals and traditions. On New Year Days they received gifts from and gave gifts to the king. Ladies often presented the king with items of clothing they had made, as in 1532 when Jane presented him with four caps, two of velvet and two of silk, and two adorned with gold buttons.[43] While noblemen generally presented the king with jewels, plate, money, or clothes, Henry Parker gave the king manuscripts of literary works he had translated. It is unknown when he started giving this kind of present. The surviving manuscripts start in the early 1530s.[44]

While the Boleyns prospered at court, Henry Parker's position in the localities was also strengthened. In 1530 he was first appointed to a commission of the peace in Essex and shortly afterwards also in Hertfordshire. This new position of local eminence was in part an acknowledgment of his good record of participation in parliament and the great councils, it was also no doubt influenced by his daughter's and in particular his son-in-law's high rank at court.

In 1532 Henry VIII's long struggle to divorce Catherine of Aragon to marry Anne Boleyn had entered a new stage: he decided to introduce his intended bride to the king of France, Francis I (1515–1547). A meeting between Francis I and Anne Boleyn that did not break any protocol or damage Henry's prospect of achieving the divorce was carefully orchestrated. As Francis I and his entourage were feasting in Calais, Anne Boleyn made her grand entrance, as one of seven masked ladies who chose partners from among the guests, Anne naturally picking king Francis himself. Jane Parker, Anne's sister-in-law, was one of the other ladies, though no record survives of who her dancing partner was.

After this successful mission, Henry VIII and Anne Boleyn finally married and Anne, already several months pregnant, was crowned in full splendour on 1 June 1533. Henry Parker and his wife Alice St John attended, as did the younger Henry Parker who was honoured by being chosen as one of the Knights of the Bath created on the eve of the coronation. Jane Parker's high status among the new queen's ladies-in-waiting was demonstrated by her riding almost immediately behind Anne in the procession from the Tower to Westminster Abbey. The younger Henry Parker with the other newly created Knights of the Bath served during the coronation feast that followed the ceremony in Westminster Abbey.[45]

So far, Jane and her family had profited from her close connection with the Boleyn clan, but fortunes changed quickly, particularly in the reign of Henry VIII. In the spring of 1536, with barely three weeks between the first arrest and the execution, Anne Boleyn lost her status as queen and her life.

Just as the fate of the Princes in the Tower has been the subject of innumerable books and fierce debate, the literature about the fall of Anne

Boleyn is extensive and comes to often contradictory conclusions. And just as in the case of the Princes in the Tower, discussing the reasons behind and the question who was the prime mover behind Anne Boleyn's fall – did Cromwell push Henry VIII or did he just enact the king's decision – is beyond the scope of this book. However, it is likewise not possible to completely bypass it. Jane Parker was not only married to one of the accused, she was also one of Anne Boleyn's ladies-in-waiting and as such, she was questioned in the process that lead up to the conviction of Anne Boleyn and her alleged lovers. In fact, Jane Parker is frequently cited as one of the key figures in the fall of Anne Boleyn, if not *the* key figure.[46]

To try to establish Jane Parker's role in these momentous events was, it is necessary to start with a report by the imperial ambassador Eustace Chapuys from the year 1534. Chapuys was a well-informed but biased witness, whose copious writings also contain rumours and sometimes misinformation. He reports that Jane Parker was banished from court in 1534 because she was involved in a conspiracy with her sister-in-law Anne Boleyn to get rid of an unnamed lady at court for whom Henry VIII had developed an interest. While some historians like David Starkey think this is a perfectly credible story others think it is not plausible. Eric Ives, for example, says the report of Jane Parker being sent from court is probably only a rumour, because Jane was 'otherwise known as Anne's enemy'.[47]

One year later, in June of 1535, a large crowd of women from London demonstrated their loyalty to and support for Princess Mary in Greenwich. Among those ordinary citizens, we are told, were two noble women, Lady Jane Parker and Lady 'William Howard' (probably William Howard's second wife Margaret Gamage). While Ives, Catherine Davies, and Diarmaid MacCullough regard this story as true, Starkey and Julia Fox argue that it is implausible that Jane Parker would participate in such a demonstration. Starkey also points out that the names of the two noblewomen involved, *'Millor de Rochesfort et millor de Guillaume'* were written in the margin of the document.[48]

All her previous and subsequent actions are seen through the lens of whether or not Jane Parker was responsible for Anne Boleyn's fall. If Jane was the key witness against the queen, she could not possibly have been part of the conspiracy with Anne Boleyn to remove her rival from court, and Jane could have been present at the demonstration for Princess

Mary. If Jane was only one of many people who provided facts or factoids that were used by the prosecution, she may very well have tried to help her sister-in-law to get rid of a women Henry VIII had fallen for and she would have stayed far away from any demonstration for the king's bastardised daughter.

Jane Parker's personal relationship with her husband and sister-in-law can only be judged by her actions. As the two instances above show, whether or not an event actually happened, is judged by many historians based on how they view these relationships. However, it is hard to imagine that Anne would have retained Jane as lady-in-waiting if, as Ives states, she was a 'known' enemy of Anne. Ives repeatedly stresses the fact that Anne had enormous influence over the personnel at court and she surely would have found a way to get rid of a troublesome lady-in-waiting who cheered the despised Lady Mary.[49] Jane Parker's father certainly had not nearly enough influence to force his daughter on an unwilling queen, nor would George Boleyn have protected his wife if she was his beloved sister's enemy.

Jane Parker was one of many men and women questioned about the goings on at court after Anne Boleyn's and her alleged lovers' arrest. Though many individual statements are known, no record of these interrogations exist. What we do know is that Jane did divulge one choice snippet which was used the proceedings. During George Boleyn's trial he was asked to *silently* read a note that was handed to him and answer whether it was true with yes or no. George however read the statement out loud. It said that Anne Boleyn had told Jane that the king 'was no good in bed with women, and that he neither had potency nor force' and that Jane in turn had told her husband George.[50] Though this was definitely an unwise statement for Anne Boleyn to have made and for Jane Parker to divulge to the prosecutors, deeply embarrassing as it was to the notoriously touchy Henry VIII, it was hardly a criminal offence and certainly did not prove anybody's adultery.

As Starkey points out, the very nature of Jane Parker's one definite contribution to the trial, the intimate details about Anne Boleyn's marital life, shows that she was on very close terms with the queen as well as with her husband, as otherwise the queen would have hardly confided such a delicate problem to her, nor would Jane in turn have told her husband. Jane Parker can also hardly be blamed for the fact that her husband read the note out in court, despite being told not to. Moreover, with the other accused already condemned it was certain George would be condemned as well.

Another record that is interpreted as proving Jane Parker was the principal witness of the prosecution is a report by the French Ambassador Lancelot de Carle. According to this report George Boleyn said to his judges, 'On the evidence of only one woman you are willing to believe this great evil of me, and on the basis of her allegations you are deciding my judgement.'[51] This vague reference need not indict his wife since several other women had provided information. According to one of the judges of the trial, John Spelman, it was Lady Wingfield's deathbed confession that first revealed Anne Boleyn's behaviour. Another source quoted as proof of Jane's guilt is the lost journal of Antony Antony, which 'probably included words to the effect that "the wife of Lord Rochford [George Boleyn] was a particular instrument in the death of Queen Anne."'[52]

Considering that lack of firm evidence of Jane Parker's guilt, the amount of criticism Jane has been subjected to is quite astounding. Jane Parker was only one of many people who were questioned and gave evidence. Anne Boleyn herself provided details useful to the prosecution during her time in the Tower, but Jane Parker is often the one person who receives all the blame.

An interesting aspect of this condemnation of Jane Parker as responsible for Anne and George Boleyn's death is that almost all historians believe that there was no substance at all to the charges made against Anne Boleyn and her alleged lovers. As Eric Ives, one of Jane Parker's critics, states, 'Under analysis, the case presented by the Crown in May 1536 collapses.'[53] If Henry VIII and/or Thomas Cromwell had decided to get rid of Anne Boleyn and her supporters and the trials were just a means to an end, what Jane Parker or anybody else said would have made little difference. All evidence was twisted and bent to allow the verdict that had already been decided upon before the first day of the process.

The question of what would have motivated Jane Parker to turn against her own husband and sister-in-law, is often answered with envy, jealousy, or spite, vices all too easily attributed to women. As mentioned above, there is little evidence that Jane hated either her husband or her sister-in-law. On the contrary the nature of her disclosure argues for a good relationship between the three, and there is no reason why Anne Boleyn would have kept a 'known enemy' at her side. Another point that Julia Fox makes repeatedly in her book about 'the infamous Lady Rochford', is that Jane's fortunes and her status as a viscountess depended completely on her husband George. She had nothing to gain and a lot to lose if he was convicted of treason.

Even today writers who believe in Jane's guilt continue to interpret all her actions in the worst possible light. When Jane Parker wrote to her husband imprisoned in the Tower that she would plead for his life with the king, Ives can even 'smell malice' in the letter, since it was sent with Henry VIII's permission.[54] One has to wonder how Jane should have succeeded sending a letter to her husband in the Tower *without* the king's permission and what would have been the point to hide the letter from the king, since she meant to beg Henry VIII for mercy on his behalf. If Jane had succeeded in corresponding with her husband without the king's knowledge we in turn certainly would not know about it. With the notable exception of Archbishop Thomas Cranmer nobody spoke up for the accused. Jane Parker's intention to plead with the king for mercy should be regarded as courageous rather than devious. Her cautious father certainly would have discouraged her from voicing any support for her husband.

Similarly MacCulloch calls her 'the *less-than-grieving* widow'.[55] He, like others, criticise Jane for complaining about her impoverished state after her husband's execution. However, as Jane Fox points out, Jane was not only short-changed in her dower arrangement but she also truly felt the loss of her income and status, being reduced from the wife of a rich and influential courtier to the widow of a convicted traitor whose lands and possessions had been confiscated. With the help of Thomas Cromwell she managed to persuade her father-in-law to improve her dower arrangement.[56]

Another piece of evidence of Jane Parker's hostility to her sister-in-law Anne Boleyn is an alleged visit she made to the king's elder daughter Mary at Whitsun 1536, only two weeks after the execution of Anne Boleyn. However, the document is so badly mutilated that it's difficult to decipher, as Starkey points out. Henry Parker was probably accompanied by his wife and unnamed daughter when he visited Mary. It is however likely that this unnamed daughter was Henry Parker's other daughter, Margaret. Margaret's father-in-law, Sir John Shelton, was in charge of

Lady Mary's household, and her mother-in-law, Lady Shelton, was lady governess of Mary.[57] Lady Shelton was born Anne Boleyn and the recently executed queen and namesake was her niece. Henry Parker's residence Great Hallingbury was only a short distance from Hunsdon where Mary stayed at the time. He was a personal friend but not a political ally and, to quote Starkey, 'nobody in power cared two hoots that Morley and Mary had met'.[58]

After the death of both Catherine of Aragon and Anne Boleyn, being on friendly terms with the Lady Mary was possible again for loyal subjects of Henry VIII, as long as one avoided calling her princess, the crime for which Lady Anne Hussey was sent to the Tower. Even Thomas Cromwell, one of the main architects of the spilt from Rome, who had also brow-beaten Mary into accepting her status as bastard, was later on good terms with her. Lady Mary was most likely godmother to his grandson Henry Cromwell.[59]

On New Year 1537, the whole family, Henry Parker and his two daughters Jane and Margaret gave Mary a present. In January 1537, Lady Mary became godmother of one of Henry Parker the younger's children, and in October, she also became godmother to Margaret Parker's child.[60] Henry Parker certainly learned to respect Mary. He admired her seriousness and religiosity, her deep reading of the psalms as well as her skills as a translator.

Henry Parker also was on very good terms with Thomas Cromwell, as several letters written by Henry Parker to Cromwell testify. His friendship with the powerful minister was not completely selfless, but the two men shared a love for books and everything Italian. In one letter Henry Parker calls Cromwell 'my singular good friend and old acquaintance Master Cromwell'.[61] Henry Parker's friendship with a wide variety of people, including the Boleyns, Lady Mary, and Cromwell did not necessarily create 'conflicting loyalties', but ensured that he had allies on all sides, a strategy that had served some of his Lovell ancestors well.[62]

His good connections to Cromwell came in useful at the time of the Pilgrimage of Grace, the rebellion that broke out in the North of England in October 1536. The rebels were violently opposed to the reformation, the dissolution of the monasteries, and in particular to Thomas Cromwell and Archbishop Thomas Cranmer. Henry Parker's association with the Catholic faction and his friendship with Lady Mary may have made him a suspect at the court as a sympathiser of the rebels. It was probably at this time that he gave Cromwell his own, carefully annotated copy of *The History of Florence* and *The Prince*, in which he highlighted the cases of undue and destructive interference of the pope in the internal affairs in Italy and the pretensions of the papacy. Henry Parker was among the nobles who sat in judgement over the rebellious noblemen who participated in the revolt.[63]

Henry Parker is criticised as a man who trimmed his sails to the prevailing winds, though a staunch Catholic by heart, he was writing – and saying – what was demanded. However, as Diarmaid MacCulloch in his biography of Thomas Cromwell does not get tired of pointing out, in the 1520s and 30s there was a lot of fluidity in religious outlooks, and Henry VIII's position veered widely from conservative to radical, depending on what aspect of doctrine was concerned and what he wanted to achieve.

How quickly attitudes changed is exemplified by the fact that Jane Seymour, after becoming pregnant in the spring of 1537, went on pilgrimage with Henry VIII to Canterbury to offer thanks to Thomas Becket. Soon afterwards the shrine was demolished and pilgrimages denounced. As yet it was unclear where the religious debate would lead, and it was far from certain that the split between the Anglican church and the Catholic church was to be permanent.[64]

In this turbulent period it is possible that Henry Parker's opinion about individual aspects of religion may have changed over time, but on the whole he remained a conservative at heart. Just like everybody else who wished to survive the rollercoaster ride of the court of Henry VIII, he kept his head down and followed wherever the king was leading, both in politics and religion.

Jane Parker's dismissal from court was of short duration and she returned as a lady-in-waiting for the new queen Jane Seymour. The following year, Jane Seymour gave birth to the longed for son for Henry VIII. At the christening of Edward, Henry Parker was given a ceremonial role when he alongside the queen's brother, Edward Seymour, aided the 4-year-old Lady Elizabeth, who was carrying her half-brother's robe.[65] Tragedy soon followed, when Jane Seymour died twelve days after the birth of Edward. Once more, the whole Parker family attended the formal function of the queen's funeral. Henry Parker the younger was one of the eleven men who carried the 'chair' with Jane Seymour's body from the hearse to the chapel. Jane Parker was one of the ladies who bore the train of the Lady Mary who was the chief mourner.[66]

Jane Parker remained a lady-in-waiting to Henry VIII's fourth queen Anne of Cleves. As it is well known, the marriage was a disaster, at least from Henry VIII's point of view. In the proceedings to have the marriage annulled, a curious exchange between the queen and some of her ladies-in-waiting is recorded to establish the fact that the marriage was never consummated. Jane Parker is given the role of pointing out that the queen must still be a virgin. After listening to the description of what happened at night when the king slept in her bed, she is said to have exclaimed: 'By Our Lady, I think your Grace is a maid still indeed.' 'How can I be a maid', the queen replied, 'and sleep every night with the King?' To which Jane Parker replied, 'There must be more than that.'[67] The marriage was soon annulled and Henry VIII quickly married his fifth wife Katherine Howard. Jane Parker retained her position as lady-in-waiting for the young queen and became her close confidant.

For some time the marriage was a happy one, until Katherine's youthful misdemeanours were discovered. When her more recent behaviour was scrutinised closely further indiscretions were discovered. What may have been excusable in another women was unacceptable for a queen. Not even the shadow of a doubt could be allowed to fall on the legitimacy of the royal offspring. In the end, this behaviour would cost Katherine Howard, Jane Parker, Thomas Culpepper, and Francis Dereham, their lives.

The whole tragic affair started when Henry VIII was informed that Katherine Howard had had an affair with Francis Dereham while she was living with her step-grandmother, the dowager duchess of Norfolk. Though strictly speaking what Katherine Howard had done before her marriage to the king should be irrelevant, Henry VIII was devastated that his idolised wife was not the unblemished flower of womanhood that he imagined her to be.

Katherine Howard reassured herself and her confidant Jane Parker that she would get away with her life, if perhaps not her position as queen, as long as her later behaviour was not discovered. However, further inquiries discovered that not only had Katherine Howard employed Francis Dereham in her household after becoming queen, she had developed a close relationship with one of her husband's Gentlemen of the Privy Chamber, Thomas Culpepper. Katherine had given him gifts on several occasions and in the one letter in her handwriting that survives she signs with 'yours as long as life endures'.[68] Not only that, the two had met clandestinely at night on several occasions with only Jane Parker present as a chaperone who had also arranged or helped to arrange the meetings.

Who initiated the often long meetings and what exactly happened was, and still is, disputed. In their responses during the interrogation, the three people at the centre of this affair, Thomas Culpepper, Katherine Howards, and Jane Parker, each tried to present their own action in as innocent a light as possible. Each of them, understandably enough, tried to shift the blame to the others: Thomas Culpepper claimed the women had led him astray and seduced him to agree to the meetings. Katherine Howard claimed that Jane Parker was the one who wanted her to befriend Thomas Culpepper. It was her lady-in-waiting who had searched out secret locations for meetings and insisted they met. Jane Parker in turn presented herself as only following the instructions of Katherine Howard. She also claimed that she did not hear or see anything during the night-time meetings, since she sat too far away from Katherine Howard and Thomas Culpepper. Moreover, she was asleep during at least one meeting. While Thomas Culpepper and Katherine Howard insisted that all that happened during these meetings was talk and a chaste kiss on the hand, Jane Parker stated that she thought the two had been lovers.[69]

In the end it is the classic and ultimately unresolvable question of whom to believe. Starkey for example thinks that Culpepper is the most credible. Josephine Wilkinson exonerates Katherine Howard completely and concludes that it was Culpepper who insisted on the meetings, which were arranged with Jane Parker's help. Lacey Baldwin Smith regards Jane Parker as the 'agent provocateur' but that the initiative came from Katherine Howard.[70]

Though Jane Parker was a mature woman with years of experience at court who knew very well how quickly even a queen could fall over rumours of sexual misconduct, she was still Katherine Howard's servant. A high-ranking and by all evidence trusted servant, but nonetheless it would have been difficult or even impossible for Jane to gainsay the headstrong young queen. Jane Parker became entangled in an affair that went quickly from innocent beginnings of taking messages from the queen to a courtier, an unremarkable and everyday occurrence at court, to clandestine meetings which were far beyond acceptable. By that time Jane Parker was already too far involved it the affair to be able to extricate herself. Perhaps the best summary of their behaviour is Starkey's: 'Catherine had behaved like the love-sick Juliet and [Jane Parker,] Lady Rochford like Juliet's pandering Nurse.'[71]

An interesting take on Jane Parker's involvement can be found in Eric Ives's biography of Anne Boleyn. He wonders 'whether the incrimination of Lady Rochford in the crimes of Katherine Howard may not have owed something to revenge', by Anne's friends and relatives.[72] However, this seems highly unlikely considering how deeply involved Jane was in the affair between Katherine Howard and Thomas Culpepper. It was hardly needed to incriminate her. She did so herself.

Like Julia Fox, I think it was the other way around. Jane was not incriminated in the 'crimes' of Katherine Howard for anything she said in Anne Boleyn's trial. Later writers indicted her as the key informant against Anne Boleyn because she was executed for her involvement with Katherine Howard's affair with Thomas Culpepper.[73]

The strain of what was no doubt harsh and relentless questioning and with the events of May 1536 probably still vividly in her mind, Jane Parker broke down. She was described as hysterical and even mad. Under the circumstances it was hardly surprising that she probably suffered what today would be called a severe nervous breakdown. Since the execution of insane people was against the law – a law that was changed just in case – Jane Parker was removed from the Tower and placed in the care of Anne Russell, wife of Admiral Lord Russell. Henry VIII even sent his own physician to look after her.[74]

As the bill of attainder that was introduced to convict Katherine Howard and Jane Parker of treason went through the House of Lords, Jane's father, Henry Parker, Lord Morley attended every reading of the bill.[75] It is impossible to know what Henry Parker's feelings were at the time. He strongly believed that a king had to be obeyed at all times, whether he was right or wrong. It would also have been folly to oppose Henry VIII in this. As with Anne Boleyn, nobody dared to speak out in favour of the convicted.

By the time the guilty sentences had been passed, Jane Parker had recovered her composure and on 13 February 1542 she was beheaded on

Tower Green, just moments after Katherine Howard. Both were buried in St Peter ad Vincula, where Jane's husband George Boleyn and his sister Anne were also buried.[76]

Relatives of Katherine Howard had been particularly quick to distance themselves from her. Her brother is reported to have ridden through London to show his unconcern with Katherine's fate. The duke of Norfolk, now with a second niece charged with adultery and treason, wrote what has been described as a hysteric letter to the king to disassociate himself from Katherine.[77]

Henry Parker distanced himself from his disgraced daughter in his own unique way. Possibly already the following New Year his gift to Henry VIII was a translation of part of Boccaccio's *De Claris Mulieribus* (About Famous Women). Most of the forty-six women whose lives were described were not so much famous as infamous. The few women who were praised were either virgins or widows who rather died than marry a second time. Chastity, the virtue Katherine Howard was accused of lacking, is seen as a woman's most praiseworthy attribute. Simpson describes 'Morley's translation [as] an act of parental severance and sacrifice'. But, in close comparison of the translation with the original, Simpson also detects some changes that indicate that Henry Parker was not completely unsympathetic towards his daughter. Some criticism both of himself as a father and Henry VIII can be read into the omission of some lives and even some changes of words. An addition to the life of Polyxena, the daughter of Priam of Troy who was sacrificed to appease the spirit of Achilles, is perhaps particularly telling: the exclamation that it was wrong for her to be sacrificed for another woman's offence. Did Henry Parker want to imply his daughter, too, was sacrificed for another woman's, namely Katherine Howard's sins?[78]

De Claris Mulieribus was just one of the translations Henry Parker made for Henry VIII, a work for which he had the necessary skills. He also wrote poetry, of which only a few pieces survive. He was noticeably proud of his achievements as a translator and recounts that Henry VIII had not been able to believe he had translated Petrach's *Triumphs* without help. However, he was also aware of his shortcomings as he could not match the brilliance of the style of his source material. He translated 'rudely, but truly'.[79]

As proud as he was of his achievements, he was not interested in making them available to a wide audience by having them printed. His translations were personal gifts. Two pieces of his work were printed but most likely not on his initiative but of others. He always chose the text he translated with the recipient in mind: Mary Tudor received translations of religious interest, Henry VIII mostly tales of heroic figures of the past. As with the translation of Boccaccio's *De Claris Mulieribus* some of the translations were influenced by the events of the time. However, they should not be read as direct commentaries of them. All his translations were about serious topics. In fact, Henry Parker was a bit of a snob in that respect, he despised (or at least claimed to despise) 'the 'merry jest' or a 'tale printed of Robin Hood, or some other dunghill matter'. Complaints about people wasting their time reading popular stories were a common phenomenon at the time.[80]

Henry Parker was not the only nobleman to take up writing in this period. The most famous were Thomas Wyatt and Henry Howard, Earl of Surrey. It has been argued that the reason behind the rise of the noble writer, whether it was poetry or history, was a sign of the decreasing importance of the nobility. Writing filled this gap and, since it was a trivial pursuit, it was also a safe one.[81] Others have argued however that while taking up writing became fashionable this did not mean that the traditional noble pursuits, their military skills, honour, and lineage, were of less importance to nobleman than they were before.[82] In fact, Henry Parker was unusual in his complete refusal to engage in all military activities, whether in war or in the mock battle of the tournament. Often, noblemen could easily combine being a poet with being a warrior. Henry VIII himself did both write poetry and was a passionate jouster and soldier. The nobleman as writer had already existed in the Middle Ages: examples are Anthony Woodville, Earl Rivers, who was a translator in the late fifteenth century, William de la Pole, Duke of Suffolk, and John Montague, wrote poetry earlier in the century. In the fourteenth century Henry, Duke of Lancaster wrote a long devotional treatise in French.[83]

Two works by Henry Parker have received particular attention: the *Exposition and Declaration of the Psalm, Deus ultionum Dominus* written in 1539 and the *Account of the Miracles of the Sacrament* written in 1555–56. In them he expresses widely different views on the papacy. The *Exposition and Declaration* is a violent and vitriolic attack on the papacy. The *Miracles of the Sacrament* are an affirmation of the supremacy of the Roman Church and the consolation of the Catholic faith. It is not surprising that he has been accused of simply writing whatever the recipient wanted to read.

What makes Henry Parker's *Exposition and Declaration* unusual is the violence of the attack on the pope and the eloquence that Henry Parker displays. Despite its title the text has little to say about the psalm. Instead it is a vindication of Henry VIII who overturned the oppression of pope and rescued the English from the Babylonian captivity of the pope's rule. No superlative is spared in the praise of Henry VIII who is compared to David and even Christ. The *Exposition and Declaration* was printed in 1539 a time of renewed antipapal propaganda, possibly on the initiative of either Henry VIII or Thomas Cromwell.[84]

Henry Parker wrote *Miracles of the Sacrament* for Queen Mary (1553–1558). It is an exceptionally personal writing. The text is not only a compilation of miracles caused by the host, but also full of reminiscences about his life which comprise two thirds of the text. Henry Parker argues vehemently for the comfort of the sacrament and confirmation of the supremacy of the pope.[85]

When looking at the two texts side by side it seems that Henry Parker did change his tune according to the prevalent mood, but he wrote the *Miracles of the Sacrament* fifteen years after the *Exposition and Declaration*. In this period the officially accepted religion had undergone repeated changes starting with Henry VIII's separation from Rome while keeping many Catholic rites, to the strong evangelical position under Edward VI, to a return to traditional Catholicism under Queen Mary. These fifteen years of change and upheaval may have persuaded Henry Parker that, despite its flaws, the papacy and the Catholic church were better than the wholesale destruction of cherished rites, venerated shrines, the looting of churches, the hardship and heartache this caused to many people, and the rebellions they had provoked.

That is not to deny that Henry Parker avoided any direct confrontation with authority and adjusted his opinion, or at least the opinion he publicly expressed. Perhaps he was swept up by the prevailing anti-papal sentiment in 1539, perhaps he expressed anti-papal sentiments more extreme than he personally held to show his loyalty and deflect accusations that he harboured sympathy for the participants in the Pilgrimage of Grace.[86] While it may be that the *Exposition and Declaration* and the *Miracles of the Sacrament* are completely contradictory, Starkey points out the different attitudes Henry Parker expressed in his writings reflected the development of opinion in England, and the effects of 'disastrous changes under Edward VI'.[87]

In the years that followed the execution of his daughter, Henry Parker continued to assiduously attend parliament and treason trials. He also acquired several smaller estates in the wake of the dissolution of the monasteries. Henry Parker's attendance of parliament decreases during the reign of Edward VI (1547–1553), a development that may have simply been due to his advanced age but possibly also to the fact that he disagreed with the reform measures of Edward Seymour, the young king's uncle and protector. While he voted for the first act of uniformity, he later opposed further reforming measures including one allowing clerical marriages. When Edward Seymour was overthrown by the Council, Henry Parker promised military aid to them. Religious conservative as he was, Henry Parker continued to acquire estates formerly belonging to the church.[88]

The accession of Queen Mary in 1553 probably came as a relief to him. Over the years he had remained her steadfast friend and had continued to present her with translations. Henry Parker, Lord Morley, died on 25 November 1556 and was buried with full Catholic pomp in St Giles's Church, Great Hallingbury. Though at this time it was hardly opportune to do anything else, for Henry Parker the splendour of the Catholic rites were certainly his preference.[89]

Since his son had died before him, it was his grandson, another Henry Parker, who inherited his estates. He was a prominent Catholic but initially firmly supported Queen Elizabeth (1558–1603) who once visited him at Great Hallingbury. However, after he had refused to subscribe the act of uniformity and after his name had been linked to the rebellion of the northern earls he fled abroad and lived in exile until his death in 1577.[90]

Henry Parker, Lord Morley's life has disappointed some historians. In the brief summary of Henry Parker's life, David Starkey calls him 'an unimportant backwoodsman', while James Kelsey McConica, writing about English humanists, describes him as an 'industrious and mediocre man'.[91] The latter assessment has been challenged in recent years. James Carley for example calls Morley 'an innovator in his choice of form and of subject matter'. The editor of Henry Parker's translation of *De Claris Mulieribus*' pointed out his unceasing interest in anything new, that included studying the Qur'an in Italian and being well-versed in the Bible including the Apocrypha.[92] As writer and translator Henry Parker had not the skill, panache and perhaps flamboyancy of some of the more famous poets of the age, but his translations and writings have their own merits.

Henry Parker obviously had no desire to become a prominent courtier or administrator.[93] Considering how many prominent men of his time ended up on the scaffold, Thomas Cromwell and Jane Seymour's brothers among them, it was safer to stay at court no longer than necessary and to keep one's head down. The execution of his daughter Jane, must surely have confirmed Henry Parker's opinion. Nevertheless, men like Parker, conscientiously doing their duties, are equally necessary for the functioning of a state as the men who lead it. Starkey calls Henry Parker a backwoodsman, but one could equally call him in less derogatory words, a backbencher.

Many if not most of the preoccupations of Tudor noblemen lived their lives very similar to their medieval forefathers. They served the king in war and peace, and just as in the previous centuries some noblemen, like William Lovell III, preferred to not involve themselves in politics and avoid the risks this could entail. As before the downside was that grants were given mainly to those who were present at court. Access to the king was still of utmost importance in the reign of Henry VIII, just as it had been in the reign of Edward III. Henry Parker received few grants, but this was a fate that he shared with the majority of noblemen. Henry VIII's grants were concentrated on a few very active courtiers.[94]

Marriage remained an important way to advancement and here the Parkers were successful. Henry Parker the younger first married an heiress and though he died before his father, he was the father of several children. Two of Henry Parker's daughters also married the heirs of important neighbouring families, the St Johns and the Boleyns.

Of the Parker family, Jane Parker's extraordinary and in the end tragic life singles her out. Like Francis Lovell, Jane Parker, Lady Rochford is relatively well known, and like her relative, her fame is based on her close connection to royalty. While it is the controversial assessment of Richard III's reign that makes Francis Lovell well known, it was Henry VIII's adventurous marital life and Jane's role in the fall of two of his queen's that made her notorious as 'the infamous Lady Rochford', a reputation that she probably does not deserve.

Conclusion

From Ascelin Goël to Jane Parker, the long history of one family has taken us from their origins as castellans in Normandy to the court of Henry VIII. In these 500 years both the family and the society they lived in changed dramatically. Over these centuries the Lovells also accumulated lands and became richer and more powerful as a consequence. From their relatively humble origins they rose into the highest tiers of the nobility.

The nobility as a whole also changed significantly. Around 1100 the focus of their ambitions was the possession of strategically placed castles and the power controlling these places gave them. It was a goal that was often achieved by violence and rebellion. In the later Middle Ages, open rebellion was no longer an accepted way to acquire possession of land and property, but violence never disappeared. The multitude of lawsuits that have been discussed bear witness to the robberies, violent break-ins, and even attempts on the owners' lives. But they were regarded as breaks of the norm and the law and redress could be sought.

The path to promotion lay increasingly in military service to the higher nobility and ultimately the king. The administration became more sophisticated and penetrated more and deeper into every aspect of life. Service in the royal administration both at court and in the localities also became an important factor for promotion and increasing status. The growing administration also produced a larger number of records allowing us more detailed knowledge of the men and women of the Lovell family.

As institutions like the Exchequer and the highest courts settled in Westminster the role of the nobility as a conduit between the centre of government and the individual counties increased. They took the decisions made at court to the localities and reported the reaction of the localities back to court. While the royal court never became completely fixed in one place, it became much more settled over time. While Henry II hardly ever spend long periods in one place, constantly travelling the length and breadth of his enormous 'empire', the Tudor court resided in and around London for most of the time. Royal progresses to different parts of the country turned into exciting and unusual occurrences. As a consequence the nobility had to come to London or the royal palaces in the surrounding area to see the king.

Primarily residing in only a few palaces in and around London allowed the royal court to become a more elaborate place. The king was attended by an increasing number of servants and courtiers and their roles within the royal household were strictly defined. The court ceremonies became more and more sophisticated and celebrations more flamboyant. The households of the nobility also became larger, the number of servants and administrators rose. Just as the royal palaces became larger and more luxurious so did the residences of the nobility. They modernised or rebuilt their favourite residences to enjoy the new standards, adding fireplaces, glass windows, and decorations, as John Lovell VII did with Wardour and William Lovell III in Minster Lovell.

The nobility also became more rigid and stratified. Though great differences in wealth and influence had always existed within the nobility these difference were now categorised. After the Norman conquest only three ranks, earls, tenurial barons, and other nobles, existed below the king. Over time more titles were added: princes, dukes, marquesses, and viscounts. The untitled nobility was increasingly strictly divided into the higher nobility who received individual summonses to parliament forming the House of Lords, and the lesser nobility, the knights and esquires, from whose ranks the knights of the shire were elected, who sat in the House of Commons.

The most profound change came at the very end of the period under discussion, the separation of the Church of England from Rome and the Reformation. It was a combination of Henry VIII's marital problems and the influence of the Reformation movements on the European continent that brought about this change. Along with several other developments (like the invention of the printing press, the 'discovery' of America, and the fall of Constantinople) the reformation is often regarded as marking the end of the Middle Ages and the beginning of the Modern Age.

However, as much as the nobility changed over the centuries, many fundamental aspects of their role remained the same.

The royal court continued to be the centre of power and patronage, whether it was itinerant or in a fixed place. It was here that the nobility were able to exercise their influence, participate in government and in the decisions taken. Here they could gain prestige, preferment and patronage.

The nobility also remained in essence a warrior elite. Just as Ascelin Goël had participated in William the Conqueror's invasion of the Vexin in 1087, Francis Lovell had served in Scotland in 1481. Henry VIII saw himself very much as a warrior king like Henry V. Henry Parker's refusal to join in either war or tournaments set him apart from his peers in the Tudor nobility. Even the idea of the crusade, which seems so quintessentially medieval, had not been completely abandoned by the Tudor period. In fact it had gained renewed urgency after the conquest of Constantinople in 1453 and the siege of Vienna in 1529.

Royal service, both in the military and at court remained dangerous. The Lovells are a good example. The family was almost extinct in the male line when John Lovell IV died in the Battle of Bannockburn and actually ended in the male line with the death of Henry Lovell, Lord Morley, in the Battle of Dixmude in 1489. Taking an important role at court could also lead to exile, as John Lovell VII experienced, or even execution, a fate suffered by Jane Parker. Every nobleman and noblewoman had to decide whether they wanted to take the risks involved. While certain expectations existed on how the nobility ought to live their lives as member of the elite, they did have a choice on how far they were willing to involve themselves. Most Lovells decided to participate fully in both military and administrative service and did so with varying levels of success, but there were others like John Lovell VIII and William Lovell III who were, by all appearances, not interested in a career at court or in the army.

The increasing stratification of the nobility never led to a complete separation of the individual segments. Younger sons of parliamentary peers, like those of the Lovells, were members of the gentry. If they were lucky enough to marry the heiress of a barony they might be included in the peerage although this was not guaranteed but depended on the good will of the king. William Lovell III's younger son William Lovell was only summoned to parliament during the readaptation of Henry VI. The richer gentry often had more in common with the poorer barons than with the men at the lower end of gentry society.

Another aspect that did not change over time was that land was and remained the basis of power for the nobility. Even men who made their riches in trade were keen to turn these riches into possession of land. Acquiring land through marrying wealthy heiresses was just as important to the Tudor nobility as it was for their medieval forefathers. In this, the Lovells did remarkably well. Almost half of the wives that married into the family were heiresses and the land they brought was the foundation of the family's increase in status within the nobility.

Women were integral and much valued members of a noble family, not only as mothers but also as representatives of their husbands administering the family estates in their absence. Unfortunately, most aspects of the lives of the women are lost to us due to a lack of records and this is no different for the women of the Lovell family, but that they were trusted and honoured members of the family has, I hope, become clear.

One important factor why the Tudor nobility seems to be different from their ancestors is that the number and variety of records surviving from this period is substantially larger than that of the medieval period, particularly from earlier medieval times. With the survival particularly of private papers and letters, the nobility of the fifteenth century and the Tudor period appear much more accessible to us. The growing number of portraits also gives the men and women faces we can relate to. While only a portrait of John Lovell VII exists from the centuries before 1500, portraits both of Henry Lovell, Lord Morley and his daughter-in-law Grace Newport survive from the Tudor period.

For 500 years, the Lovell family advanced within the society, reaping the benefits of service in war and peace as well as profiting from their marriages with rich heiresses. However, their advancement was not steady. They experienced turmoil and upsets. But for several centuries, they were able to overcome these setbacks. Only at the very end of the Middle Ages the successful history of the Lovells came to an end, when the family died out in the male line. The family survived in the female line, and the offspring of Alice Lovell, the Parker Lords Morley retained it status within the nobility and their place in the tumultuous history of their days.

The family participated in many of the most famous events of these five centuries. They fought in battles from Bourgtheroulde to Dixmude, joined two crusades, participated in sieges including the siege of Calais, and witnessed revolts and the overthrow of kings. The history of the Lovell family and of their Parker descendants allows us interesting insights into the developments and changes which occurred during this time.

Glossary

benefice = church office

commission of array = commission to gather the military troops in a county or area

commission of gaol delivery = commissions to try all prisoners held in gaol

commission of oyer and terminer = commission to hear and determine court cases

enfeoffments to use = grant of land to a group of trustees (feoffees) to hold for the use of the actual owner or other specified beneficiary, avoiding a minor heir becoming a ward of the king or noble from which the land was held

familia = household of a noblemen, including servants and soldiers

feet of fines = government records of land transactions. Three copies of the agreement were made, two were given to the parties involved, one, the stump (foot) of the entries remained in government archives

fee tail = land held in fee tail could be inherited by one's heirs, regardless of their sex

jointure = land held jointly by husband and wife, which after the death of one spouse remained in the hands of the surviving partner

indenture = contract, usually for military service

itinerant justices = justices sent to visit the country to try legal cases

prebend = church stipend given for example to a canon

recognizance = acknowledgment

tail male = land which could only be inherited by the male heirs

tallage = land tax

view of frankpledge = right to check (view) the frankpledge, in which a group of men (a tithing) swore to stand surety for each other. Originally held by sheriffs twice a year to collect the tithing penny and other fines. By the later Middle Ages often appropriated by landowners

writ of *mort d'ancestor* = the defendant is accused of illegally depriving an heir of his rightful inheritance

writ of *novel disseisin* = the defendant is accused of illegally depriving an owner of his land

Genealogies

Genealogy 1: The Ancestors of the Lovells in Normandy

Guillaume Longue Épée *m.* (1) Sprote (2) *m.* l'Eperlan

Herfast

Gonnor *m.* Richard I Duke of Normandy

Ralph Count of Bayeux *m.* Aubrée

Yves de Bellême *m.* Godehaut

Osbern Steward of William I

Emma *m.*

Hugh, Bishop of Bayeux

Basle *m.* Richard

Aubert *m.* Hildeburge le Rich de Gallardon

Adeliza de Tosny *m.* William fitz Osbern

Aubrée *m.* Robert d'Ivry

Robert

m.

Beatrix *m.* Herve de Gallardon

Hildeburge

William

Roger the Obstinate Earl of Hereford

Emma *m.* Ralph Gael

William de Breteuil (*d.* 1103)

Eustace de Breteuil *m.* Juliana

Isabel *m.*

Robert Goël (*d.* before 1123)

Ascelin Goël (*d.* 1116/19)

Robert Rufus

William Gael

Ralph Gael

William de Pacy

William Lovell I (*d.* 1166/70)

Richard* *m.* (1) Amice Gael (2) Robert Beaumont

Genealogy 2: The Beaumont Connection

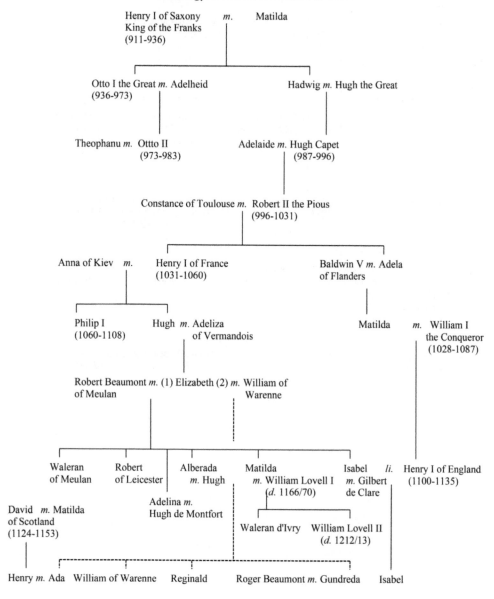

Genealogy 3: The Basset Family

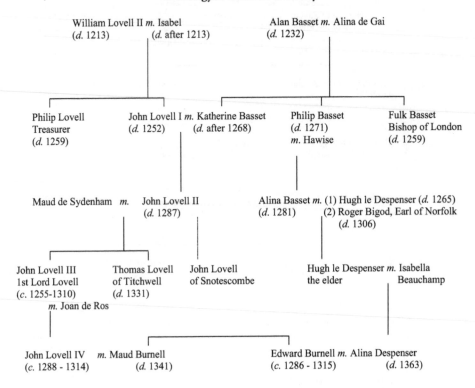

William Lovell II *m.* Isabel
(*d.* 1213)   (*d.* after 1213)

Alan Basset *m.* Alina de Gai
(*d.* 1232)

Philip Lovell
Treasurer
(*d.* 1259)

John Lovell I *m.* Katherine Basset
(*d.* 1252)   (*d.* after 1268)

Philip Basset
(*d.* 1271)
m. Hawise

Fulk Basset
Bishop of London
(*d.* 1259)

Maud de Sydenham *m.* John Lovell II
(*d.* 1287)

Alina Basset *m.* (1) Hugh le Despenser (*d.* 1265)
(*d.* 1281)   (2) Roger Bigod, Earl of Norfolk
(*d.* 1306)

John Lovell III
1st Lord Lovell
(*c.* 1255-1310)
m. Joan de Ros

Thomas Lovell
of Titchwell
(*d.* 1331)

John Lovell
of Snotescombe

Hugh le Despenser *m.* Isabella
the elder   Beauchamp

John Lovell IV *m.* Maud Burnell
(*c.* 1288 - 1314)   (*d.* 1341)

Edward Burnell *m.* Alina Despenser
(*c.* 1286 - 1315)   (*d.* 1363)

Genealogy 4: The de la Zouche Family

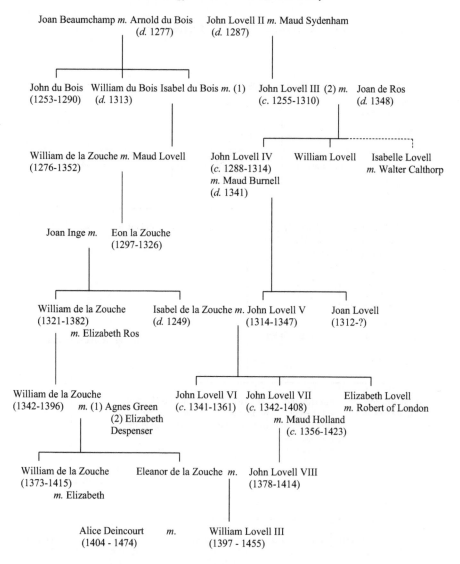

Genealogy 5: The Holland Family

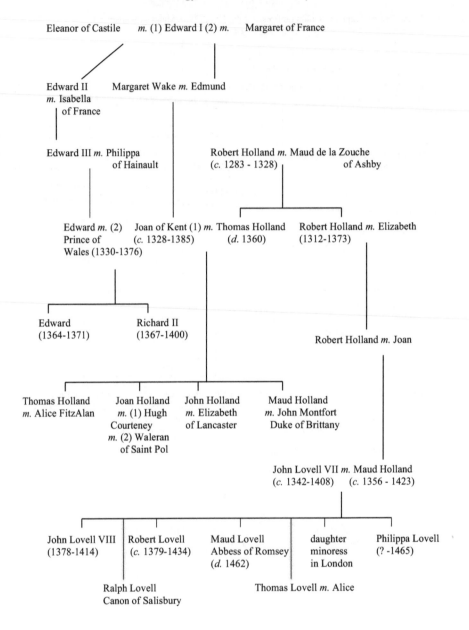

Eleanor of Castile   *m.* (1) Edward I (2) *m.*   Margaret of France

Edward II   Margaret Wake *m.* Edmund
m. Isabella
  of France

Edward III *m.* Philippa   Robert Holland *m.* Maud de la Zouche
        of Hainault   (*c.* 1283 - 1328)   of Ashby

Edward *m.* (2)   Joan of Kent (1) *m.* Thomas Holland   Robert Holland *m.* Elizabeth
Prince of   (*c.* 1328-1385)   (*d.* 1360)   (1312-1373)
Wales (1330-1376)

Edward   Richard II
(1364-1371)   (1367-1400)   Robert Holland *m.* Joan

Thomas Holland   Joan Holland   John Holland   Maud Holland
m. Alice FitzAlan   *m.* (1) Hugh   *m.* Elizabeth   *m.* John Montfort
            Courteney   of Lancaster   Duke of Brittany
         m. (2) Waleran
          of Saint Pol

John Lovell VII *m.* Maud Holland
(*c.* 1342-1408)   (*c.* 1356 - 1423)

John Lovell VIII | Robert Lovell   Maud Lovell   daughter   Philippa Lovell
(1378-1414) | (*c.* 1379-1434)   Abbess of Romsey   minoress   (? -1465)
                (*d.* 1462)   in London

     Ralph Lovell   Thomas Lovell *m.* Alice
     Canon of Salisbury

Genealogy 6: The Burnell Family

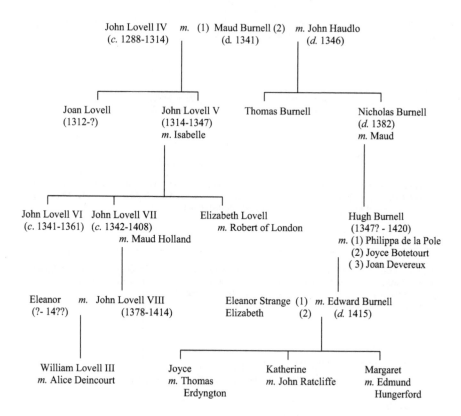

John Lovell IV   *m.*   (1)   Maud Burnell (2)   *m.* John Haudlo
(*c.* 1288-1314)   (*d.* 1341)   (*d.* 1346)

Joan Lovell   John Lovell V   Thomas Burnell   Nicholas Burnell
(1312-?)   (1314-1347)   (*d.* 1382)
                 m. Isabelle   *m.* Maud

John Lovell VI   John Lovell VII   Elizabeth Lovell   Hugh Burnell
(*c.* 1341-1361)   (*c.* 1342-1408)   *m.* Robert of London   (1347? - 1420)
              m. Maud Holland   *m.* (1) Philippa de la Pole
                                                   (2) Joyce Botetourt
                                                   (3) Joan Devereux

Eleanor   *m.*   John Lovell VIII   Eleanor Strange (1)   *m.* Edward Burnell
(?- 14??)   (1378-1414)   Elizabeth   (2)   (*d.* 1415)

William Lovell III   Joyce   Katherine   Margaret
m. Alice Deincourt   *m.* Thomas   *m.* John Ratcliffe   *m.* Edmund
                     Erdyngton   Hungerford

Genealogy 7: The Deincourt and Grey of Rotherfield Families

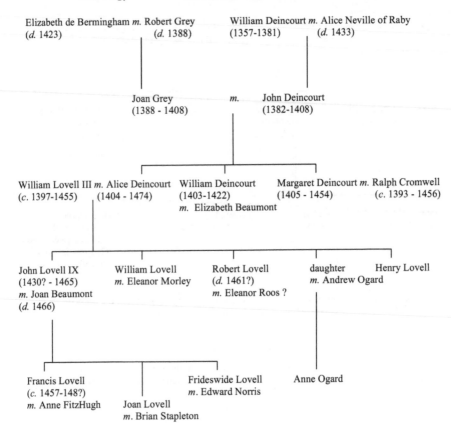

Elizabeth de Bermingham *m.* Robert Grey
(*d.* 1423)   (*d.* 1388)

William Deincourt *m.* Alice Neville of Raby
(1357-1381)   (*d.* 1433)

Joan Grey   *m.*   John Deincourt
(1388 - 1408)   (1382-1408)

William Lovell III *m.* Alice Deincourt   William Deincourt   Margaret Deincourt *m.* Ralph Cromwell
(*c.* 1397-1455)   (1404 - 1474)   (1403-1422)   (1405 - 1454)   (*c.* 1393 - 1456)
                                            m. Elizabeth Beaumont

John Lovell IX   William Lovell   Robert Lovell   daughter   Henry Lovell
(1430? - 1465)   *m.* Eleanor Morley   (*d.* 1461?)   *m.* Andrew Ogard
m. Joan Beaumont   *m.* Eleanor Roos ?
(*d.* 1466)

Francis Lovell   Frideswide Lovell   Anne Ogard
(*c.* 1457-148?)   *m.* Edward Norris
m. Anne FitzHugh   Joan Lovell
                      m. Brian Stapleton

Genealogy 8: The Bryan Family

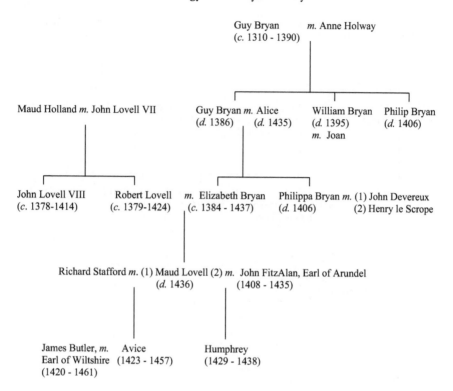

Guy Bryan *m.* Anne Holway
(*c.* 1310 - 1390)

Maud Holland *m.* John Lovell VII

Guy Bryan *m.* Alice   William Bryan   Philip Bryan
(*d.* 1386)   (*d.* 1435)   (*d.* 1395)   (*d.* 1406)
                           m. Joan

John Lovell VIII   Robert Lovell   *m.* Elizabeth Bryan   Philippa Bryan *m.* (1) John Devereux
(*c.* 1378-1414)   (*c.* 1379-1424)   (*c.* 1384 - 1437)   (*d.* 1406)   (2) Henry le Scrope

Richard Stafford *m.* (1) Maud Lovell (2) *m.* John FitzAlan, Earl of Arundel
                        (*d.* 1436)   (1408 - 1435)

James Butler, *m.*   Avice   Humphrey
Earl of Wiltshire   (1423 - 1457)   (1429 - 1438)
(1420 - 1461)

Genealogy 9: The Morley Family

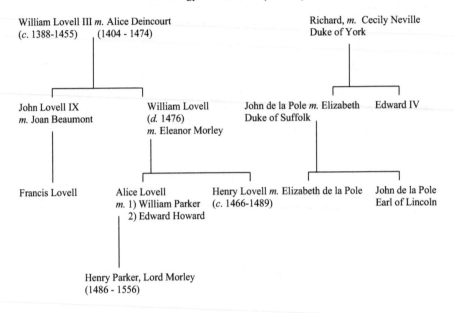

William Lovell III *m.* Alice Deincourt
(*c.* 1388-1455)   (1404 - 1474)

Richard, *m.* Cecily Neville
Duke of York

John Lovell IX
m. Joan Beaumont

William Lovell
(*d.* 1476)
m. Eleanor Morley

John de la Pole *m.* Elizabeth
Duke of Suffolk

Edward IV

Francis Lovell

Alice Lovell
m. 1) William Parker
2) Edward Howard

Henry Lovell *m.* Elizabeth de la Pole
(*c.* 1466-1489)

John de la Pole
Earl of Lincoln

Henry Parker, Lord Morley
(1486 - 1556)

Genealogy 10: The Parker Family

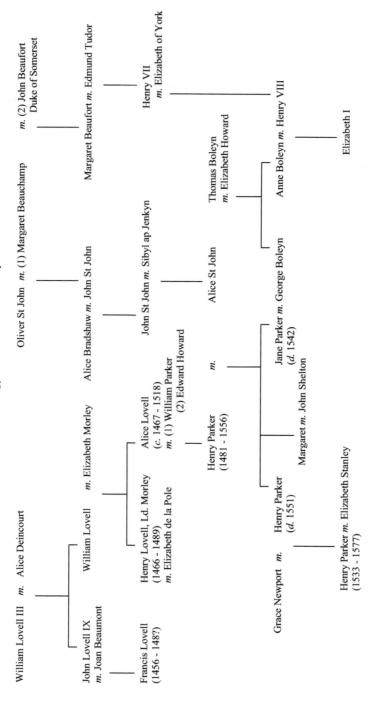

Genealogy 11: The Parker, Boleyn and Shelton Families

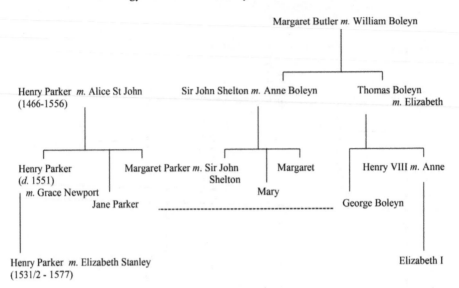

Notes

Introduction

1. R. Fabyan, *The New Chronicles of England and France in to Parts* (London, 1811), p. 672.

Chapter 1: The Lords of Bréval, the Castle of Ivry, and the Profits of Rebellion

1. *CP*, vol. viii, pp. 208–10.
2. Impey, 'The Ancestry of the White Tower', in Edward Impey (ed.), *The White Tower* (New Haven, 2008), pp. 240–41.
3. OV, vol. iv, pp. 290–91; *Cartulaire de L'Abbaye de Saint-Martin de Pontoise*, J. Depoin (ed.) (Pontoise, 1895), p. 50.
4. See also Depoin's references to charters Robert witnessed as Robert 'd'Ivry', ibid., p. 471.
5. *CP*, vol. viii, p. 209; OV, vol. 3, pp. 208–09; Depoin, p. 472.
6. Depoin, p. 50.
7. Chibnall, *The World of Orderic Vitalis* (Oxford, 1984), p. 80; 'Vie de la B. Hildeburge de Gallardon, châtelaine d'Ivry, religieuse à St Martin', in Depoin, pp. 50–54.
8. Depoin, p. 50. and p. 473, n. 930.
9. *CP*, vol. viii, p. 208.
10. *ODNB*, Orderic Vitalis.
11. OV, vol. iv, p. 78; Vaughn, *Anselm of Bec and Robert of Meulan: The Innocence of the Dove and the Wisdom of the Serpent* (Berkeley, 1987), p. 95.
12. OV, vol. iv, pp. 112–14.
13. OV, vol. iv, p. 114.
14. Vaughn, *Anselm*, pp. 95, 98; Judith Green, 'Robert Curthose Reassessed', *Anglo-Norman Studies* 22 (2000), p. 105.
15. *ODNB*, Roger Breteuil.
16. OV, vol. iii, p. 209; Daniel Power, *The Norman Frontier in the Twelfth and Early Thirteenth Century*, Cambridge Studies in Medieval Life and Thought, 4th series, 62 (2004), p. 207.
17. C.W. David, *Robert Curthose, Duke of Normandy* (Cambridge, Mass., 1920), p. 78.
18. OV, vol. iv, p. 287.
19. OV, vol. iv, p. 286.
20. *GND*, vol. ii, p. 229; OV, vol. iii, p. 209; vol. iv, p. 286.
21. OV, vol. iv, pp. 288.
22. OV, vol. iv, pp. 286–88.
23. OV, vol. iv, p. 199.
24. David Crouch, *The Beaumont Twins* (Cambridge, 1986), p. 108.
25. OV, vol. iv, p. 40. C. Warren Hollister, *Henry I* (New Haven and London, 2003), p. 178.

26. OV, vol. iv, p. 46.
27. Depoin, pp. 54, 343–5. I am grateful to Dan Power for information about this grant.
28. OV, vol. iv, p. 202.
29. OV, vol. iv, p. 203.
30. Depoin, p. 55, p. 474, n. 935; *CP*, vol. viii, p. 210.
31. Crouch, *Beaumont Twins*, p. 4; Green, 'King Henry and the Aristocracy of Normandy', in *La 'France Anglaise' au Moyen Âge. Colloque des historiens médiévistes français et britanniques* (Paris, 1988), p. 163.
32. *ODNB*, Orderic Vitalis.
33. OV, vol. vi pp. 218–19, 228–31; Hollister, *Henry I*, p. 260.
34. Depoin, p. 474, n. 936.
35. OV, vol. vi, pp. 228–31; Hollister, *Henry I*, pp. 247–48.
36. OV, vol. vi, p. 333.
37. Crouch, *Beaumont Twins*, p. 14.
38. Crouch, *Beaumont Twins*, pp. 4; OV, vol. vi, p. 333.
39. OV, vol. vi, pp. 232–33.
40. Crouch, *Beaumont Twins*, p. 16.
41. OV, vol. vi, p. 333.
42. Green, *Henry I: King of England and Duke of Normandy* (Cambridge, 2006), pp. 183–85.
43. OV, vol. vi, pp. 348–49.
44. OV, vol. vi, pp. 350–51.
45. OV, vol. vi, p. 352; Bradbury, *The Medieval Archer* (Woodbridge, 1985), p. 50.
46. Hollister, *Henry I*, p. 300.
47. OV, vol. vi, p. 358.
48. Crouch, *Beaumont Twins*, pp. 23–25; Hollister, *Henry I*, pp. 304, 334, n. 31.
49. Crouch, *Beaumont Twins*, pp. 36, 60, 69, 75; *GND*, vol. ii, pp. 228–29.
50. Chibnall, *World of Orderic Vitalis*, p. 21; Green, 'King Henry I and the Aristocracy of Normandy', p. 167.
51. Green, *Henry I*, p. 73; Power, *Norman Frontier*, p. 200.

Chapter 2: The First Lovells in England

1. Crouch, *Beaumont Twins*, pp. 24–26.
2. *Liber Feodorum: The Book of Fees Commonly called Testa de Nevill* (PRO, 1920–31), vol. i, p. 134.
3. Newman, *The Anglo-Norman Nobility in the Reign of Henry I: The Second Generation* (University of Pennsylvania Press, Philadelphia, 1988), p. 72.
4. *The Pipe Roll of 31 Henry I: Michaelmas 1130*, Joseph Hunter (ed.) (orig. publ. 1833, facsimile London, 1929), pp. 5, 23, 95, 99.
5. A.J. Taylor, 'The Alien Priory of Minster Lovell', *Oxoniensia* 2 (1937), p. 103.
6. Alison McHardy, 'The Effects of War on the Church: The Case of the Alien Priories in the Fourteenth Century', in Michael Jones and Malcom Vale (eds.) *England and her Neighbours, 1066–1453. Essays in Honour of Pierre Chaplais* (London and Roncerverte, 1989), p. 279; Marjorie Morgan, 'The Suppression of the Alien Priories', *History* 26 (1941), p. 205.
7. Taylor, 'Alien Priory', p. 103.
8. Grant of Minster Lovell to John Lovell VII, *CFR*, 1368–1377, p. 225; to Maud Holland, *CFR*, 1405–1408, p. 130; to William Lovell III, *CFR*, 1437–1445, p. 39.

9. *VCH*, Buckinghamshire, vol. ii, p. 153.
10. A.J. Taylor, *Minster Lovell Hall* (1985), p. 16.
11. Crouch, *Beaumont Twins*, p. 36.
12. Crouch, *Beaumont Twins*, 31–32, 38.
13. C. Warren Hollister, 'The Anglo-Norman Succession Debate of 1126: Prelude to Stephen's Anarchy', in C. Warren Hollister, *Monarchy, Magnates and Institutions in the Anglo-Norman World* (London and Ronceverte, 1986), pp. 164–66.
14. Crouch, *Beaumont Twins*, pp. 50–51.
15. *Regesta Regum Anglo-Normannorum, 1066–1154*, H.A. Cronne and R.H.C. Davis (eds.), vol. iii (Oxford, 1968), pp. xxxviii–xxix, 106; Charles Homer Haskins, *Norman Institutions* (1918), p. 140.
16. *Regesta Regum Anglo-Normannorum*, vol. iii, pp. 268–69; Crouch, *Beaumont Twins*, p. 69.
17. *Chronicles of the Reign of Stephen, Henry II and Richard I*, Richard Howlett (ed.) (London, 1889) vol. iv, p. 175; Crouch, *Beaumont Twins*, pp. 74–5; *ODNB*, Waleran Beaumont, Count of Meulan and Earl of Worcester.
18. *CP*, vol. viii, pp. 212–13.
19. Newman, *Anglo-Norman Nobility*, p. 21; George Garnett, '"Ducal" Succession in Early Normandy', in G. Garnett and J. Hudson (eds.), *Law and Government in Medieval England and Normandy: Essays in Honour of Sir James Holt* (Cambridge, 1994), 80–110; E.Z. Tabuteau, 'The Role of Law in the Succession to Normandy and England, 1087', *Haskins Society Journal* 3 (1992), pp. 141–69.
20. *CP*, vol. viii, p. 214.
21. Crouch, *Beaumont Twins*, pp. 8–9.
22. *CP*, vol. viii, p. 212.
23. *CP*, vol. viii, p. 214.
24. *CP*, vol. viii, pp. 213–14.
25. *Book of Fees*, vol. I, p. 137; *CP*, vol. viii, pp. 213–14.
26. *ODNB*, Alan Basset; King John's Evil Councillors.
27. *CPR*, 1258–1266, p. 638; *CP*, vol. viii, p. 214; Philip Lovell, *DNB*, vol. xii, pp. 164–65; *ODNB*, Alan Basset.
28. *CP*, vol. viii, p. 214.
29. D.A. Carpenter, *The Minority of Henry III* (London, 1990), p. 311; *CP*, vol. viii, p. 213.
30. *Rotuli Litterarum Clausarum in Turri Londiniensi asservati*, vol. ii, London 1844, p. 10.
31. Grant G. Simpson, 'The *Familia* of Roger de Quincy, Earl of Winchester and Constable of Scotland', in K.J. Stringer (ed.), *Essays on the Nobility of Medieval Scotland* (Edinburgh, 1985), p. 118.
32. *CCR*, 1385–1389, p. 629.
33. *CCR*, 1247–1251, p. 405 (John Lovell), p. 203 (Philip Lovell).
34. *CPR*, 1216–1225, pp. 567–68.
35. *CCR*, 1234–1237, p. 231; *CCR*, 1247–1251, p. 141.
36. *CPR*, 1225–1231, p. 356.
37. *CIPM*, vol. i, Henry III, no. 269.

Chapter 3: Law and Connections

1. *ODNB*, Philip Lovel.
2. Simpson, p. 110; Lewis C. Loyd and Doris Mary Stanton (eds.), *Sir Christopher Hatton's Book of Seals to which is Appended a Select List of the Works of Frank Merry Stenton* (Oxford, 1950), nos. 18, 418.

3. *ODNB*, Philip Lovel.
4. Emma Mason (ed.), *The Beauchamp Cartulary Charters 1100–1268* (Publications of the Pipe Roll Society, LXXXI, New Series, XLIII, London, 1980), no. 251; Emma Mason, 'A Truth Universally Acknowledged', in David Baker (ed.), *The Church in Town and Countryside: Papers Read at the Seventeenth Summer Meeting and the Eighteenth Winter Meeting of the Ecclesiastical History Society* (Oxford, 1979), p. 177.
5. Matthew Paris, *Chronica Majora*, Henry R. Luard (ed.), Rolls Series 57 (London, 1880), vol. v, p. 270,
6. *ODNB*, John Mansel; Matthew Paris, vol. v, pp. 261–62; 320; *CPR*, 1247–1258, p. 149.
7. *CLP*, vol. iv, pp. 104, 145, 154, 180, 264, 336–67, 362, 371, 401.
8. *CPR*, 1247–1258, pp. 60, 80, 263, 406.
9. *CCR*, 1247–1251, pp. 177, 298; *CCR*, 1251–1453, pp. 333, 367; *CCR*, 1253–1254, pp. 29, 84.
10. *VCH*, Staffordshire, vol. iv, p. 116; *VCH*, Warwickshire, vol. iv, p. 64.
11. *ODNB*, Phillip Lovel.
12. *ODNB*, Alan Basset; Fulk Basset; Gilbert Basset; Philip Basset.
13. Anthony R. Wagner, *Heralds and Heraldry in the Middle Ages*, (London, 1956), p. 19.
14. J. Bain, 'Note of a Grant of Lands at Docking (co. Norfolk?) and Seal With Unusual Inscription Appended', Archaeological Journal 37 (1880), p. 328.; Gerard J. Brault (ed.), *Rolls of Arms Edward I (1272–1307): Heralds Roll, Dering Roll, Camden, Roll, St George's Roll, Charles' Roll, Segar's Roll, Lord Marshal's Roll, Collins' Roll, Falkirk Roll, Guillim's Roll, Caerlaverock Poem, Galloway Roll, Smallpece's Roll, Stirling Roll, Nativity Roll, Fife Roll, Sir William le Neve's Roll* (London, 1997), vol. ii, p. 266.
15. Taylor, 'Alien Priory', p. 108; *CPR*, 1266–1275, pp. 658, 672, 727; 'Annales Londonienses and Annales Paulini', *Chronicles of the Reigns of Edward I and Edward II*, William Stubbs (ed.), RS 76 (London 1882), p. 89.
16. The chantry was one of several ill-endowed chantries in the cathedral that were combined in 1391, *CPR*, 1388–1392, p. 413.
17. *CPR*, 1247–1258, p. 402; *Foedera*, vol. i, 1, 1, p. 361.
18. *VCH*, Northamptonshire, vol. iii, p. 144; Burke, *The General Armory of England, Scotland, Ireland, and Wales: Comprising a Registry of Armorial Bearings from the Earliest to the Present Time* (London, 1884, reprint 1969), p. 992; Monika E. Simon, 'Who is Buried in the Tomb in St Kenelm's Church, Minster Lovell?', *The Ricardian* 19 (2009), 84–94.
19. *CPR*, 1247–1258, p. 590; J.R. Maddicott, *Simon de Montfort* (Cambridge, 1994), p. 136.
20. Matthew Paris, vol. v, pp. 714–19, 731; *CPR*, 1258–1266, p. 1; Maddicott, *Simon de Montfort*, p. 171.
21. Matthew Paris, vol. v, p. 270; Maddicott, *Simon de Montfort*, p. 171; see also *DNB*, vol. xii, pp. 164–65.
22. *ODNB*, Philip Lovel.
23. *CPR*, 1258–1266, p. 163–64, 410 and *Lists of Sheriffs for England and Wales*, PRO Lists and Indexes 9 (repr. with amendments, 1963), p. 106.
24. *CPR*, 1258–1266, pp. 165, 300.
25. D.A. Carpenter, *The Battles of Lewes and Evesham, 1264/65* (Keele, 1987); *CPR*, 1258–1266, p. 410.
26. *CPR*, 1258–1266, p. 495.

27. *CP*, vol. iv, pp. 261–62.
28. *CPR*, 1258–1266, p. 488.
29. *CPR*, 1258–1266, p. 638.
30. *CPR*, 1258–1266, p. 537.
31. *CPR*, 1258–1266, pp. 490–91; *CPR*, 1266–1275, p. 113.
32. *CChR*, 1257–1300, p. 93.
33. Prestwich, *Edward I* (London, 1988), pp. 66–68.
34. *CPR*, 1266–1275, pp. 425, 440.
35. Prestwich, *Edward I*, pp. 78–85.
36. *CP*, vol. viii, p. 215. *Parl. Writs*, vol. i, pp. 195, 202, 226.
37. *CCR*, 1272–1279, p. 539; *CCR*, 1279–1288, pp. 79, 173, 213.
38. *CCR*, 1279–1288, pp. 111, 344, 365, 406; *CCR*, 1279–1288, pp. 405, 465.
39. *CP*, vol. viii, p. 215.

Chapter 4: The Profit and Peril of Service

1. *CP*, vol. viii, p. 217; vol. ii, p. 202; *CIPM*, vol. v. 263; *ODNB*, du Bois family.
2. Francis Blomefield, *Essay Towards a Topographical History of the County of Norfolk, Containing A Description...* (London, 1769), p. 717. Thanks to Florian Doyle for making me aware of this reference; *CIPM*, vol. v, no. 520.
3. *CPR*, 1281–1292, pp. 271–72, 295–96.
4. *CCR*, 1288–1296, p. 126.
5. *CPR*, 1292–1301, pp. 44–45.
6. *CPR*, 1281–1292, p. 321; *CPR*, 1292–1301, p. 29.
7. Dugdale, pp. 8–9.
8. *CPR*, 1292–1301, pp. 73, 76.
9. *Chancery Warrants*, A.D. 1244–1326 (London, 1927), p. 61.
10. *Calendar of Documents related to Scotland Preserved in Her Majesty's Public Record Office*, Joseph Bain (ed.),(Edinburgh, 1884), vol. ii, A.D. 1272–1307, pp. 190–92.
11. Dugdale, pp. 18–19; see also *Parl. Writs*, vol. i, p. 52.
12. M. Prestwich, 'Magnate Summonses in England in the Later Years of Edward I', *Parliaments, Estates and Representation* 5 (1985), pp. 100–01.
13. *Parl. Writs*, vol. i, pp. 282, 56, 303, 393; *CP*, vol. viii, p. 216.
14. *CPR*, 1292–1301, p. 271; *Calendar of Documents related to Scotland*, vol. ii, pp. 252–55.
15. *Documents Illustrating the Crisis of 1297–98 in England*, Michael Prestwich (ed.), Camden Society 4th series, 24 (1980), pp. 8, 31, 157.
16. *CChR*, 1300–1326, p. 31, 34; *CCR*, 1307–1313, p. 111; *Chancery Warrants*, 1244–1326, pp. 217–18.
17. Prestwich, *Edward I*, p. 394.
18. *Documents and Records Illustrating the History of Scotland and the Transactions between the Crowns of Scotland and England*, Francis Palgrave (ed.) (London, 1837), vol. i, pp. 213, 217, 263, 268; Prestwich, *The Three Edwards. War and State in England 1272–1377* (London, 1980), p. 49; *Foedera*, vol. i, p. 966.
19. *CPR*, 1301–1307, pp. 145–46, 166, 230.
20. *CCR*, 1302–1307, p. 24; see also chapter 7.
21. *CPR*, 1301–1307, pp. 348–49, 405.
22. *CPR*, 1301–1307, p. 321; *CP*, vol. viii, pp. 216–17.
23. *Parl. Writs*, vol. i, pp. 42–43.
24. *CPR*, 1301–1307, p. 290; *CChR*, 1300–1326, p. 49.

25. *Parl. Writs*, vol. ii, p. 17.
26. A. Tomkinson, 'The Retinues at the Tournament of Dunstable, 1309', *EHR* 74 (1959), pp. 70–72.
27. *CCR*, 1307–1313, p. 253; *Munimenta Gildhallae Londoniensis*, Henry T. Riley (ed.), vol. ii, *Liber Custumarum*, Rolls Series 12 (London, 1860).
28. *CIPM*, vol. v, no. 263; *CFR*, 1307–1319, pp. 73–76.
29. *CIPM*, vol. ix, no. 128.
30. TNA, PRO 30/26/69, no. 210.
31. Phillips, *Aymer de Valence. Earl of Pembroke, 1207–1324: Baronial Politics in the Reign of Edward II* (Oxford, 1972), p. 300; *CPR*, 1307–1313, p. 101.
32. For William de la Zouche see Phillips, *Aymer de Valence*, pp. 300–03; for William de Ros see *CP*, vol. xi, pp. 96–97.
33. *ODNB*, Robert Burnell.
34. *ODNB*, Robert Burnell; *CP*, vol. ii, p. 434.
35. Phillips, *Aymer de Valence*, p. 75.
36. *CIPM*, vol. v, nos. 520, 545.
37. It seems that his name was copied to the new list of summonses even though he had died three months earlier. The entry was later cancelled, *Parl. Writs*, vol. ii, p. 138.
38. *CP*, vol. viii, p. 218.
39. *CFR*, 1307–1319, p. 206; *CFR*, 1307–1319, pp. 211–12; *CPR*, 1323–1327, pp. 163, 267.
40. *CCR*, 1313–1318, p. 208.
41. Kathryn Warner, *Hugh Despenser the Younger & Edward II: Downfall of a King's Favourite* (Barnsley, 2018), p. 6.
42. Nigel Saul, 'The Despensers and the Downfall of Edward II', *EHR* 99 (1984), pp. 6, 19.
43. Monika Simon, 'Of Lands and Ladies: The Marriage Strategies of the Lords Lovell (*c.* 1200–1487)', *Southern History Review* 23 (2011), pp. 19–20.
44. Warner, *Hugh Despenser*, p. 49; *CPR*, 1327–30, p. 188.
45. Simon, 'Lands and Ladies', pp. 19–20.
46. *CPR*, 1327–1330, p. 134.
47. Saul, 'An Early Private Indenture of Retainer: The Agreement Between Hugh Despenser the Younger and Sir Robert De Shirland', *EHR* 128 (2013), pp. 56–58.
48. R.M. Haines, *Edward II: Edward of Caernarfon, his Life, his Reign, and its Aftermath, 1284–1330* (Montreal and Kingston, 2003), pp. 144–45; Saul, 'Private Indentures', p. 57, n. 44.
49. *CPR*, 1321–1324, p. 175; *CFR*, 1319–1327, p. 157, p. 323; *CPR*, 1325–1327, p. 193.
50. G.O. Sayles, 'The Formal Judgements on the Traitors of 1322', *Speculum* 16 (1941), p. 63.
51. *CCR*, 1333–1337, p. 74.
52. E.B. Fryde, 'The Deposits of Hugh Despenser the Younger with Italian Bankers', *Econ. Hist. Rev.*, 2nd series, iii (1951), p. 371; *CFR*, 1327–1337, p. 333.
53. Warner, *Hugh Despenser*, pp. 155–56.
54. *CPR*, 1327–1330, pp. 13, 37–38.
55. *CIPM*, vol. vii, no. 304.
56. *CCR*, pp. 555, 563; *CIPM*, vol. viii, no. 8.
57. *ODNB*, Henry of Lancaster.
58. *CPR*, 1327–1330, p. 546.

59. Anthony Goodman, *Joan, the Fair Maid of Kent: A Fourteenth-Century Princess and her World* (Woodbridge, 2017), p. 16.
60. *CIPM*, vol. xix, no. 406.
61. *CCR*, 1333–1337, pp. 47, 79; *CFR*, 1327–1337, pp. 343–44.
62. *CPR*, 1330–1334, p. 556.
63. *CPR*, 1334–1338, p. 324.
64. *CPR*, 1340–1343, p. 86; *CFR*, 1337–1347, pp. 283, 286.
65. *CP*, vol. viii, p. 218.
66. PRO 30/26/69, nos. 175, 164, 176, 183.
67. *CIPM*, vol. ix, no. 44.
68. *CPR*, 1343–1345, pp. 407–08; *CPR*, 1348–1350, p. 457.
69. *CCR*, 1347–1349, p. 353.
70. *CIPM*, vol. ix, nos. 464, 664.
71. *CFR*, 1347–1356, pp. 63, 73.
72. *CPR*, 1350–1354, p. 46.
73. *CPR*, 1361–1364, pp. 10, 113, 138.
74. *CPR*, 1348–1350, pp. 343, 358, 479.
75. *CFR*, 1347–1356, p. 244.
76. *CIPM*, vol. ix, no. 664; Taylor, *Minster Lovell Hall*, p. 2.
77. *CIPM*, vol. xi, no. 358.

Chapter 5: Luck, Service, and Opportunism

1. *CPR*, 1364–1367, pp. 365, 431.
2. *Foedera*, vol. iii, 2, pp. 731, 844.
3. *ODNB*, John Lovell.
4. *Foedera*, vol. iii, 2, p. 1011.
5. *CPR*, 1381–85, pp. 284, 452.
6. *CCR*, 1369–1374, p. 309.
7. Simon, 'Of Lands and Ladies', pp. 7–8.
8. J. Enoch Powell and Keith Wallis, *The House of Lords in the Middle Ages* (London, 1968), p. 437.
9. David Starkey, *Six Wives. The Queens of Henry VIII* (London, 2003), p. 13.
10. Monika E. Simon, 'The Lovells of Titchmarsh: An English Baronial Family, 1297–148?' (unpubl. DPhil thesis, York, 1999), pp. 222–23.
11. Goodman, *Joan of Kent*, p. 24; *ODNB*, Thomas Holland.
12. Dugdale, p. 289; *ODNB*, John Lovell, fifth Baron Lovell.
13. *Parl. Rolls*, Edward III: 1376, items 29–30; Powell and Wallis, p. 374.
14. *Munimenta Gildhallae Londoniensis*, vol. ii, p. 479.
15. *The Anonimalle Chronicle. 1333–1381*, V.H. Galbraith (ed.)(Manchester, 1927), p. 126; *CPR*, 1377–1381, pp. 409, 458.
16. *Testamenta Vetusta*, Nicholas H. Nicolas (ed.), 2 vols. in one (London, 1826), p. 112; *CIPM*, vol. xv, nos. 541, 542.
17. *CFR*, 1377–1383, p. 86.
18. For a recent study see Juliet Baker, *England Arise* (London, 2015), which also discusses why the name 'Peasants' Revolt' is a misnomer.
19. *CPR*, 1381–1385, pp. 71, 72–73, 84, 86, 140, 141.
20. *CPR*, 1381–1385, pp. 62; *CFR*, 1377–1383, p. 280. The grant was renewed in 1391, *CFR*, 1383–1391, p. 353.

21. e.g. *CCR*, 1381–1385, p. 176, *CPR*, 1381–1385, pp. 202, 247, 252.

22. 'An Account of the Army with which King Richard the Second Invaded Scotland in the Ninth Year of his Reign, A.D. 1385', N.H. Nicolas (ed.), *Archaeologia* 22 (1879), p. 17; *CCR*, 1381–1385, p. 555.

23. G.D. Squibb, *The High Court of Chivalry: A Study of the Civil Law in England* (Oxford, 1959), pp. 14–15; A.S. Ellis, 'On the Arms of de Aton', *Yorkshire Archaeological Journal* 12 (1893), 263–66.

24. For the Scrope-Grosvenor case see, Nicholas H. Nicolas (ed.), *The Controversy between Sir Richard Scrope and Sir Robert Grosvenor in the Court of Chivalry. AD. 1385–1390*, (London, 1832), 2 vols.; for the trial of Grey vs. Hastings see: Jack, 'Entail and Descent: The Hastings Inheritance, 1370–1436', *Bulletin of the Institute of Historical Research* 38 (1965), 1–19.

25. Andrew Ayton, 'Knights, Esquires and Military Service: The Evidence of the Armorial Case before the Court of Chivalry', in A. Ayton and J.L. Price (eds.), *The Medieval Military Revolution. State, Society and Military Change in Medieval and Early Modern Europe* (London and New York, 1995), p. 83.

26. TNA, C47/6/1, no. 23, 40.

27. TNA, PRO 30/26/69, nos. 186, 210.

28. TNA, PRO 30/26/69, no. 223; TNA C47/6/1, m. 38.

29. The depositions in favour of Morley were studied by Philip Caudry, 'War, Chivalry and Regional Society: East Anglia's Warrior Gentry before the Court of Chivalry', in *Fourteenth Century England* 8 (2014), 119–45.

30. Thomas Willement (ed.), *Rolls of Arms of the Reign of Richard the Second* (London, 1834). p. 9.

31. TNA PRO 30/26/69, no. 210; TNA, C47/6/1, nos. 18, 92, 298.

32. *ODNB*, John Lovell, *CPR*, 1385–1388, pp. 80, 82, 128, 169, 546.

33. *Parl. Rolls*, Richard II: April 1384, item 9.

34. *CCR*, 1385–1389, p. 230, *CPR*, 1385–1388. p. 239.

35. *CPR*, 1385–1388, p. 276.

36. *CFR*, 1383–1391, p. 201.

37. E. G. F. Stanes, 'Sir Guy de Brian, K.G., *Report and Transactions of the Devonshire Association for the Advancement of Science, Literature and Art* 92 (1960), 248–78.

38. *ODNB*, John Lovell.

39. John L. Leland, 'The Abjuration of 1388', *Medieval Prosopography* 15 (1994), 115–38.

40. Margaret Aston, *Thomas Arundel: A Study of Church Life in the Reign of Richard II* (Oxford, 1967), pp. 181, 194, 197, 198, 200, 202 and 182, n. 1.

41. Muster Rolls, www.medievalsoldier.org.

42. *CPR*, 1388–1392, p. 107.

43. *CPR*, 1391–1396, p. 488–89.

44. Chris Given-Wilson, 'Richard II and the Higher Nobility', in A. Goodman and J.L. Gillespie, (eds.), *Richard II: The Art of Kingship* (Oxford 1999), p. 115; Given-Wilson, 'Royal Charter Witness Lists 1327–1399', *Medieval Prosopography* 12 (1991), Tables 6 and 7; *CPR*, 1392–1396, p. 552.

45. *CPR*, 1391–1396, pp. 71, 306, 390, 576 589; *CPR*, 1396–1399, p. 28.

46. *Parl. Rolls*, Richard II: 1991, item 17; *CPR*, 1391–1396, pp. 79, 238.

47. *CPR*, 1388–1391, pp. 520–21.

48. *CPR*, 1388–1391, p. 21; *VCH*, Wiltshire, vol. xii, p. 49 ; Loyd, *Book of Seals*, no. 384.

49. *CCR*, 1402–1405, pp. 412–13; 461–62.

50. *CCR*, 1402–1405, pp. 412–13, 461–62; *CCR*, 1409–1413, p. 75; J.S. Roskell, Linda S. Clark, and Carole Rawcliffe (eds.), *The House of Commons, 1386–1421* (Stroud, 1993), vol. iv, p. 114.

51. *CPR*, 1391–1396, p. 261.

52. *CCR*, 1392–1396, pp. 294–95.

53. *CCR*, 1392–1396, p. 368.

54. *CPR*, 1391–1396, pp. 488–89.

55. *CPR*, 1391–1396, pp. 482, 486.

56. *CPR*, 1396–1399, p. 208.

57. C.D. Fletcher, *Richard II: Manhood, Youth, and Politics, 1377–99* (Oxford, 2008); Richard Hutton Jones, *The Royal Policy of Richard II. Absolutism in the Later Middle Ages* (Oxford, 1968).

58. *CPR*, 1396–1399, pp. 406, 416.

59. *CPR*, 1396–1399, pp. 545, 563.

60. *Chronicles of the Revolution 1377–1421*, Chris Given-Wilson (ed. and trans.) (Manchester, 1993), p. 219.

61. *Parl. Rolls*, Henry IV: 1399 (Rolls), items 73–74.

62. *CPR*, 1399–1401, pp. 182, 267–68; Michael M.N. Stansfield, 'The Holland Family, Dukes of Exeter, Earls of Kent and Huntingdon, 1352–1475' (unpubl. PhD thesis, Oxford University, 1987), p. 153.

63. *Proceedings and Ordinances of the Privy Council of England*, N.H. Nicolas (ed.) (London, 1834), vol. i., pp. 177–78.

64. *CPR*, 1399–1401, pp. 213; 269.

65. *CCR*, 1402–1405, p. 82–83.

66. *Parl. Rolls*, Henry IV: 1402, item 7; 1404, item 6; item 1404, item 6; 1406, item 6; 1407, item 10.

67. *Parl. Rolls*, Henry IV: 1404, item 37.

68. Edward Powell, 'Law and Justice', in R. Horrox (ed.), *Fifteenth Century Attitudes* (Cambridge, 1995), p. 39.

69. *Parl. Rolls*, Henry IV: 1406, Introduction and item 35; 1410 item 43.

70. Gwilym Dodd, 'Henry IV's Council, 1399–1405', in: Gwilym Dodd and Douglas Biggs (eds.), *Henry IV: The Establishment of the Regime, 1399–1406* (York, 2003), pp. 103–5; J.L. Kirby, 'Council and Councillors of Henry IV, 1399–1413' *TRHS*, 5th series, 14 (1963), p. 45.

71. Hugh E.L. Collins, *The Order of the Garter, 1348–1461: Chivalry and Politics in Late Medieval England* (Oxford, 2000), p. 292.

72. *CPR*, pp. 121, 140; *CCR*, 1402–1405, pp. 461–62.

73. Magdalen College, Oxford, Adds. 99; P.S. Lewis, 'Sir John Fastolf's Lawsuit over Titchwell, 1448–55', *Historical Journal* 1 (1958), pp. 12–13.

74. Oxford, Magdalen College, 36/9 (Estate Papers) and Oxford, Magdalen College, Misc. 315.

75. Simon, 'The Lovells of Titchmarsh', Appendix 4.

76. K.B. McFarlane, *Fifteenth Century* (London, 1981), p. 62.

77. British Library, Harley 7026.

78. Kathleen L. Scott, *Later Gothic Manuscripts. 1390–1490* (London, 1996), vol. ii, p. 62.

79. Janet Backhouse, 'The Lovel Lectionary: a Memorial Offering to Salisbury', in J. Backhouse (ed.), *The Medieval English Cathedral: Papers in Honour of Pamela Tudor-Craig. Proceedings of the 1998 Harlaxton Symposium* (Donington, 2003), 112–25.
80. *CIPM*, vol. xix, nos. 404–17.
81. A. Emery, *Dartington Hall* (Oxford, 1970), p. 117.
82. *CP*, vol. vi, p. 531.

Chapter 6: Family Tradition and Individual Choices

1. *CCR*, 1405–1409, pp. 430, 445; *CFR*, 1405–1413, p. 128.
2. Roskell, et al., vol. ii, p. 632; *CPR*, 1391–1396, pp. 482, 712; *CPR*, 1396–1399, p. 145; *CPR*, 1406–1408, p. 159.
3. *Parl. Rolls*, Henry IV: 1410, item 43.
4. *CPR*, 1405–1408, pp. 496, 499; *CPR*, 1413–1416, p. 422.
5. *CIPM*, vol. xix, nos. 417, 415.
6. *CIPM*, vol. xvi, nos. 959–62, nos. 988–990; Roskell et al, p. 632. Division of land granted to Christina Kentcombe by Guy Bryan; *CIPM*, vol. xviii, no. 215; division of estates of Philip Bryan in 1406, *CCR*, 1405–1409, p. 160.
7. Ffiona Swabey, *Medieval Gentlewoman: Life in a Widow's Household in the Later Middle Ages* (Stroud, 1999), p. 43. *CCR*, 1385–1389, p. 624.
8. *CIPM*, vol. xviii, no. 314.
9. Roskell et al., vol. ii, p. 632; see previous chapter.
10. *CP*, vol. viii, p. 221.
11. Backhouse, p. 120.
12. Simon, 'Who is Buried', pp. 85–87.
13. *CIPM*, vol. xix, nos. 228–32.
14. Roskell, et al., vol. ii, pp. 632–33.
15. J.L. Kirby, *Henry IV of England* (London, 1970), p. 234.
16. *CCR*, 1405–1409, pp. 245, 269; J.S. Roskell, *The Commons in the Parliament of 1422: English Society and Parliamentary Representation under the Lancastrians* (Manchester, 1954), p. 200.
17. *CCR*, 1413–1419, pp. 58, 62.
18. Gwilym Dodd, 'Henry V's Establishment: Service, Loyalty and Reward in 1413', in: Gwilym Dodd (ed.), *Henry V. New Interpretations* (Woodbridge, 2013), pp. 75, 76. The entry here reads 'Roger Lovell', but this is certainly a misreading for Robert Lovell.
19. Roskell et al., vol. ii, pp. 633–34.
20. Dugdale, pp. 393–94.
21. *CCR*, 1429–1435, pp. 57–58.
22. Roskell et al, vol. ii, p. 633.
23. *CPR*, 1416–1422, p. 229, 233, *CPR*, 1422–1429, p. 312.
24. Roskell et al., vol. ii, p. 633.
25. *CPR*, 1422–1426, pp. 319, 323, 452; *CPR*, p. 1422–1426, p. 562; Roskell et al, pp. 632–33.
26. Ffiona Swabey, 'The Letter Book of Alice de Bryene and Alice de Sutton's List of Debts', *Nottingham Medieval Studies* 42 (1998), p. 123; *CIPM*, vol. xxiv, nos. 248–53.
27. Roskell et al, p. 634.
28. Swabey, Letter Book, p. 124.

29. Nicholas Orme, *From Childhood to Chivalry: The Education of English Kings and Aristocracy 1066–1530* (London and New York, 1984), pp. 125–26.
30. Swabey, Letter Book, pp. 133–34, 143; Swabey, *Gentlewoman*, pp. 46–47.
31. *CPR*, 1416–1422, p. 9–10.
32. *CPR*, 1416–1422, pp. 9–10, 37.
33. Muster Rolls, www.medievalsoldier.org.
34. Roskell, et al., vol. iv, p. 157.
35. Roskell, et al., vol. iii, p. 446; vol. iv, p. 157.
36. *CIPM*, vol. xxi, no. 653.
37. Roskell, et al., vol. iv, p. 157; *CPR*, 1436–1441, pp. 544, 563; *CCR*, 1435–1441, pp. 414, 424; 1441–1447, pp. 10–11; *CIPM*, vol. xxv, no. 494.
38. *CIPM*, Henry VII, vol. i, no. 137; *CIPM*, Henry VII, vol. iii, no. 629.
39. *CFR*, 1422–1430, p. 42.
40. *CFR*, 1422–1430, p. 31.
41. *CFR*, 1422–1430, p. 68; Simon, 'Lands and Ladies', p. 9.
42. Simon, 'Lovells of Titchmarsh', Appendix 4.
43. *CPR*, 1436–1441, p. 544; *CPR*, 1441–1446, p. 392.
44. *CIPM*, vo. xxiv, nos. 25–26; Grey, 'Incomes from Land in England in 1436', *EHR* 49 (1934), p. 615.
45. *CPR*, 1422–1426, pp. 559–72; *CPR*, 1429–1436, pp. 613–28; *CPR*, 1436–1441, pp. 578–94.
46. *CCR*, 1429–1435, p. 71; *Annales Monasterii S Albani a Johanne Amundesham. Monacho. A.D. 1421–1440*, T. Riley (ed.), Rolls Series 28 (London, 1870, repr. Wiesbaden, 1965), vol. i, p. 62.
47. *CPR*, 1446–1452, p. 523.
48. S.J. Payling, 'A Disputed Mortgage: Ralph, Lord Cromwell, Sir John Gra and the Manor of Multon Hall', in R. Archer and S. Walker (eds.), *Rulers and Ruled in Late Medieval England: Essays presented to Gerald Harris* (London and Rio Grande, 1995), p. 117.
49. *ODNB*, Ralph Cromwell.
50. *Parl. Rolls*, Henry VI: 1433, item 8.
51. *CPR*, 1429–1436, pp. 50, 354, 467, 521, 529.
52. *CPR*, 1436–1441, p. 376.
53. *CPR*, 1446–1452, p. 333.
54. McFarlane, *Fifteenth Century*, pp. 233–34.
55. *CPR*, 1452–1461, pp. 74–75; 169.
56. *CPR*, 1446–1452, pp. 180–81.
57. *CIPM*, xxvi, no. 492; *CPR*, 1446–1452, p. 385; *CIPM*, xxxvi, no. 322, 328.
58. Josiah C. Wedgewood and Ann D. Holt, *History of Parliament. Biographies of the Members of the Commons, 1436–1509* (London, 1936), pp. 556–57.
59. *CP*, vol. ix, p. 219; *CIPM*, xxvi, no. 70; *CFR*, 1461–1471, p. 208.
60. K.M. Phillips, *Medieval Maidens: Young Women and Gender in England, 1370–1540* (Manchester, 2003), p. 109.
61. N.J.G. Pounds, *The Medieval Castle in England and Wales: A Social and Political History* (Cambridge, 1990), p. 296; Christine Carpenter, *Locality and Polity: A Study of Warwickshire Landed Society, 1401–1499* (Cambridge, 1992), p. 229–31.
62. Given-Wilson, *The English Nobility in the Late Middle Ages, The Fourteenth-Century Political Community* (London and New York, 1987), p. 11.

63. *VCH*, Oxfordshire, vol. 4, The City of Oxford, p. 367; Simon, 'Who is Buried', pp. 84–94.
64. *A Short Guide to the Church of St Mary the Virgin Titchmarsh* (no author or publication date, no pagination).
65. Margaret Wood, *The English Medieval House* (London, 1965), pp. 78, 185, 132; Taylor, *Minster Lovell Hall* (1947), pp. 2–3.
66. *CPR*, 1301–1307, p. 290; Taylor, *Minster Lovell Hall*, p. 2; see also N. Pevsner, *Northamptonshire* (London, 1961), p. 432.
67. H.E.L. Dryden, 'The Castle of Tichmarsh, Northamptonshire', *Associated Architectural Societies, Reports and Papers* 21 (1891), pp. 243–52.
68. *CPR*, 1391–1396 , p. 261.
69. Mark Girouard, 'Wardour Old Castle - I', *Country Life*, 14 Feb. 1991, p. 46.
70. Simon, 'The Lovells of Titchmarsh', p. 195.
71. Mary D. Lobel and W.H. Johns (eds.), *The British Atlas of Historic Towns*, vol. iii, *The City of London from Prehistoric Times to c. 1520* (Oxford, 1989), p. 79.
72. *The Paston Letters, 1422–1509 A.D.*, J. Gairdner (ed.) (London, 1895), vol. i, pp. 442–43.
73. *CIPM*, xxii, no. 30. Interestingly in one of the letters from Francis Lovell to his 'cousin' William Stonor, he asks him to look after his game at Rotherfield, *Kingsford's Stonor Letters and Papers*, 1290–1483, Christine Carpenter (ed.) (Cambridge, 1996), p. 150.
74. IPM of William Lovell III, TNA C139/158, no. 28.

Chapter 7: Wives, Widows, and Daughters

1. Joel Rosenthal, 'Aristocratic Widows in Fifteenth-Century England', in B.J. Harris and J.K. McNamara (eds.), *Women and the Structure of Society* (Durham, N. C., 1984), pp. 36–47.
2. Rowena E. Archer, 'Rich Old Ladies: The Problem of Late Medieval Dowagers', in A.J. Pollard (ed.), *Property and Politics: Essays in Later Medieval English History* (Gloucester, 1984), p. 22; Carpenter, 'The Fifteenth Century English Gentry and their Estates', M. Jones (ed.), *Gentry and the Lesser Nobility in Later Medieval Europe* (Gloucester, 1986), p. 41.
3. K.B. McFarlane, *The Nobility of Later Medieval England* (Oxford, 1973), p. 2.
4. Rosenthal, 'Aristocratic Widows'; Rowena E. Archer, '"How ladies… who live on their manors ought to manage their household and estates": Women Landholders and Administrators in the Later Middle Ages', in P.J.P. Goldberg (ed.), *Woman is a Worthy Wight: Women in English Society c. 1200–1500* (Stroud, 1992), 149–81.
5. H.L. Grey, 'Incomes from Land, p. 615.
6. Joanna L. Laynesmith, *The Last Medieval Queens: English Queenship 1445–1503* (Oxford, 2004).
7. *CIPM*, xxii, nos. 30, 219.
8. *ODNB*, Ralph Cromwell.
9. Archer, 'Rich Old Ladies', p. 22.
10. M. Hicks, *Warwick the Kingmaker*, p. 29, states that the Earl of Salisbury's land would 'be immune from waste because enfeoffed or held by his countess in her own right, jointure and dower'.
11. *CIPM*, vol. ix, no. 128; *CCR*, 1346–1349, p. 573.
12. *CCR*, 1405–1409, pp. 412–15, 422.
13. *CCR*, 1429–1435, pp. 57–58.
14. Simon, 'Lovells of Titchmarsh', Appendix 4, table 6.

15. Joanna Laynesmith, *Cecily, Duchess of York* (London et al., 2017), p. 72.
16. *CPR*, 1485–1494, p. 100.
17. *Parl. Rolls*, Henry VII: 1495, item 38.
18. *CPR*, 1485–1494, p. 304; *Letters and Papers of the Reign of Richard III and Henry VII*, J.G. Gairdner (ed.), Rolls Series 24 (London, 1861–3), vol. ii, p. 71; Simon, 'Lands and Ladies, p. 18.
19. *Lincoln Diocesan Documents, 1450–1544*, Andrew Clark (ed.), Early English Text Society, orig. series, 149 (London, 1914), pp. 73–75.
20. *Testamenta Vetusta*, p. 173; British Library, Add. Ms. 39,992 N.
21. *CCR*, 1419–1422, pp. 105, 125–26; *Calendar of Entries in the Papal Registers Relating to Great Britain and Ireland. Papal Letters* (London, 1904), vol. vi, 1404–1415, p. 294.
22. *VCH*, Northamptonshire, vol. ii, n. 15.
23. Barbara J. Harris, *English Aristocratic Women and the Fabric of Piety, 1450–1550* (Amsterdam, 2018), pp. 58–60, 75.
24. Aston, *Thomas Arundel*, p. 182, n. 2.
25. J. Bridges, *History and Antiquities of the County of Northamptonshire* (1791), vol. i, p. 151.
26. *VCH*, Oxfordshire, vol. iv, The City of Oxford, p. 194.
27. *CCR*, 1302–1307, p. 24; *CPR*, 1327–1330, p. 188; *CPR*, 1446–1452, p. 523.
28. *The Paston Letters and Papers of the Fifteenth Century*, N. Davis (ed.),(Oxford, 1971), vol. ii, pp. 455–56.
29. *Paston Letters*, Gairdner (ed.), p. 443.
30. *CPR*, 1452–1461, p. 567.
31. Orme, *Childhood*, p. 13; Katherine Lewis, *Kingship and Masculinity in Late Medieval England* (London and New York, 2013), p. 143.
32. Nicholals Orme, 'The Education of Edward V', *Bulletin of the Institute of Historical Research* 57: 136 (1984), p. 120; R.A. Griffiths, *The Reign of King Henry VI The Exercise of Royal Authority, 1422–1461* (London, 1981), p. 52.
33. *CPR*, 1454–1462, p. 433.
34. Griffith, *Henry VI*, p. 52.
35. Laynesmith, *Last Queens*, pp. 147–48; Myers, 'Household', p. 148.
36. Archer, 'How ladies…', p. 168.
37. *CIPM*, Henry III, vol. i, no. 670.
38. *CCR*, 1454–1461, p. 93; *CPR*, 1452–1461, p. 278.
39. *CPR*, 1461–1467, p. 222.
40. John Ashdown-Hill, *Eleanor, The Secret Queen: The Woman Who put Richard III on the Throne* (Stroud, 2009), p. 53.
41. Charles Ross, *Richard III* (London, 1981), p. 15; *ODNB*, Ralph Boteler.
42. Ashdown-Hill, *Secret Queen*, p. 89.
43. Ashdown-Hill, *Secret Queen*, p. 37.
44. McFarlane, *Nobility*, p. 11.
45. *ODNB*, Joan of Acre.
46. McFarlane, *Nobility*, p. 153.
47. Oxford, Magdalen College, Adds. 99.
48. *Lincoln Diocesan Documents*, p. 74.

49. J.S. Roskell, *Parliament and Politics in Late Medieval England* (London, 1981–3), vol. ii, p. 187; P.A. Johnson, *Duke Richard of York, 1411–1460* (Oxford, 1988), p. 17; McFarlane, *Nobility*, p. 35, and again pp. 183–84.

50. A.R. Myers (ed.), 'The Household of Queen Margaret of Anjou, 1452–3', *Bulleting of the John Rylands Library* 40 (1957–58), pp. 79–113, 181–82, n. 6, 391–431; Roskell, *Parliament and Politics*, vol. i, p. 191; *CFR*, 1452–1461, p. 99.

51. Archer, 'How ladies...', pp. 165–67.

Chapter 8: The Wars of the Roses

1. *ODNB*, John, first Viscount Beaumont.

2. Nicholas Orme, *Medieval Children*, (New Haven and London, 2001), p. 37.

3. Orme, *Childhood*, p. 28.

4. *CPR*, 1452–1461, pp. 379, 660–69.

5. *Parl. Rolls*, Henry IV: 1459, item 4.

6. Colin Richmond, 'The Nobility and the Wars of the Roses, 1459–1461', *Nottingham Medieval Studies* 21 (1977), p. 74.

7. *CPR*, 1454–1461, pp. 534–35.

8. *CPR*, 1452–1461, pp. 603, 613–14.

9. Anthony Goodman, *The Wars of the Roses* (London, 1990), p. 38; Anthony Pollard, *The Wars of the Roses* (3rd ed., 2013), p. 47; Laynesmith, *Cecily*, pp. 75–76.

10. *CPR*, 1461–1467, pp. 35, 43–44.

11. *CPR*, 1461–1467, p. 87.

12. *CPR*, 1461–1467, pp. 549–50; J.M. Williams, 'The Political Career of Francis Viscount Lovell (1456–?)', *The Ricardian* 8 (1990), p. 38.

13. *CCR*, 1461–1468, p. 139; *VCH*, Shropshire, vol. iv, p. 79; *VCH*, Shropshire, vol. viii, p. 201.

14. J.R. Lander, *Government and Community. England 1450–1509* (London, 1980), p. 46; Loyd, *Book of Seals*, no. 32.

15. *CPR*, 1461–1467, p. 346.

16. *CFR*, 1461–1471, p. 127; C140/13 no. 27; Simon, 'Who is Buried'.

17. *CFR*, 1461–1471, p. 177. C140/19 no. 20; C140/40 no. 7. Barbara Coulton's claim that Joan Beaumont had three children with Sir William Stanley, William, Joan, and Catherine, and died on 24 August 1469 can be dismissed. B. Coulton, 'The Wives of Sir William Stanley: Joan Beaumont and Elizabeth Hopton', *The Ricardian* 9 (1992), 315–18.

18. *ODNB*, Francis Lovell, Viscount Lovell.

19. *CPR*, 1467–1477, p. 51; *Paston Letters*, Davis (ed.), vol. ii, p. 375. I am indebted to Joe Ann Ricca who first made me aware of the time lag between the death of John IX and the grant of the wardship to Richard Neville.

20. For example David Hipshon, *Richard III* (Abingdon, 2011), pp. 56–57.

21. Paul Murray Kendall, *Richard III: Der letzte Plantagenet auf dem englischen Königsthron 1452–1485* (München, 1980), pp. 53–54; Ross, *Richard III*, p. 7, n. 9.

22. A.J. Pollard, 'Lord FitzHugh's Rising in 1470', *BIHR* 53 (1979), 170–75; Hicks, *Warwick*, p. 295; *CPR*, 1467–1477, pp. 215–16.

23. *CCR*, 1468–1476, pp. 115–16.

24. Dugdale, p. 469.

25. Ashdown-Hill, *Secret Queen*, p. 151.

26. Dugdale, p. 471.

27. *CPR*, 1467–1477, pp. 261, 312, 440, 257.
28. *The Registrum of the Guild of Corpus Christi in the City of York*, R.H. Skaife (ed.), Surtees Society 57 (1872), p. 86.
29. *CPR*, 1467–1477, p. 468. Francis is called her son and heir in this entry; *CFR*, 1471–1485, pp. 87, 88.
30. *CPR*, 1476–1485, p. 62.
31. *CP*, vol. viii, p. 224; *CPR*, 1476–1485, pp. 213, 343.
32. *Parl. Rolls*, Edward IV: 1483, item 4; Richard III: 1484, item 1.
33. McFarlane, *Fifteenth Century*, p. 250.
34. British Library, Add Ms. 6113, fol. 126d; a transcript of most of this text can be found in *CP*, vol. viii, p. 224, n. h.
35. Charles Ross, *Edward IV* (London, 1974), p. 66.
36. *British Library Harleian Manuscript. 433*, R. Horrox and P. Hammond (eds.) (Gloucester, 1983), vol. iii, pp. 3–4.
37. Nigel Saul, *The Three Richards: Richard I, Richard II and Richard III* (London and New York, 2006), p. 219.
38. Ashdown-Hill, *Secret Queen*, p. 107.
39. I am grateful to Dianne Penn who made me aware of the legend.
40. That Francis Lovell supported 'Edward, Earl of Warwick' in 1487, whether real or an imposter called Lambert Simnel, does not preclude that he rescued the princes since he would have still considered them as excluded from the line of succession.
41. Rosemary Horrox, *Richard III. A Study in Service* (Cambridge, 1989), p. 249. Chris Given-Wilson, *The Royal Household and the King's Affinity, 1360–1413* (New Haven and London, 1986), p. 72–74.
42. Given-Wilson, *Royal Household*, pp. 72–73; *The Household of Edward IV: The Black Book and the Ordinance of 1478*, A.R. Myers (ed.)(Manchester, 1959), pp. 105–06.
43. Given-Wilson, *Royal Household*, p. 73.
44. *The Coronation of Richard III: The Extant Documents*, Anne F. Sutton and P.W. Hammond (eds.) (Gloucester, 1983), pp. 32, 34, 218, 224, 249–50.
45. *CPR*, 1477–1485, p. 365; *British Library Harleian Manuscript*, vol. i, pp. 78–80.
46. N.S.B. Gras, *The Early English Custom System. A Documentary Study of the Institutional and Economic History of the Customs from the Thirteenth to the Sixteenth Century* (Cambridge, 1918), p. 258; Given-Wilson, *Royal Household*, p. 43.
47. Given-Wilson, *Royal Household*, p. 96.
48. *CPR*, 1476–1485, pp. 374, 465.
49. *CPR*, 1477–1485, p. 365.
50. *CP*, vol. ii, Appendix B.
51. *CPR*, 1476–1485, pp. 370–71.
52. *Kingsford's Stonor Letters*, no. 333.
53. *British Library Harleian Manuscript*, vol. iii, p. 148–49.
54. J.S. Roskell, 'William Catesby, Counsellor to Richard III', *Bulletin of the John Ryland's Library* 42 (1959), p. 285; *British Library Harleian Manuscript*, vol. i, pp. 3, 252, 282; vol. iii, pp. 148–49, *CPR*, 1476–1485, pp. 483, 508; *CCR*, 1476–1485, pp. 381, 358.
55. *CPR*, 1476–1485, pp. 553–79.
56. Horrox, *Richard III*, p. 222.
57. *CPR*, 1476–1485, p. 519.
58. Williams, 'Political Career', p. 382.

59. 'Historical Notes of a London Citizen', Richard Firth Green (ed.), *EHR* 96 (1981) 585–590; Polydore Vergil, *The Anglicana Historia, 1485–1537*, Denys Hays (ed. and trans.), Camden Society, 3rd series, 74 (1950), pp. 10–24.

60. *ODNB*, William Hastings; Williams, 'Political Career', p. 387; Colin Richmond, 'Patronage and Polemic', in J.L. Watts, *The End of the Middle Ages? England in the Fifteenth and Sixteenth Centuries* (Thrupp, Stroud, 1998), p. 70.

61. *British Library Harleian Manuscript*, vol. ii, p. 53.

62. *The Croyland Chronicle*, part ix, online source; *CPR*, 1476–1485, p. 547; Williams, 'Political Career', p. 393.

63. *A Descriptive Catalogue of Ancient Deeds in the Public Record office: Prepared under the Superintendence of the Deputy Keeper of the Records*, H.C. Maxwell Lyte (ed.), vol. iii (London, 1990), p. 106, no. A4790.

64. John Ashdown-Hill, *The Dublin King: The True Story of Edward, Earl of Warwick, Lambert Simnel and the 'Princes in the Tower'* (Stroud, 2015), p. 92.

65. A prose version of the later poem about the battle also states that he was at fighting at Richard's side. Williams, 'Political Career', p. 393; Bennett, *Bosworth*, pp. 155–56; *ODNB*, Richard Ratcliffe.

66. *Parl. Rolls;* Henry VII: 1485, item 7; *CPR*, 1485–1494, pp. 133–35; *CP*, vol. ii, Appendix B, p. 581.

67. Grant Jasper Tudor, *CPR*, 1485–1494, p. 64; John de Vere, *ibid.*, p. 121. Thomas Lovel, ibid., pp. 25–26.

68. Simon, 'Lovells of Titchmarsh', p. 76.

69. Williams, 'Political Career', pp. 393–95; S. O'Connor, 'Francis Lovell and the Rebels of Furness Fells', *The Ricardian* 7 (1987), p. 366; *Paston Letters*, Davis (ed.), vol. ii, p. 447–48.

70. Ashdown-Hill, *The Dublin King*, passim.

71. O'Connor, 'Francis Lovell', p. 367; Williams, 'Political Career', p. 395; 'Historical Notes of a London Citizen', p. 589.

72. *ODNB*, Francis Lovell.

73. *Minster Lovell Hall*, p. 19; For arguments in favour of the truthfulness in this scenario see D. Baldwin, 'What Happened to Lord Lovell?', *The Ricardian* 7 (1985), 60–65.

74. *Parl. Rolls*, Henry VII: 1495: item 38.

75. *Letters and Papers*, vol. ii, p. 71.

76. Williams, 'Political Career', p. 397.

77. Anne Crawford, *Yorkist Lord: John Howard, Duke of Norfolk, c. 1425–1485* (London, 2010); *Kingsford's Stonor Letters and Papers*, nos. 318, 333.

Chapter 9: Beyond the Lovells of Titchmarsh

1. TNA, C140/759, no. 73.

2. *CPR*, 1476–1485, pp. 3, 5, 14, 15,16, 48.

3. Orme, *Childhood*, pp. 28–29.

4. Orme, *Childhood*, p. 52.

5. *CP*, vol. ix, p. 220.

6. *Coronation of Richard III*, p. 32.

7. *CP*, vol. ix, p. 220.

8. *British Library Harleian Manuscript*, p. 114.

9. *CPR*, 1485–1494, p. 268.

10. Christine Weightman, *Margaret of York, Duchess of Burgundy* (Stroud, 1989), p. 159; *CIPM*, vol. i (2nd series), nos. 499–509.

11. *CIPM*, Henry VII, i , no. 469

12. Laynesmith, *Last Queens*, pp. 199, 207, 217–18.

13. *CP*, vol. viii, p. 220.

14. McFarlane, *Fifteenth Century*, p. 258.

15. *CIPM*, Henry VII, vol. i, no. 97.

16. Ross, *Richard III*, p. 108; M. Bennett, *Lambert Simnel and the Battle of Stoke*, (Stroud, 1987), p. 83, 136.

17. *ODNB*, Francis Lovell; Helen Miller, *Henry VIII and the English Nobility* (Oxford, 1986), pp. 211, 214, 218.

18. *CP*, vol. ii, p. 63.

19. *ODNB*, Henry Norris; *DNB*, vol. xiv, p. 566.

20. *VCH*, Berkshire, vol. iv, p. 127.

21. *CIPM*, Henry VII, vol. i, 491, 499–509.

22. David Starkey, 'An Attendant Lord? Henry Parker, Lord Morley', in Marie Axton and James P. Carley (eds.), *'Triumphs of English': Henry Parker, Lord Morley, Translator to the Tudor Court* (London, 2000), p. 7.

23. Horrox, *Richard III*, p. 300; *ODNB*, Henry Parker, tenth Lord Morley.

24. Retha M. Warnicke, 'Lord Morley's Statements about Richard III', *Albion* 15 (1983), p. 174; Starkey, 'Attendant Lord', p. 7.

25. Richard Hutton Jones and Michael K. and Malcolm Underwood, *The King's Mother: Lady Margaret Beaufort, Countess of Richmond and Derby* (Cambridge, 1992), p. 114.

26. *CFR*, 1485–1509, pp. 125–27; *CPR*, 1485–1494, pp. 298, 304, 305, 307, 309–10.

27. Warnicke, 'Lord Morley's Statement', p. 174.

28. Julia Fox, *Jane Boleyn. The Infamous Lady Rochford* (London, 2007), p. 116.

29. Katherine J. Lewis, 'Women and Power', in Stephen H. Rigby (ed.), *Historians on John Gower* (Woodbridge, 2019), p. 334; Starkey, 'Attendant Lord', p. 2; *ODNB*, Henry Parker.

30. Starkey, 'Attendant Lord', p. 6; Elizabeth Norton, *Margaret Beaufort: Mother of the Tudor Dynasty* (Stroud, 2010), pp. 24–25.

31. Retha M. Warnicke, *Rise and Fall of Anne Boleyn* (Cambridge, 1989), p. 30; McFarlane, *Nobility*, p. 42.

32. *ODNB*, Edward Howard; Starkey, *Six Wives*, pp. 134–35.

33. Fox, *Infamous Lady*, p. 7.

34. Starkey, 'Attendant Lord', p. 4.

35. Miller, *Henry VIII*, p. 157.

36. McFarlane, *Nobility*, p. 212.]

37. Fox, *Infamous Lady*, pp. 15, 18.

38. Fox, *Infamous Lady*, pp. 28–30; Starkey, 'Attendant Lord', p. 12

39. Fox, *Infamous Lady*, p. 33; Starkey, 'Attendant Lord', p. 11; Warnicke, *Rise and Fall*, p. 46, says 1526.

40. Warnicke, *Rise and Fall*, p. 46; according to the *ODNB*, Shelton Family Margaret was the older of the two sisters, however, Starkey says that Jane was the older daughter, 'Attendant Lord', pp. 11–12.

41. *ODNB*, Jane Parker.

42. James P. Carley, 'The Writings of Henry Parker, Lord Morley: A Biographical Survey', in Marie Axton and James P. Carley (eds.), *'Triumphs of English': Henry Parker, Lord Morley, Translator to the Tudor Court* (London, 2000), pp. 37–39.

43. Fox, *Infamous Lady*, pp. 78, 83, 85.

44. Carley, 'Writing', p. 27.

45. Fox, *Infamous Lady*, pp. 99–114; Eric Ives, *The Live and Death of Anne Boleyn: 'The Most Happy'* (Oxford, 2004), pp. 175–80.

46. 'Morley's daughter Jane, was principal witness against her husband, George Boleyn, Lord Rochford, at the time of his trial in 1536'. Carley, 'Writings', p. 43.

47. Ives, *Anne Boleyn*, p. 194.

48. *ODNB*, Jane Parker; Ives, *Anne Boleyn*, p. 293; Diarmaid MacCullough, *Thomas Cromwell: A Life* (Milton Keynes, 2018), p. 304; Starkey, 'Attendant Lord', p. 14, Fox, *Infamous Lady*, p. 172.

49. Ives, *Anne Boleyn*, pp. 202, 210–11 and passim.

50. Starkey, *Six Wives*, p. 580.

51. Ives, *Anne Boleyn*, p. 331.

52. My italics, Ives, *Anne Boleyn*, p. 331.

53. Ives, *Anne Boleyn*, p. 348.

54. Ives, *Anne Boleyn*, p. 332.

55. My italics, MacCulloch, *Thomas Cromwell*, p. 347.

56. Fox, *Infamous Lady*, 211–17.

57. Starkey, 'Attendant Lord', p. 14; Fox, *Infamous Lady*, p. 224.

58. Starkey, 'Attendant Lord', p. 17.

59. MacCullough, *Thomas Cromwell*, pp. 440–41.

60. Carley, 'Writing', p. 44. Since Henry Parker, the eldest grandson was born in 1531/32, *ODNB*, Parker, Henry eleventh Baron Morley, this must have been a younger grandson. Starkey, 'Attendant Lord', p. 15.

61. H.G. Wright (ed.), *Forty-six Lives: Translated from Boccaccio's 'De Claris Mulieribus' by Henry Parker, Lord Morley*, (=EETS OS 214, 1943 [for 1940]), pp. xxv–vi; MacCulloch, *Thomas Cromwell*, pp. 28, 347.

62. James P. Carley, '"Plutarch's" Life of Agesilaus: A Recently Located New Year's Gift to Thomas Cromwell by Henry Parker, Lord Morley', in Felicity Riddy (ed.), *Prestige, Authority and Power in Late Medieval Manuscripts and Texts* (York, 2000), p. 160.

63. K.R. Bartlett, 'Morley, Machiavelli, and the Pilgrimage of Grace', in Marie Axton and James P. Carley (eds.), *'Triumphs of English': Henry Parker, Lord Morley, Translator to the Tudor Court* (London, 2000), p. 78–82.

64. MacCullough, *Thomas Cromwell*, pp. 35, 120 and throughout.

65. MacCulloch, *Thomas Cromwell*, p. 436.

66. Fox, *Infamous Lady*, pp. 243.44; *CP*, vol. ix, p. 224.

67. Starkey, *Six Wives*, p. 633.

68. Josephine Wilkinson, *Katherine Howard: The Tragic Story of Henry VIII's Fifth Queen* (London, 2016), pp. 124–25.

69. Starkey, *Six Wives*, pp. 673–84; *Letters and Papers, Foreign and Domestic of the Reign of Henry VIII. Preserved in the Public Record Office, The British Museum and Elsewhere in England*, vol. xvi (London, 1898), p. 619.

70. Starkey, *Six Wives*, p. 675; Wilkinson, *Katherine Howard*, p. 246; Lacey Baldwin Smith, *A Tudor Tragedy: The Life and Times of Catherine Howard* (London, 1961), p. 167–69.
71. Starkey, *Six Wives*, p. 674; Fox, *Infamous Lady*, p. 288.
72. Ives, *Anne Boleyn*, p. 418, n. 73.
73. Fox, *Infamous Lady*, p. 315.
74. Fox, *Infamous Lady*, pp. 301–02.
75. Miller, *Henry VIII*, p. 181.
76. *ODNB*, Boleyn [née Parker], Jane, Viscountess Rochford.
77. Smith, *Tudor Tragedy*, p. 199.
78. James Simpson, 'The Sacrifice of Lady Rochford: Henry Parker, Lord Morley's Translation of *De claris mulieribus*', in Marie Axton and James P. Carley (eds.), *'Triumphs of English': Henry Parker, Lord Morley, Translator to the Tudor Court* (London, 2000), pp. 154, 159, 163–65.
79. Wright, *Forty-Six Lives*, pp. c, cii.
80. Jeremy Maule, 'What Did Morley Give when he Gave a 'Plutarch' *Life*?', in Marie Axton and James P. Carley (eds.), *'Triumphs of English': Henry Parker, Lord Morley, Translator to the Tudor Court* (London, 2000), p. 107; Wright, p. lxxvii; Orme, *Medieval Children*, pp. 288–89.
81. David R. Carlson, 'Morley's Translations from Roman Philosophers and English Courtier Literature', in: Marie Axton and James P. Carley (eds.), *'Triumphs of English': Henry Parker, Lord Morley, Translator to the Tudor Court* (London, 2000), pp. 135–40.
82. G.W. Bernard, 'The Tudor Nobility in Perspective', in G.W. Bernard (ed.), *The Tudor Nobility* (Manchester and New York, 1992), p. 3.
83. Orme, *Childhood*, p. 127; McFarlane, *Nobility*, p. 46.
84. Richard Rex, 'Morley and the Papacy. Rome, Regime, and Religion', in Marie Axton and James P. Carley (eds.), *'Triumphs of English': Henry Parker, Lord Morley, Translator to the Tudor Court* (London, 2000), pp. 87–90.
85. Rex, 'Morley and the Papacy', pp. 93–95.
86. Rex, 'Morley and the Papacy', p. 89.
87. Starkey, 'Attendant Lord', pp. 19–22.
88. *ODNB*, Henry Parker, eleventh Baron Morley; Rex, 'Morley and Papacy', pp. 96–97; Chris Skidmore, *Edward VI: The Lost King of England* (London, 2007), p. 138.
89. Axton, 'Lord Morley's Funeral', 213–24.
90. *ODNB*, Henry Parker.
91. Starkey, 'Attendant Lord', p. 10, McConica J.K., English Humanists and Reformation Politics under Henry VIII and Edward VI (Oxford, 1965), p. 152.
92. Carley, 'Life Of Agesilaus', p. 159; Wright, *Forty-Six Lives*, p. lxxi.
93. Wright, *Forty-six Lives*, p. xcii.
94. Steven J. Gunn, 'Henry Bourchier, Earl of Essex (1472–1540)', in: G.W. Bernard (ed.), *The Tudor Nobility* (Manchester & New York, 1992), p. 154; Miller, *Henry VIII*, p. 139.

Abbreviations

BIHR	*Bulletin of the Institute of Historical Research*
CChR	*Calendar of Charter Rolls*
CCR	*Calendar of Close Rolls*
CFR	*Calendar of Fine Rolls*
CIPM	*Calendar of Inquisitions post mortem*
CLP	*Calendar of Liberate Rolls*
CPR	*Calendar of Patent Rolls*
CP	*Complete Peerage*
DNB	*Dictionary of National Biography*
Dugdale	William Dugdale, *A perfect copy of all summons of the nobility to the great councils and parliaments of this realm from the XLIX of King Henry the IIId until these present times: with catalogues of such noblemen as have been summoned to Parliament in right of their wives, and of such other noblemen as derive their titles of honour from the heirs-female from whom they are descended, and of such noblemens eldest sons as have been summoned to Parliament by some of their fathers titles* (London, 1685)
EHR	*English Historical Review*
Foedera	*Foedera, conventiones, literæ, et cujuscunque generis acta publica, inter reges Angliæ et alios quosvis imperatores, reges, pontifices, principes, vel communitates, ab ineunte sæculo duodecimo, viz. ab anno 1101, ad nostra usque tempore habita aut tractata; ex autographis, infra secretiores Archivorum regiorum thesaurarias, per multa sæcula reconditis, fideliter exscripta ...,* Thomas Rymer (ed.), 3 vols. (1816–1869). [https://catalog.hathitrust.org/]
GND	*Gesta Normannorum Ducum*
ODNB	*Oxford Dictionary of National Biography* [online source]
OV	Orderic Vitalis, *The Ecclesiastical History of Orderic Vitalis,* ed. and trans. Marjorie Chibnall, 6 vols., (Oxford, 1972–1980)
Parl. Writs	Francis Palgrave, *Parliamentary Writs and Writs of Military Summons, together with Records and Muniments relating to the suit and service due and performed to the King's High Court of Parliament and the councils of the realm, or affording evidence of attendance given at Parliament and Councils,* 2 vols. (London, 1827–30)
Parl. Rolls	*The Parliament Rolls of Medieval England,* ed. C. Given-Wilson et al. http://www.sd-editions.com/PROME/home.html
VCH	*Victoria County History*

Bibliography

Unprinted Sources:
The National Archives (TNA), PRO 30/26/69
TNA, C 47/6/1
TNA, C 140
British Library, Add. Ms. 39,992 N
British Library, Add Ms. 6113, fol. 126d
British Library, Harley 7026
Oxford, Magdalen College, Adds. 99
Oxford, Magdalen College, Misc. 315

Printed Sources:
'An Account of the Army with which King Richard the Second Invaded Scotland in the Ninth Year of his Reign, A.D. 1385', N.H. Nicolas (ed.), *Archaeologia* 22 (1879), 13–19

Annales Monasterii S Albani a Johanne Amundesham. Monacho. A.D. 1421–1440, T. Riley (ed.), Rolls Series 28, vol. i (London, 1870, repr. Wiesbaden, 1965)

'Annales Londonienses and Annales Paulini', *Chronicles of the Reigns of Edward I and Edward II*, William Stubbs (ed.), Rolls Series 76 (London, 1882)

The Anonimalle Chronicle. 1333–1381, V.H. Galbraith (ed.)(Manchester, 1927)

British Library Harleian Manuscript 433, Rosemary Horrox and P. Hammond (eds.), 4 vols. (Gloucester, 1979–83)

Calendar of Documents Related to Scotland Preserved in Her Majesty's Public Record Office, Joseph Bain (ed.)(Edinburgh, 1884), vol. ii, A.D. 1272–1307

Calendar of Entries in the Papal Registers Relating to Great Britain and Ireland. Papal Letters, vol. vi, 1404–1415 (London, 1904)

Cartulaire de L'Abbaye de Saint-Martin de Pontoise, Depoin, J. (ed.) (Pontoise, 1895)

Chancery Warrants, A.D. 1244–1326 (London, 1927)

Chronicles of the Reign of Stephen, Henry II and Richard I, Richard Howlett (ed.), vol. iv (London, 1889)

Chronicles of the Revolution 1377–1421, Chris Given-Wilson (ed. and trans.) (Manchester, 1993)

The Controversy between Sir Richard Scrope and Sir Robert Grosvenor in the Court of Chivalry. AD. 1385–1390, Nicholas H. Nicolas (ed.), 2 vols. (London, 1832)

The Coronation of Richard III: The Extant Documents, Anne F. Sutton and P.W. Hammond (eds.) (Gloucester, 1983)

The Croyland Chronicle. The Croyland Chronicle: Part IX. The Third Continuation of the History of Croyland Abbey: July, 1485 – April, 1486. https://web.archive.org/web/20051226030956/http://www.r3.org/bookcase/croyland/croy9.html

A Descriptive Catalogue of Ancient Deeds in the Public Record Office: Prepared under the Superintendence of the Deputy Keeper of the Records, H.C. Maxwell Lyte (ed.), vol. iii (London, 1990)

Documents and Records illustrating the Affairs and History of Scotland and the Transactions between the Crowns of Scotland and England, Francis Palgrave (ed.), vol. i (London, 1837)

Documents Illustrating the Crisis of 1297–98 in England, Michael Prestwich (ed.), Camden Society, 4th series, 24 (1980)

The Gesta Normannorum Ducum of William of Jumiéges, Orderic Vitalis, and Robert of Torigny, Elizabeth M.C. van Houts (ed. and trans.), 2 vols. (Oxford, 1995)

'Historical Notes of a London Citizen, 1483–1488', Richard Firth Green (ed.), *EHR* 96 (1981), 585–590

The Household of Edward IV: The Black Book and the Ordinance of 1478, A.R. Myers (ed.) (Manchester, 1959)

Kingsford's Stonor Letters and Papers, 1290–1483, Christine Carpenter (ed.) (Cambridge, 1996)

Letters and Papers of the Reign of Richard III and Henry VII, J.G. Gairdner (ed.), 2 vols., Rolls Series 24 (London, 1861–3)

Letters and Papers, Foreign and Domestic of the Reign of Henry VIII. Preserved in the Public Record Office, The British Museum and Elsewhere in England, vol. xvi (London, 1898)

Liber Feodorum: The Book of Fees Commonly called Testa de Nevill, 3 vols. (PRO, 1920–31)

Lincoln Diocesan Documents. 1450–1544, Andrew Clark (ed.), Early English Text Society, orig. ser., 149 (London, 1914)

Lists of Sheriffs for England and Wales, PRO Lists and Indexes 9 (repr. with amendments, 1963)

Loyd, Lewis C. and Doris Mary Stanton (eds.), *Sir Christopher Hatton's Book of Seals to which is Appended a Select List of the Works of Frank Merry Stenton* (Oxford, 1950)

Mason, Emma (ed.), *The Beauchamp Cartulary Charters 1100–1268* (Publications of the Pipe Roll Society, LXXXI, New Series, XLIII, London, 1980)

Matthew Paris, *Chronica Majora*, Henry R. Luard (ed.), 7 vols., Rolls Series 57 (London, 1872–1882)

Munimenta Gildhallae Londoniensis, Henry T. Riley (ed.), 3 vols., Rolls Series 12 (London, 1859–62)

Myers, A.R. (ed.), 'The Household of Queen Margaret of Anjou, 1452–3', *Bulleting of the John Rylands Library* 40 (1957–58), pp. 79–113, 391–431

Orderic Vitalis, *The Ecclesiastical History of Orderic Vitalis*, ed. and trans. Marjorie Chibnall, 6 vols., (Oxford, 1972–1980)

The Paston Letters and Papers of the Fifteenth Century, N. Davis (ed.), 2 vols. (Oxford, 1971)

The Paston Letters. 1422–1509 A.D., J. Gairdner (ed.), 3 vols. (London, 1895)

The Pipe Roll of 31 Henry I. Michaelmas 1130, Joseph Hunter (ed.) (orig. publ. 1833, facsimile London, 1929)

Proceedings and Ordinances of the Privy Council of England, N.H. Nicolas (ed.), vol. I, (London, 1834)

Regesta Regum Anglo-Normannorum, 1066–1154, H.A. Cronne and R.H.C. Davis (eds.), vol. iii (Oxford, 1968)

The Registrum of the Guild of Corpus Christi in the City of York, R.H. Skaife (ed.), Surtees Society 57 (1872)

Rotuli Litterarum Clausarum in Turri Londiniensi asservati, vol. ii (London 1844)

Testamenta Vetusta, Nicholas H. Nicolas (ed.), 2 vols. in one (London, 1826)

Vergil, Polydore, *The Anglicana Historia, 1485–1537*, Denys Hay (ed. and trans.), Camden Society, 3rd series, 74 (1950)

Wright, H.G. (ed.), *Forty-six Lives: Translated from Boccaccio's 'De Claris Mulieribus' by Henry Parker, Lord Morley*, (=EETS OS 214, 1943 [for 1940])

Secondary Literature:

A Short Guide to the Church of St Mary the Virgin Titchmarsh (no author or publication date)

Archer, Rowena E., 'Rich Old Ladies: The Problem of Late Medieval Dowagers', in A.J. Pollard (ed.), *Property and Politics: Essays in Later Medieval English History* (Gloucester, 1984), 15–33

——— '"How ladies… who live on their manors ought to manage their household and estates": Women Landholders and Administrators in the Later Middle Ages', in: P.J.P. Goldberg (ed.), *Woman is a Worthy Wight: Women in English Society c. 1200–1500* (Stroud, 1992), 149–181

Ashdown-Hill, John, *Eleanor, The Secret Queen: The Woman who put Richard III on the Throne* (Stroud, 2009)

——— *The Dublin King: The True Story of Edward, Earl of Warwick, Lambert Simnel and the 'Princes in the Tower'* (Stroud, 2015)

Aston, Margaret, *Thomas Arundel: A Study of Church Life in the Reign of Richard II* (Oxford, 1967)

Axton, Richard, 'Lord Morley's Funeral', in M. Axton and J.P. Carley, *Triumphs of English: Henry Parker, Lord Morley, Translator to the Tudor Court, New Essays in Interpretation* (London, 2000), 213–224

Ayton, Andrew, 'Knights, Esquires and Military Service: The Evidence of the Armorial Case before the Court of Chivalry', in A. Ayton and J.L. Price (eds.), *The Medieval Military Revolution. State, Society and Military Change in Medieval and Early Modern Europe* (London and New York, 1995), 81–104

Backhouse, Janet, 'The Lovel Lectionary: A Memorial Offering to Salisbury', in J. Backhouse (ed.), *The Medieval English Cathedral: Papers in Honour of Pamela Tudor-Craig. Proceedings of the 1998 Harlaxton Symposium* (Donington, 2003), 112–125

Bain, J., 'Note of a Grant of Lands at Docking (co. Norfolk?) and Seal With Unusual Inscription Appended, *Archaeological Journal* 37 (1880), 328

Baldwin, D., 'What happened to Lord Lovell?', *The Ricardian* 7 (1985), 60–65

Baker, Juliet, *England Arise* (London, 2015)

Barlow, Frank, *William Rufus* (New Haven and London, 1983, 2nd slightly updated version, 2000)

Bartlett, K.R., 'Morley, Machiavelli, and the Pilgrimage of Grace', in Marie Axton and James P. Carley (eds.), *'Triumphs of English': Henry Parker, Lord Morley, Translator to the Tudor Court* (London, 2000), 77–85

Bennett, Michael, *Lambert Simnel and the Battle of Stoke* (Stroud, 1987)

Bernard, G.W., 'The Tudor Nobility in Perspective', in G.W. Bernard (ed.). *The Tudor Nobility* (Manchester and New York, 1992), 1–48

Blomefield, Francis, *Essay Towards a Topographical History of the County of Norfolk, Containing A Description…* (London, 1769), p. 717

Bradbury, Jim, *The Medieval Archer* (Woodbridge, 1985)

Brault, Gerard J. (ed.), *Rolls of Arms Edward I (1272–1307); Herald's Roll, Dering Roll, Camden, Roll, St George's Roll, Charles' Roll, Segar's Roll, Lord Marshal's Roll, Collins' Roll, Falkirk Roll, Guillim's Roll, Caerlaverock Poem, Galloway Roll, Smallpece's Roll, Stirling Roll, Nativity Roll, Fife Roll, Sir William le Neve's Roll*, 2 vols. (London, 1997)

Bridges, J., *History and Antiquities of the County of Northamptonshire* (1791), vol. i

Burke, Bernhard, *The General Armory of England, Scotland, Ireland, and Wales; Comprising a Registry of Armorial Bearings from the Earliest to the Present Time* (London, 1884, reprint 1969)

Carley, James P., '"Plutarch's" Life of Agesilaus: A Recently Located New Year's Gift to Thomas Cromwell by Henry Parker, Lord Morley', in Felicity Riddy (ed.), *Prestige, Authority and Power in Late Medieval Manuscripts and Texts* (York, 2000), 159–169

—— 'The Writings of Henry Parker, Lord Morley: A Biographical Survey', in Marie Axton and James P. Carley (eds.), *'Triumphs of English': Henry Parker, Lord Morley, Translator to the Tudor Court* (London, 2000), 27–68

Carlson, David R., 'Morley's Translations from Roman Philosophers and English Courtier Literature', in Marie Axton and James P. Carley (eds), *'Triumphs of English': Henry Parker, Lord Morley, Translator to the Tudor Court* (London, 2000), 131–151

Carpenter, Christine, 'The Fifteenth Century English Gentry and their Estates', M. Jones (ed.), *Gentry and the Lesser Nobility in Later Medieval Europe* (Gloucester, 1986), 36–60

—— *Locality and Polity: A Study of Warwickshire Landed Society. 1401–1499* (Cambridge, 1992)

Carpenter, David, *The Battles of Lewes and Evesham, 1264/65* (Keele, 1987)

—— *The Minority of Henry III* (London, 1990)

Caudry, Philip, 'War, Chivalry and Regional Society: East Anglia's Warrior Gentry before the Court of Chivalry', in *Fourteenth Century England* 8 (2014), 189–145

Chibnall, Marjorie, *World of Orderic Vitalisi* (Oxford, 1984)

Collins, Hugh E.L., *The Order of the Garter, 1348–1461: Chivalry and Politics in Late Medieval England* (Oxford, 2000)

Coulton, Barbara, 'The Wives of Sir William Stanley: Joan Beaumont and Elizabeth Hopton', *The Ricardian* 9 (1992), 315–18

Crawford, Anne, *Yorkist Lord. John Howard, Duke of Norfolk, c. 1425–1485* (London, 2010)

Crouch, David, *The Beaumont Twins* (Cambridge, 1986)

David, C.W., *Robert Curthose, Duke of Normandy* (Cambridge, Mass., 1920)

Dodd, Gwilym, 'Henry IV's Council, 1399–1405', in: Gwilym Dodd and Douglas Biggs (eds.), *Henry IV: The Establishment of the Regime, 1399–1406* (York, 2003), 95–115

—— 'Henry V's Establishment: Service, Loyalty and Reward in 1413', in Gwilym Dodd (ed.), *Henry V: New Interpretations* (Woodbridge, 2013)

Dryden, H.E.L., 'The Castle of Tichmarsh, Northamptonshire', *Associated Architectural Societies, Reports and Papers* 21 (1891), 248–52

Ellis, A.S., 'On the Arms of de Aton', *Yorkshire Archaeological Journal* 12 (1893), 263–266

Emery, A., *Dartington Hall* (Oxford, 1970)

Fletcher, C.D., *Richard II: Manhood, Youth, and Politics, 1377–99* (Oxford, 2008)

Fox, Julia, *Jane Boleyn: The Infamous Lady Rochford* (London, 2007)

Fryde, E.B., 'The Deposits of Hugh Despenser the Younger with Italian Bankers', *Econ. Hist. Rev.*, 2nd series, iii (1951), 344–362

Garnett, George, '"Ducal" Succession in Early Normandy', in G. Garnett and J. Hudson (eds.), *Law and Government in Medieval England and Normandy. Essays in Honour of Sir James Holt* (Cambridge, 1994), 80–110

Girouard, Mark, 'Wardour Old Castle - I', *Country Life*, 14 Feb. 1991, 44–49

Given-Wilson, Chris, *The Royal Household and the King's Affinity, 1360–1413* (New Haven and London, 1986)

—— *The English Nobility in the Late Middle Ages, The Fourteenth-Century Political Community* (London and New York, 1987)

—— 'Royal Charter Witness Lists 1327–1399', *Medieval Prosopography* 12 (1991), 35–59

—— 'Richard II and the Higher Nobility', in A. Goodman and J.L. Gillespie (eds.), *Richard II: The Art of Kingship* (Oxford 1999), 107–28

Goodman, Anthony, *The Wars of the Roses* (London, 1990)

—— *Joan, the Fair Maid of Kent: A Fourteenth-Century Princess and her World* (Woodbridge, 2017)

Gras, N.S.B., *The Early English Custom System: A Documentary Study of the Institutional and Economic History of the Customs from the Thirteenth to the Sixteenth Century* (Cambridge, 1918)

Green, Judith, 'King Henry I and the Aristocracy of Normandy', in *La 'France Anglaise' au Moyen Âge: Colloque des historiens médiévistes français et britanniques* (Paris, 1988), 161–173

—— ,Robert Curthose Reassessed', *Anglo-Norman Studies* 22 (2000), 95–116

—— *Henry I: King of England and Duke of Normandy* (Cambridge, 2006)

Grey, H.L., 'Incomes from Land in England in 1436', *EHR* 49 (1934), 607–39

Griffith, R.A., *The Reign of King Henry VI. The Exercise of Royal Authority, 1422–1461* (London, 1981)

Gunn, Steven J., 'Henry Bourchier, Earl of Essex (1472–1540)', in G.W. Bernard (ed.). *The Tudor Nobility* (Manchester and New York, 1992), 134–179

Haines, R.M., *Edward II: Edward of Caernarfon, his Life, his Reign, and its Aftermath, 1284–1330* (Montreal and Kingston, 2003)

Harris, Barbara J., *English Aristocratic Women and the Fabric of Piety, 1450–1550* (Amsterdam, 2018)

Haskins, Charles Homer, *Norman Institutions*, (1918)

Hicks, M., *Warwick the Kingmaker* (Oxford, 1999)

Hipshon, David, *Richard III* (Abingdon, 2011)

Hollister, C. Warren, 'The Anglo-Norman Succession Debate of 1126: Prelude to Stephen's Anarchy', in C. Warren Hollister, *Monarchy, Magnates and Institutions in the Anglo-Norman World* (London and Ronceverte, 1986), 145–69

—— *Henry I* (New Haven and London, 2003)

Horrox, Rosemary, *Richard III: A Study in Service* (Cambridge, 1989)

Impey, Edward, 'The Ancestry of the White Tower', in Edward Impey (ed.), *The White Tower* (New Haven, 2008), 227–241

Ives, Eric, *The Live and Death of Anne Boleyn: 'The Most Happy'* (Oxford, 2004)

Jack, R.I., 'Entail and Descent: The Hastings Inheritance, 1370–1436', *Bulletin of the Institute of Historical Research* 38 (1965), 1–19

Johnson, P.A., *Duke Richard of York, 1411–1460* (Oxford, 1988)

Jones, Michael K. and Malcolm Underwood, *The King's Mother: Lady Margaret Beaufort, Countess of Richmond and Derby* (Cambridge, 1992)

Jones, Richard Hutton, *The Royal Policy of Richard II: Absolutism in the Later Middle Ages* (Oxford, 1968)

Kendall, Paul Murray, *Richard III: Der letzte Plantagenet auf dem englischen Königsthron 1452–1485* (München, 1980)

Kirby, J.L., 'Council and Councillors of Henry IV, 1399–1413', *TRHS*, 5th series, 14 (1963), 35–65

—— *Henry IV of England* (London, 1970)

Lander, J.R., *Government and Community: England 1450–1509* (London, 1980)

Laynesmith, Joanna L., *The Last Medieval Queens: English Queenship 1445–1503* (Oxford, 2004)

—— *Cecily, Duchess of York* (London et al., 2017)

Leland, John L., 'The Abjuration of 1388', *Medieval Prosopography* 15 (1994), 115–38

Lewis, Katherine J., *Kingship and Masculinity in Late Medieval England* (London and New York, 2013)

—— 'Women and Power', in Stephen H. Rigby (ed.), *Historians on John Gower* (Woodbridge, 2019), 323–350

Lewis, P.S., 'Sir John Fastolf's Lawsuit over Titchwell, 1448–55', *Historical Journal* 1 (1958), 1–20

Lobel, Mary D. and Johns, W.H. (eds.), *The British Atlas of Historic Towns*, vol. iii, *The City of London from Prehistoric Times to c. 1520* (Oxford, 1989)

MacCullough, Diarmaid, *Thomas Cromwell: A Life* (Milton Keynes, 2018)

Maddicott, J.R., *Simon de Montfort* (Cambridge, 1994)

Mason, Emma, 'A Truth Universally Acknowledged', in David Baker (ed.), *The Church in Town and Countryside. Papers read at the Seventeenth Summer Meeting and the Eighteenth Winter Meeting of the Ecclesiastical History Society* (Oxford, 1979), 171–186

Maule, Jeremy, 'What did Morley Give when he Gave a 'Plutarch' *Life*?', in Marie Axton and James P. Carley (eds.), *'Triumphs of English': Henry Parker, Lord Morley, Translator to the Tudor Court* (London, 2000), 107–130

McConica, J.K., *English Humanists and Reformation Politics under Henry VIII and Edward VI* (Oxford, 1965)

McFarlane, K.B., *The Nobility of Later Medieval England* (Oxford, 1973)

—— *England in the Fifteenth Century* (London, 1981)

McHardy, Alison, 'The Effects of War on the Church: The Case of the Alien Priories in the Fourteenth Century', in Michael Jones and Malcom Vale (eds.) *England and her Neighbours, 1066–1453: Essays in Honour of Pierre Chaplais* (London and Roncerverte, 1989)

Miller, Helen, *Henry VIII and the English Nobility* (Oxford, 1986)

Morgan, Marjorie, 'The Suppression of the Alien Priories', *History* 26 (1941)

Newman, Charlotte A., *The Anglo-Norman Nobility in the Reign of Henry I: The Second Generation* (Philadelphia, 1988)

Norton, Elizabeth, *Margaret Beaufort: Mother of the Tudor Dynasty* (Stroud, 2010)

O'Connor, S., 'Francis Lovell and the Rebels of Furness Fells', *The Ricardian* 7 (1987)

Orme, Nicholas, *From Childhood to Chivalry. The Education of English Kings and Aristocracy 1066–1530* (London and New York, 1984)

—— 'The Education of Edward V', *Bulletin of the Institute of Historical Research*, 57: 136 (1984), 119–130

—— *Medieval Children* (New Haven and London, 2001)

Payling, S.J., 'A Disputed Mortgage: Ralph, Lord Cromwell, Sir John Gra and the Manor of Multon Hall', in R. Archer and S. Walker (eds.), *Rulers and Ruled in Late Medieval England: Essays presented to Gerald Harris* (1995), 117–36

Pevsner, N., *Northamptonshire* (London, 1961)

Phillips, J.R.S., *Aymer de Valence. Earl of Pembroke, 1207–1324. Baronial Politics in the Reign of Edward II* (Oxford, 1972)

Phillips, K.M., *Medieval Maidens: Young Women and Gender in England, 1370–1540* (Manchester, 2003)

Pollard, Anthony, *The Wars of the Roses* (3rd ed., 2013)

Pollard, A.J., 'Lord FitzHugh's Rising in 1470', *BIHR* 53 (1979), 170–75

Pounds, N.J.G., *The Medieval Castle in England and Wales: A Social and Political History* (Cambridge, 1990)

Powell, Edward, 'Law and Justice', in R. Horrox (ed.), *Fifteenth Century Attitudes* (Cambridge, 1995), 29–41

Powell, J. Enoch and Keith Wallis, *The House of Lords in the Middle Ages* (London, 1968)

Power, Daniel, *The Norman Frontier in the Twelfth and Early Thirteenth Century*, Cambridge Studies in Medieval Life and Thought, 4th series, 62 (2004)

Prestwich, Michael, *The Three Edwards. War and State in England 1272–1377* (London, 1980)

—— 'Magnate Summonses in England in the Later Years of Edward I', *Parliaments, Estates and Representation* 5 (1985), 97–101

—— *Edward I* (London, 1988)

Rex, Richard, 'Morley and the Papacy. Rome, Regime, and Religion', in Marie Axton and James P. Carley (eds.), *'Triumphs of English': Henry Parker, Lord Morley, Translator to the Tudor Court* (London, 2000), 87–105

Richmond, Colin, 'The Nobility and the Wars of the Roses, 1459–1461', *Nottingham Medieval Studies* 21 (1977), 71–86

—— 'Patronage and Polemic', in J.L. Watts, *The End of the Middle Ages? England in the Fifteenth and Sixteenth Centuries* (Thrupp, Stroud, 1998), 65–87

Rosenthal, Joel, 'Aristocratic Widows in Fifteenth-Century England', in B.J. Harris and J.K. McNamara (eds.), *Women and the Structure of Society* (Durham, N.C., 1984), 36–47

Roskell, J.S., *The Commons in the Parliament of 1422: English Society and Parliamentary Representation under the Lancastrians* (Manchester, 1954)

—— 'William Catesby, Counsellor to Richard III' *Bulletin of the John Ryland's Library* 42 (1959–60), 145–74

—— *Parliament and Politics in Late Medieval England*, 3 vols. (London, 1981–3)

Roskell, J.S., Linda S. Clark and Carole Rawcliffe (eds.), *The House of Commons, 1386–1421*, 4 vols. (Stroud, 1993)

Ross, C.D., *Edward IV* (London, 1974)

—— *Richard III* (London, 1981)

Saul, Nigel, 'The Despensers and the Downfall of Edward II', *EHR* 99 (1984), 1–133

—— *The Three Richards: Richard I, Richard II and Richard III* (London and New York, 2006)

—— 'An Early Private Indenture of Retainer: The Agreement Between Hugh Despenser the Younger and Sir Robert De Shirland', *EHR* 128 (2013), 519–534

Sayles, G.O., 'The Formal Judgements on the Traitors of 1322', *Speculum* 16 (1941), 57–63

Scott, Kathleen L., *Later Gothic Manuscripts, 1390–1490*, 2 vols. (London, 1996)

Simon, Monika E., 'The Lovells of Titchmarsh: An English Baronial Family, 1297–148?' (unpubl. DPhil thesis, York, 1999)

—— 'Who is Buried in the Tomb in St Kenelm's Church, Minster Lovell?', *The Ricardian* 19 (2009), 84–94

—— 'Of Lands and Ladies': The Marriage Strategies of the Lords Lovell (c. 1200–1487)', *Southern History Review* 23 (2011), 1–29

Simpson, G.G., 'The *Familia* of Roger de Quincy, Earl of Winchester and Constable of Scotland', in K.J. Stringer (ed.), *Essays on the Nobility of Medieval Scotland* (Edinburgh, 1985), 102–29

Simpson, James, 'The Sacrifice of Lady Rochford: Henry Parker, Lord Morley's Translation of *De claris mulieribus*', in Marie Axton and James P. Carley (eds), *'Triumphs of English': Henry Parker, Lord Morley, Translator to the Tudor Court* (London, 2000), 153–69

Skidmore, Chris, *Edward VI: The Lost King of England* (London, 2007)

Smith, Lacey Baldwin, *A Tudor Tragedy: The Life and Times of Catherine Howard* (London, 1961)

Squibb, G.D., *The High Court of Chivalry: A Study of the Civil Law in England* (Oxford, 1959)

Stanes, E.G.F., 'Sir Guy de Brian, K.G.', *Report and Transactions of the Devonshire Association for the Advancement of Science, Literature and Art* 92 (1960), 248–78

Stansfield, Michael M. N., 'The Holland Family, Dukes of Exeter, Earls of Kent and Huntingdon, 1352–1475' (unpubl. PhD thesis, Oxford University, 1987)

Starkey, David, 'An Attendant Lord? Henry Parker, Lord Morley', in Marie Axton and James P. Carley (eds), *'Triumphs of English': Henry Parker, Lord Morley, Translator to the Tudor Court* (London, 2000), 1–25

—— *Six Wives. The Queens of Henry VIII* (London, 2003)

Swabey, Ffiona, 'The Letter Book of Alice de Bryene and Alice de Sutton's List of Debts', *Nottingham Medieval Studies* 42 (1998), 121–145

—— *Medieval Gentlewoman: Life in a Widow's Household in the Later Middle Ages* (Sutton Publishing, Stroud, 1999)

Tabuteau, E.Z., 'The Role of Law in the Succession to Normandy and England, 1087', *Haskins Society Journal* 3 (1992), 141–69

Taylor, A.J., ,The Alien Priory of Minster Lovell', *Oxoniensia* 2 (1937), 103–117

—— *Minster Lovell Hall* (1985)

Tomkinson, A., 'The Retinues at the Tournament of Dunstable, 1309', *EHR* 74 (1959), 70–89

Vaughn, Sally N., *Anselm of Bec and Robert of Meulan: The Innocence of the Dove and the Wisdom of the Serpent* (Berkeley, 1987)

Wagner, Anthony R, *Heralds and Heraldry in the Middle Ages* (London, 1956)

Warner, Kathryn, *Hugh Despenser the Younger & Edward II: Downfall of a King's Favourite* (Barnsley, 2018)

Warnicke, Retha M., 'Lord Morley's Statements about Richard III', *Albion* 15 (1983), 173–8

—— *The Rise and Fall of Anne Boleyn* (Cambridge, 1989)

Wedgewood, Josiah C. and Ann D. Holt, *History of Parliament: Biographies of the Members of the Commons, 1436–1509* (London, 1936)

Weightman, Christine, *Margaret of York, Duchess of Burgundy* (Stroud, 1989)

Wilkinson, Josephine, *Katherine Howard: The Tragic Story of Henry VIII's Fifth Queen* (London, 2016)

Willement, Thomas (ed.), *Rolls of Arms of the Reign of Richard the Second* (London, 1834)

Williams, J.M. 'The Political Career of Francis Viscount Lovell (1456–?)', *The Ricardian* 8 (1990), 382–402

Wood, Margaret, *The English Medieval House* (London, 1965)

Index